W9-CMG-537

Other books by
HARRY EMERSON FOSDICK

THE SECOND MILE
THE ASSURANCE OF IMMORTALITY
THE MANHOOD OF THE MASTER
THE MEANING OF PRAYER
THE MEANING OF FAITH
THE MEANING OF SERVICE
CHRISTIANITY AND PROGRESS
TWELVE TESTS OF CHARACTER
THE MODERN USE OF THE BIBLE
ADVENTUROUS RELIGION
A PILGRIMAGE TO PALESTINE
AS I SEE RELIGION
THE HOPE OF THE WORLD
THE SECRET OF VICTORIOUS LIVING
THE POWER TO SEE IT THROUGH
SUCCESSFUL CHRISTIAN LIVING
A GUIDE TO UNDERSTANDING THE BIBLE
LIVING UNDER TENSION
ON BEING A REAL PERSON
A GREAT TIME TO BE ALIVE
ON BEING FIT TO LIVE WITH
THE MAN FROM NAZARETH
RUFUS JONES SPEAKS TO OUR TIMES, AN ANTHOLOGY
GREAT VOICES OF THE REFORMATION, AN ANTHOLOGY
MARTIN LUTHER (LANDMARK SERIES)
A FAITH FOR TOUGH TIMES
WHAT IS VITAL IN RELIGION
THE LIVING OF THESE DAYS (AN AUTOBIOGRAPHY)

RIVERSIDE SERMONS

RIVERSIDE SERMONS

by

Harry Emerson Fosdick

Introduction by Henry Pitney Van Dusen

HARPER & BROTHERS

PUBLISHERS NEW YORK

Printed in the United States of America

FIRST EDITION

C-H

Library of Congress catalog card number: 58-7093

Contents

Introduction

FOR close to two decades, from October 5, 1930, when the first service was held in the newly completed Riverside Church, until May, 1946, when Dr. Fosdick formally retired as its Senior Minister, the pulpit of that church was the locus of what is widely recognized as the most influential preaching ministry in the United States in the current century. Sunday by Sunday, throngs crowded into the church, not only from every section of Metropolitan New York but from every corner of the nation and distant parts of the world, overflowing its cathedral-like sanctuary into its chapel and auditorium, filling every room into which the service could be amplified. Sunday after Sunday, following an uplifting service of worship, a short, stocky, dynamic figure, ruddy cheeks crowned by bushy graying hair, mounted that pulpit and a clear, strong, resonant voice with an arresting metallic ring and almost mesmeric command launched forth on the discourse for which all had been eagerly waiting and which held every listener in alert attention until its end. Such was the setting of these Riverside sermons.

However, the congregation was far vaster than those assembled in the church. On Sunday afternoons through most of those years, that same voice reached out across the continent through the "National Vespers" of the National Broadcasting Company and by short-wave to far places of the earth. Indeed, those two congregations were closely interrelated. It was a well-known fact that visitors to New York by the thousands, whatever the attractions of the city's theaters, museums and skyscrapers, placed first on their calendars attendance Sunday morning at Riverside Church, that they might see with their own eyes the man whose voice had spoken to them week by week over the air across the years.

From time to time, selections from these sermons have been gathered into published volumes; most of these are now out of print. This book contains forty sermons chosen as most likely to have continuing relevance and value, and is issued in honor of Dr. Fosdick's eightieth birthday.

The secret of the power of this extraordinary preaching ministry, no one could fully explain. Undoubtedly, it has lain in part in native equipment of mind and soul of the highest potential, nurtured to maturity within a solid, frontier Christian community and under the influence of parents to whom the dedications of two early books pay eloquent tribute. In part, it was the result of "solid learning, true piety, and enlightened experience" in professional preparation; despite a severe nervous breakdown at the end of his first year, young Fosdick drained the best from the Union Theological Seminary of that day. In no small measure, it was the fruit of unremitting self-discipline in habits of work exactingly determined and rigorously adhered to; sixteen hours was the normal allowance for preparation of each sermon. Linked to this were lofty standards of craftsmanship. Just before an Ordination Service at which he was to preach, Dr. Fosdick inquired if twenty-eight minutes would be an excessive allowance for the sermon; stop-watch timing revealed that the sermon concluded within thirty seconds of the self-imposed limit. In part, the secret lay in a mysterious gift of which Dr. Fosdick was aware but which escaped the attention of others; not once but repeatedly, he speaks of "clairvoyance" into the problems of individuals. He himself would attribute the effectiveness of his preaching to one other factor which grew in importance with him over the years—grounding his sermons directly in the problems and perplexities disclosed to him in personal counseling. Behind all these, of course, lay the basic intangibles of life dedication to Christ's ministry through His church.

In his autobiography, *The Living of These Days*, Dr. Fosdick has told the story of the launching and development of the Riverside Church during his ministry. There is much about the circumstances of the conception and planning of the church, about the erection and architecture of its sanctuary and tower, about the dream of welding a nonsectarian inclusive congregation drawn from all races and classes and many nations, about its manifold and many-sided progam of service to its own people, to the great educational and cultural center of Morningside Heights where it is located, and to the countless organizations and groups to which it offers prodigal hospitality of its facilities, about its principles of membership and its ideals of worship, about its problems and fulfillments, about its generous support of good causes thoughout the world, about the central place of personal counseling in the ministry of the church. Characteristically, relatively little is said about the *preaching* ministry of its pulpit. Yet all who shared with him in its life and all who observed its growth as sympathetic neighbors would agree that that preaching was the keystone of this great and complex arch of activity and Christian fellowship.

Scattered through the autobiography, however, are fragments of self-revelation disclosing his conception of the preacher's task, of the secret of sound and effective preaching and of the making of the sermons of which this is a representative collection. Far more appropriate as an introduction than the comments of another is Dr. Fosdick's own account of how these sermons came to be.

Of his first beginning as a preacher, in all its agony and frustration, he writes: "Preaching for me has never been easy, and at the start it was often exceedingly painful. My road as a preacher was very rough at the beginning, but little by little I saw clearly what I verily believed and wanted to say and, as clairvoyance into the needs of those to whom I spoke increased, I discovered, at least occasionally, the satisfaction of preaching so that something creative happened in the listener. I do not recall that I ever cherished any ambition to be an author. But I do not see how any man can preach without writing. I always have thought with my pen in hand."

He reveals the alteration of focus which he considers the secret of his mature preaching: "I floundered until personal counseling gradually led me into an approach to preaching which made it an exciting adventure.

"I am commonly thought of as a preacher, but I should not put preaching central in my ministry. Personal counseling has been central. My preaching at its best has itself been personal counseling on a group scale.

"Indeed, I distrust a preacher to whom sermons seem the crux of his functioning. The temptations of a popular preacher—if he is only that—are devastating. To preach a 'successful' sermon, to feel the rouse of a responsive audience, to hold in one's hands the concentrated attention of spellbound congregations, is a thrilling experience. Let any preacher who has such an experience go humbly home and pray to be delivered from its seductions!

"The Bible came alive to me—an amazing compendium of every kind of situation in human experience with the garnered wisdom of the ages to help in meeting them.

"Every sermon should have for its main business the head-on constructive meeting of some problem which was puzzling minds, burdening consciences, distracting lives, and no sermon which so met a real human difficulty, with light to throw on it and help to win a victory over it, could possibly be futile.

"A good sermon is an engineering operation by which a chasm is bridged so that spiritual goods on one side—the 'unsearchable riches of Christ'—are actually transported into personal lives upon the other." This he calls "project preaching."

"My silent prayer rose each Sunday before the sermon started: 'O God, some one person here needs what I am going to say. Help me to reach him!'

"Without this creative experience of personal counseling I never could have preached for twenty years in Riverside Chuch."

Of his radio ministry, he says:

"When I began radio preaching, I had no idea of the possibilities involved. Frankly skeptical of its effect, I undertook it rather listlessly. I used to go down to the studio on Sunday afternoons and sitting at a table, talk into that strange contrivance, the microphone, with no vivid sense of contact with the unseen audience. Later the microphone became to me almost as stirring as a great congregation, no longer a thing but an almost living symbol of multitudes of individual people.

"A deep impression that years of radio preaching made on me was the intense, intimate and influential meaning it has for multitudes of individuals. The steady stream of letters—grateful, intimate, presenting vital personal and domestic problems—made the unseen audiences very real and human to me. Take a letter like this from San Quentin prison in California: 'Did you know that the quietest thirty minutes in this large "Bay View Hotel" is on Sunday evening when your sermon is rebroadcast? It is a pleasure to hear you, you make it so plain, so easy to understand. I am sure that all the fellows appreciate you as much as I do.'

"Whatever the effect of radio preaching may be on the listener, the effect on the preacher is salutary. He is speaking to all kinds of persons from all the social, racial and religious backgrounds there are. Nothing narrow, sectarian, exclusive and merely partisan will do. He must strike a universal note and deal with elemental human problems. He must be fair, inclusive in his understanding and sympathy, always a human being first and not a partisan. I am profoundly grateful for the opportunity the radio has given me to help others; I am just as grateful for what the radio ministry has done for me."

His final word is this:

"Many a time as I went into the pulpit I recalled Hugh Latimer's experience that Sunday morning when, headed toward the royal chapel, he heard a voice within him say: 'Latimer, Latimer, be careful what you preach today because you are going to preach before the king of England'; then another voice said: 'Latimer, Latimer, be careful what you preach today since you are going to preach before the King of kings.'

"Looking back on my twenty years as a minister at the Riverside Church I often wonder how I got through them. The opportunities were always greater than I could compass, the demands heavier than I could carry. Whether my nerves would much longer stand the strain seemed at times questionable. Being a minister can seem 'a heartbreaking way of making a living,' but always I knew that I 'would not give it up for all the world.'"

Doubtless, some day a definitive study of "Harry Emerson Fosdick as Preacher" will be undertaken. It will reveal, I suspect, not a little change in both the content and manner of his preaching across the years, from those early trial-heats in his first parish in Montclair when solid theological substance, much of which found its way into his great trilogy of "Meanings," was more marked than in the latter years, through the intermediate period at the First Presbyterian and Park Avenue Baptist churches, to the climactic phase in the Riverside pulpit, when the continuous interplay of his mind and spirit with his hearers through the intimate revelations of what he was bold to call his "confessional" dominated his sermons and gave to all of them a more immediate, directly personal character. It is from this later period that the sermons in this volume are drawn. As they reappear here on the printed page, thousands of those who felt the power of their first delivery from the Riverside pulpit or on the "National Vespers" will hear again that inimitable voice and once more be caught within the contagion of its clarity of thought, honesty of self-confrontation and power of faith. May it prove true that countless more, who have not known the privilege of hearing him speak, will, through these pages, come to share in that experience and join in gratitude to one whom many would hail as the most winsome and convincing interpreter of Christian Faith in our time.

HENRY PITNEY VAN DUSEN

Publisher's Note

The publishers desire to express their appreciation to Professor Charles L. Wallis of Keuka College, Keuka Park, New York, editor of *Pulpit Preaching* and compiler and editor of *Worship Resources for the Christian Year*, who did the major work of selecting the forty sermons included in this volume.

The basis of selection was largely one of timelessness; sermons that endure should have relevance and value beyond their date of delivery.

Some of Dr. Fosdick's most notable sermons, however, were evoked by specific situations and events, and three of them are here included: "God Talks to a Dictator," dealing with Adolf Hitler; "The Unknown Soldier," an Armistice Day sermon, 1933, voicing the preacher's indignation against war; and "The Church Must Go Beyond Modernism," dealing with the theological crisis in the middle nineteen thirties. These three sermons close the volume.

RIVERSIDE SERMONS

The Ideas That Use Us

ONE of the most extraordinary eras in human life was the first century of the Christian movement. Our calendars still are dated from its beginning and, any way one looks at it, it was an amazing turning point in mankind's journey. To one, however, who knows that era well and without romantic illusions looks on what happened there, nothing is more surprising than the ordinary character of most of the men who helped lead mankind around that corner. The records of the New Testament are realistically frank about the first followers of Jesus, their crudity, their slowness of comprehension, their downright self-seeking even, and yet these were the men who helped inaugurate one of the great, new eras of human life.

Behind this fact there is a major principle. Victor Hugo was right in his belief that nothing is so powerful in this world as an idea whose time has come. Repeatedly in history that truth has been vindicated. As though its hour had struck, a new idea emerged. The special men and women who happened to represent it were often not remarkable in themselves, not by any means the most brilliant and able of their time. Only this was their distinction: they were the implements and instrumentalities of an idea whose time had come.

As a picturesque illustration of this, consider Peter and John after the death of Jesus, haled into court in Jerusalem and threatened with condign punishment if they did not cease preaching the new gospel. No one who realistically visualizes Peter and John can have illusions about them. They had been fishermen; they were Galileans, of the common people, and to the educated and aristocratic gentlemen of the court they seemed, as it is written, to be "unlearned and ignorant men." As one imagines the scene, with the best minds and names of Judea on one side and on the other the unprepossessing prisoners, the one incredible absurdity would seem to be that the future should belong to Peter and John. But it did. They were the representatives of an idea which possessed and used them. "We cannot but speak," they said, "the things which we saw and heard." The tremendous power which was going to change the course of centuries was not primarily in them, but lay deeper. They were being used by an idea whose hour had struck.

As we pursue the significance of this truth into our present situation, it is evident that a man need not be in himself very great to be used by a great idea. By no stretch of imagination can Simon Peter be considered an extraordinary man. St. Peter, indeed! One feels, as one reads the record, that he was a long way from a saint. Reluctant at the first to follow Jesus, stupidly unable to understand some of the Master's simplest ideas, so much on the wrong side of the major issue in Jesus' life, sacrificial saviorhood, that Jesus had to say to him, "Get thee behind me, Satan," and, when danger threatened, wilting before a serving maid in Pilate's court, denying he had ever known the Lord—he was a very ordinary man. Had we been able to apply to him our psychological tests to reveal his intelligence quotient and suchlike, I suspect he would still have turned out to be an ordinary man. Yet he was and is St. Peter. He belonged to that little group of men who led mankind around one of the most crucial corners in history. If he himself were to explain how this almost incredible thing happened to him, I can imagine his saying something like this: It was not due to what I was in myself; the world of my time was full of men more able, more brilliant, more capacious, of better character than I; how I came to be St. Peter can be put into a single phrase: an ordinary man used by an idea whose time had come.

This is the explanation of some of the most shining names in history. They were ordinary men used by extraordinary ideas. Here, indeed, is both the truth and the falsity of the new school of biographers who recently have been stripping the glamour from our long-loved heroes and heroines. A great character in history, long idealized, now stands before us with his court clothes taken from him, left in dishabille. He does not seem to us an extraordinary person and we are irritated by our disillusionment. One naturally thinks that Columbus, for example, must have been an extraordinary man. Now, however, he is portrayed to us as not remarkable at all. His generation had many mariners brave and daring like himself. Even our intelligence tests probably would not have explained his eminence. So far the new biographers have the right of the matter; that much is true. But let us not forget that an idea which had knocked in vain at many a mariner's mind knocked at Columbus' mind and was let in. A great idea whose time had come used him. That is glory enough for one lifetime on this earth.

I defy the cynicism of these new biographers. They cannot take my heroes from me. They picture Florence Nightingale with the faults of an uncertain temperament. They show her under strain, losing her self-control. They quote her when she was impatient, tempestuous, and petulant. They leave her just like ourselves. Of course she was like ourselves. If every time God wanted to do great business he had to perform a miracle and make perfect persons, the world would be hopeless. We ought to know that Florence Nightingale, carrying the load she carried, facing the administrative stupidity she had to deal with, had moods and tempers, petulances and tricks of character that would not appear ideal in biographical portraiture. But let them not forget that other matter—being what she was, a great idea that has made this earth ever since a more decent and humane place for sick people used her. That is glory enough for one lifetime.

When we take this principle out of other people's biography into our own, it brings a challenge to all of us. One need not in himself be very great to be used by a great idea. Even some of us who do not think much of ourselves may have this high distinction that the supreme ideas of our time use us.

Let us go deeper into this truth and consider that if up to date some one has been resistant to this sermon, not wishing to assume the responsibility of such a life as our thought suggests, not so easily can he evade it. Willy-nilly we *are* used by ideas. That is not an ideal simply; it is an inescapable fact.

Take selfishness, for example. When one sees a person conducting his life selfishly, how one would like to talk to him in some such way as this: The principle on which you are living is an old one; as far back in history as one can go one finds homes ruined, friendships broken, wars waged, and every evil thing that has made man's record hideous and cruel sustained by that idea. Now it is using you. In every generation ideas have to find people they can use or they could not go on. So your selfishness is not an individual matter as you think. It is cosmic. Generation after generation, men come and go. They pass. But ideas do not; they abide. On each new life when it arrives they knock and say, Let me use you in your time. The ultimate meaning of our lives, therefore, lies in the ideas which we allow to use us.

Well, there are some ideas I should hate to have use me now. Drunkenness, for example, the supposition that one can solve real problems or escape from real perplexities by the swift and facile road of intoxication. That is an old idea, ancient as the legends of Noah, and its trail across history, as it has found in multitudes of people a vehicle and implement, is one of the saddest portions of the human record. I should hate to have that idea use me.

Or, turning to the social realm, race prejudice. That is an old idea too, ancient as the story of the Tower of Babel, and still, I think, it has in it more concentrate evil, more poison to cause human agony than almost any other cruelty of man. I should hate to have that idea use me.

Or coming to the intellectual realm, cynicism, the loss of faith that life has meaning, the conviction, as Theodore Dreiser, the novelist, puts it, that man is only an accidental mechanism, undevised and uncreated, living a life that gets us nowhere spiritually and has no importance after all. That is an old idea that has sucked the sap from life for centuries. I should hate to have it use me.

This way of picturing the matter is quite different from our ordinary method of imagining it. We commonly think that a man gets his ideas, that they are his private property, his interior possession. No, ideas get us. They are historic, not we. They last on from age to age. They need representatives and witnesses. They use us. No man ever can understand what sin means until he sees this. Some old idea that for ages has thrown its influence like vitriol across mankind finds in us an instrument. We give it gangway in our time. We prolong its life by our embodiment. We betray humanity from within by giving one of its ancient enemies the use of us. That is the fact and the shame of sin. So, you see, there is no use trying to escape this truth. We *are* being used by ideas. All we can do is to choose which ones shall use us.

Going deeper into this matter, consider what happens to a man when he takes this philosophy of life earnestly, makes constructive employment of it, and knows at last that, being what he is, he is being used in his day by some ideas to which the future belongs. Have you never seen a young man or woman made all over by that? One of our seers has said that the greatest hour in a man's life is when he turns the corner of a street and runs into a new idea. That is certainly the greatest hour in many a youth's life, especially if, as the youth faces that truth or cause, there rises in him the invincible conviction that he belongs to it.

Dean Wicks of Princeton, watching boys grow up in college, said that the sign that a boy had passed out of his childish stage and had become a man lay in the discovery of some important enterprise or undertaking concerning which he said, I belong to that. Commonly we miss this glory which lies within our reach. We think that life consists in saying of many things, These belong to me. We gather instruments that we can use and say, All this belongs to me, Then, some day, like Paul or Peter, Columbus or Florence Nightingale, or like some humbler folk whom history has forgotten but God has not, we come to our crucial turning point, the revolutionary upset and conversion of our lives, and find our fate in something concerning which we say, not, That belongs to me, but, I belong to that.

This is so much the deepest experience in life that if it could come to some one here it might mean the swinging of the door of a new era for multitudes; it certainly would mean the swinging of the door of a new era for that life. For while it is true, as we have said, that one does not need in himself to be very great to be used by a great idea, it is also true that no man can be used by a great idea without becoming greater himself.

Consider one item in our common human problem which this

experience crucially affects. I mean dealing with our inward self-contempt. Even in a congregation as large as this there is, I suspect, no one who in his own solitariness does not deal with self-contempt. Because of our inside information about ourselves and the mortifying situations which outwardly we face, every person confronts the lurking devil of self-contempt. That is one reason why we welcome praise so eagerly; the approval of our friends helps to lift us above our low self-estimate. That is why we are so pleased by position, office, and prestige; they re-establish our uncertain self-confidence.

A boy in one of our church families came home the other day from the school where he is getting started and made this glad announcement: "I am the assistant to the assistant manager of the third football team." Every man here with lively memories of his boyhood feels his heart go out to that lad. So, sometimes wholesomely, by welcoming the trust of our friends, and sometimes less wholesomely, we try to handle our self-contempt. But only one deepest way exists of dealing with it, one supreme experience where utter humility and utter self-respect are blended, and that is when a man, being what he is, no larger than God made him, recognizes that in his time he is being used by ideas on which man's welfare depends and to which the future belongs.

Felix Adler expressed it in the very phraseology we are employing today. Looking back over his life work, he said, "I am grateful for the Idea that has used me." We modern preachers do not talk so much as our forefathers did about preparing to die, and doubtless by that we have escaped morbidity. Nevertheless, death remains a fact and the days do come when a man must see his life in retrospect, and, since this is so realistically true that no honest man should wish to evade the issue, he may well recognize that, when the signs of evening gather in his western sky, it would be a triumph, looking back, to be able thus to say, I am grateful for the idea that has used me.

There lies the victory of some souls who seemed to be defeated. Mozart died in poverty and was buried in a pauper's grave, but when recently I heard Kreisler play from Mozart I felt the victory that has been his despite the world which so mistreated him. If he could come back again, he would be grateful for the idea that had used him.

They made Socrates drink the hemlock and outside the gates of Jerusalem they nailed to a cross the Son of man. Yes, but the triumph refused to stay in the hands of those who afterward went comfortably home to dinner. How elusive triumph is! How it slips through the fingers of the men who grasp it and flies to the defeated! For in the end there is no victory without being used by an idea whose time has come.

That truth belongs to the humblest soul. As water is represented not only by a great lake or a sea but by a brook, so supreme ideas use humble people. The potential value of our lives, so often circumscribed and apparently unimportant, is that great ideas can use us.

Finally, pursue this idea into its special meaning in this distracted and often disheartened generation. At one stage in his career William Wilberforce was so downcast about the British Empire and the world at large that he hesitated to marry and so give hostages to fortune in so dreadful a world. He was as low in his mind as that. Moreover, he was not unjustified in being discouraged about social evil in general and the slave trade in particular. Was not the slave trade a cruel and towering fact? Had it not existed through all history so that the memory of man went not back to the time when it had not cursed the race? Did not the world's wisest statesmen say that they foresaw slavery's indefinite continuance? Even Edmund Burke said that. Well, then, with the existent facts, the inveterate history and the cynicism of the worldly-wise on the side of slavery's continuance, what was there to give a man hope? Nothing much. Only an idea, which spread like fire from mind to mind, that slavery was wrong, that it never could be harmonized with the principles of Christ, that it was, as well, economically self-defeating, that it was as degrading to the masters and as impoverishing to the wage-earners as it was brutal to the slaves—an idea which kept using more and more people, with Wilberforce pre-eminent among them, until before he died he was assured of the abolition of the British slave trade. Once more in history the statement was vindicated: there is nothing so powerful in this world—not existent facts, nor inveterate history, nor the selfishness of ruling classes, nor the reluctance of apathetic governments—nothing so powerful as an idea whose day has dawned.

My soul, gird yourself with that truth now! None will doubt the perilous posture of the world's affairs. When one asks what there is to give us social hope, the answer—ideas in the air—seems vague and tenuous. Yes, but they are ideas that spread from mind to mind—that war is wrong and stupid; that mankind is one family, woven more inextricably together by each new scientific invention, and that it is insane to try to evade the spiritual and governmental implications of that fact; that as democracy could not exist if a multitude of the people were illiterate, so democracy cannot exist if a multitude of the people are economically insecure, and that society therefore must take responsibility for at least a minimum economic security as it does for a minimum education; that in consequence the old, brutal, economic "catch-as-catch-can" must go and a more decently humane and co-operative order be established; that on this continent, lured by the most amazing opportunities for material success which any people ever faced, we have been deceived by the outward shows of prosperity and must learn again that unless a people's faith and character, their shared good fortune and mutual goodwill are healthy, there can be nothing sound at all.

Well, this audience does not need from me a long rehearsal of true ideas in the air. What we do need is a fresh vision of the overcoming power in those ideas if we will have it so. In every generation the future has belonged to ideas in the air. They crucified Jesus but one thing they could not do—injure his idea. Not a nail they drove pierced it; not a stone they rolled before his tomb imprisoned it. Here is the realistic basis of social hope that, when once a great idea is started, no one can stop it. If you crucify it, you glorify it. If you bury it, you give it an Easter Day. If you postpone its victory, you only make the more overwhelming its victory when it comes.

My chief concern is not for the ultimate victory of good. My chief concern is lest in my generation I should somehow miss being used by the great ideas. For at this sermon's end, as at its beginning, one is haunted by that court scene in Jerusalem. How typical it is of history! All the educated, well-born, worldly-wise, prosperous men there were on the wrong side of the supreme issue of their time, and on the right side were two humble men of lowly station whom in retrospect we honor now because they helped lead mankind around one of the most significant corners in its history, and who, somewhere today, I trust, are grateful for the idea that used them.

The Great Hours of a Man's Life

IN THE twelfth chapter of Second Corinthians, Paul describes one of the great hours in his experience: "I know a man in Christ, fourteen years ago (whether in the body, I know not; or whether out of the body, I know not; God knoweth), such a one caught up even to the third heaven. And I know such a man (whether in the body, or apart from the body, I know not; God knoweth), how that he was caught up into Paradise, and heard unspeakable words, which it is not lawful for a man to utter." That must have been a high hour of insight and vision, and described though it is in ancient symbolism, we all know at least a little what it means. Our spiritual lives, too, have times when vision clears, and doubt and cynicism go, and our souls are kindled and aflame. We may prefer Browning's way of describing them—

moments,
Sure tho' seldom, ...
When the spirit's true endowments
Stand out plainly from its false ones—

but however we may describe them, we know what such experiences mean.

Now at the time when Paul recalled that great hour of his he was in one of the most despondent periods of his life—not having a great hour at all. In the verses immediately preceding, he recounts his tribulations—labor and travail, hunger and thirst, cold and nakedness, and, "Besides those things that are without," he adds, "that which presseth upon me daily, anxiety for all the churches." Paul is in a down hour. In words that suggest our situation now, he describes his time. "Quarrels," he says, "jealousy, temper, rivalry, slanders, gossiping, arrogance, and disorder." Such, in this very chapter, is Paul's list of the evils of his time.

Then into the midst of his discouraging present he interjects a factor that makes all the difference in the world to him. His high hours and what they have taught him, come back to him. Fourteen years before, he recalls one of them when vision cleared and the eternal verities were surely seen. Like a sailor on a foggy day having a tough time, he remembers his clear days when far horizons could be seen. And as one reads this worried letter, written out of a disheartening present, one sees this thing at least that is saving the man and making him rememberable yet across the centuries: he is believing the testimony of his best hours against the testimony of his worst hours as to what life really means.

Is not that one of the central problems of human life? Which are we to believe, our best hours or our worst? We have them both. We may be a long way from mystics, not given to spiritual raptures but, matter of fact and pedestrian though our temperaments may be, we do have hours when life seems meaningful, goodness beautiful, love the greatest thing in the world, God real, and the victory of righteousness a possibility worth living and dying for. But then low hours also come. Man's stupidity and brutality are dreadful; they dishearten us. Good plans for peace and decency go awry; wars are won, but disillusionment follows victory, and cynicism seems at times the only realism. This alternation of mood characterizes every life. As the Negro spiritual says,

> Sometimes I'se up, sometimes I'se down,
> Oh, yes, Lord.

A decisive question rises, therefore, on whose answer depends the total meaning of one's life—which do we really believe and trust and base our lives upon, the testimony of the high hours, or of the low?

Surely, we need Paul's secret now. Many of us here are in a low mood, in a depressing year. We have won a war, but what a mess! It is foggy weather on a rough sea for all of us who care about the world, and I, for one, need to remember the clear days when I could see better. This morning let us consider what that might mean to us.

First of all, recall those better hours so that they may be real to us. I do not mean simply happy hours, when all was going well, but better hours, when great things seemed great and life was purposeful, when worth-while endeavors challenged us, and we were our best selves.

One of my boyhood's recollections is my father dealing with me when I was in a bad temper. "Where's Harry?" he would say, and I would answer, "Why, here he is." And he would say to me, "No! You are not Harry. Harry is lost. Go find him. I want Harry!" So, catching his meaning, I would wander off through the house, getting myself under control until, returning, I could face him again, saying, "I've found him. Here he is." Thus my father said to me, as a child, what modern psychology is saying now—that we are not just one self, but varied selves, high and low, good and bad, and that the art of life is to identify oneself with one's best self, and believe and be what that best self affirms. What my father said to me long ago I am trying now to say to myself, in a depressing year when one's best self is sometimes hard to find.

Biography is a running commentary on this matter. Wordsworth, for example, had great hours:

> I have felt
> A presence that disturbs me with the joy
> Of elevated thoughts;—

hours like that!

> While with an eye made quiet by the power
> Of harmony, and the deep power of joy,
> We see into the life of things—

hours like that!

> There are times,
> I doubt not, when to you it doth impart
> Authentic tidings of invisible things—

hours like that!

Wordsworth, however, did not always have such hours. The French Revolution aroused his ardent hopes. To it his faith was given; a brave new era, so he thought, was coming. Then postwar letdown came, disillusioning, frightening, and Wordsworth cried:

I lost
All feeling of conviction, and, in fine,
Sick, wearied out with contrarieties,
Yielded up moral questions in despair.

That's Wordsworth, too! Well, in Wordsworth, as in all of us, there is plenty to criticize—he did not make a perfect score—yet, thinking now of his life's total meaning, here is his glory, that on the whole he stands in mankind's recollection for his best hours, that in the long run what his great days said he believed and caused to be remembered. That is the mark of high character.

Here is a strange mystery in human nature, that with an inner certainty none can deny, we do distinguish our best hours from our worst. Sir Edward Elgar wrote a lot of music, more or less good, but once, in "The Dream of Gerontius," he composed something that he knew was his very best. "This is the best of me," he wrote to a friend, "for the rest, I ate, and drank, and slept, and loved and hated, like another; my life was as the vapour, and is not; *but this I saw and knew*; this, if anything of mine, is worth your memory." Every one of us knows what Elgar meant, and his was Paul's experience over again. Paul knew his best when it came. What he saw on the Damascus Road; what he felt when he wrote the thirteenth chapter of First Corinthians; what he knew when he answered the call of the man of Macedonia, "Come over and help us"; what he beheld when he was, as it were, caught up into the third heaven—that was his best and, come what low moods might, he would believe that, take that for the interpretation of his life. How we need now to make our own that secret of great character!

See now that when we talk thus about what our best hours reveal, we are really talking about essential Christianity. The Christian view of God and man and life's meaning, is the outlook of our best hours. It is when we are crushed and cynical that we say, I cannot believe in a good God and in the Christian way of life. Sometimes we consider that an argument against Christianity. But, friends, that is an argument for Christianity. It is when we are down and out, beaten in spirit and at our worst, that we say we cannot believe in God and his Christ. But when great hours come, and the fog departs and vision clears, then the higher the mood reaches the more possible and real Christian faith appears. This is the stubborn fact on which all attacks on Christianity ultimately go to pieces, that in our best hours the Christian view of life is most real.

So Ernest Renan said, "Man is most religious in his best moments." So Browning sang:

> Faith is my waking life:
> One sleeps, indeed, and dreams at intervals,
> We know, but waking's the main point with us.

So even Tyndall, the nineteenth century scientist, regarded by Christians of his day as a materialist and their mortal enemy, said once about the materialistic philosophy, "I have noticed during years of self-observation, that it is not in hours of clearness and vigor that this doctrine commends itself to my mind."

I should say not! We have low hours when nothing seems real except the physical, but then great hours come and lo! the soul is real again. We have low hours when we feel like crying, There is no God! but then high hours come, when we know that life must be purposeful, divine meaning in it, Providence over it, God in control of it. We have low hours when man seems only an educated brute, but then great hours come when love of man grows real again and we see him as a child of God, appallingly wayward, but with his sonship still the deepest fact about him. I am appealing now to no ecclesiastical or creedal authority but to the authority of our own enlightened hours. It is they which bear witness to the truth of Christ.

One of the strangest statements from an early church father is Tertullian's saying that the human soul is "naturally Christian." What can he mean by that? Does not Christianity teach that man is naturally corrupt? Are not the doctrines of original sin and of total depravity, orthodox Christian teaching? How can Tertullian, seeing human nature as he saw it in the brutal days of the Roman Empire, say that the human soul is naturally Christian? But he said it, and what he meant we are trying to say today. Catch man in his best hours and see how Christian his thoughts, his ideals, his aspirations, his convictions are!

We ask too much if we expect not to have low hours. In every realm they come. Would you not say that of all men who ever lived Wordsworth most surely would always respond to nature's beauties? But he didn't!

> There was a time when meadow, grove, and stream,
> The earth, and every common sight,
> To me did seem
> Appareled in celestial light,
> The glory and the freshness of a dream.
> It is not now as it hath been of yore;—
> Turn whereso'er I may,
> By night or day,
> The things which I have seen I now can see no more.

Even in his love of nature Wordsworth had low hours. The question is not whether such times come, but whether, when they come, we are at their mercy. We need not be at their mercy. When they come we can still trust and base our lives upon our hours of insight.

Ah, Paul, you were up against this! "Fourteen years ago," you wrote, remembering back so far to a day of clear vision you could trust. You were a Christian through thick and thin, "in season and out of season," as the letter to Timothy says, because you trusted your enlightened not your darkened hours.

Very pertinent to us now is the third truth with which our theme confronts us, namely, that it is crisis that often calls the great hours out. Throughout this sermon we have spoken of these present days as depressing, but that is not the whole truth. Again and again in history, it is the critical periods that have called out the great hours.

In personal life this is true. Some of us never rise to our great hours until we are up against something difficult. Sidney Lanier, stricken with tuberculosis, was banished from his work to win his hard battle if he could, and there in the crisis of his life he had an unforgettable experience, which he made immortal in his lines about the hour when

> . . . belief overmasters doubt, and I know that I know,
> And my spirit is grown to a lordly great compass
> within.

Crisis can call out great hours.

In every realm this is about the most encouraging aspect of history. We are still playing Hamlet in New York City. We go back yet to that amazing outburst of creative literature in the Elizabethan era. But what an unsettled age it was! Columbus discovered America, and a whole new world was opened up. Twenty-five years after that, Luther nailed his theses to the Cathedral doors at Wittenberg, and the Reformation began its tumultuous career. Wars raged, new adventures were called for, new adjustments demanded. It was an uproarious century. And then, out of that tremendous era came what Tennyson called

> Those melodious bursts that fill
> The spacious times of great Elizabeth
> With sounds that echo still.

What is true in literature is true in every creative realm of the spirit, Crisis can call out great hours.

Let us say this to ourselves now! This is a time for greatness. God grant us statesmen to measure up to it! But if our children, looking back on our days, are going to think of them as a great era in history —crisis turned into opportunity—there must be at the heart of this generation enough individuals who make that response in their own living.

Our Lord himself faced this. He had low hours too. If ever a soul might have been expected to live always on the heights it was he. But not even he could do it. "Now is my soul troubled; and what shall I say? Father, save me from this hour." He too had days of fog on a dangerous sea. He had memorized—mark it—he had memorized the Psalm which begins,

> My God, my God, why hast thou forsaken me?
> Why art thou so far from helping me, and from
> the words of my groaning?

Our Lord was transfigured, we say, until the fashion of his countenance was altered—yes—but only once—once!

> Tasks in hours of insight will'd
> Can be through hours of gloom fulfill'd.

Matthew Arnold said that, but Jesus knew its meaning. To follow in his steps means this too—to believe in our enlightened hours when days are dark and to use crisis, even though it be a cross, to make the great hours come.

So may God grant this inward victory to each of us!

The Mystery of Life

THE older a man grows the more mysterious life becomes to him. We sometimes say to a youth that when he grows up he will know more, but that is a half-truth. In general, an increasing experience of life only deepens the sense of its mystery.

Professor Palmer of Harvard tells of receiving from one of his young students a manuscript with an accompanying letter in which the youth said that he intended to write several books and that this was only the first of them, in which, wrote the youth, "I have explained the universe." You see what it would mean to tell such a youth that when he grows up he will know more. It really means that when he grows up he will know less. He will discover, if he is wise, that life is set in a limitless sea of mystery.

Indeed, in every realm, the more we know the more the mystery grows. The popular idea that science clears up mysteries in the sense that the more science there is the less mystery is left, is a strange inversion of the facts. Modern science makes even the physical universe increasingly mysterious. Our ancient forefathers thought they lived upon a flat and stationary earth, and they were content with simple explanations, while we are on a planet flying eighteen and a half miles per second, with the nearest star twenty-five trillion miles away. There has been an increase of knowledge, but also an increase of mystery. And when one turns from the extensive aspect of science to the intensive and tries to keep up with modern physics and chemistry, what an access of information and what an access of mystery! In one of the last treatises on the new quantum theory of physics, the first sentence is this: "The series of concepts which we now approach are difficult to grasp and still more difficult to explain." I should say so! Professor Jeans, in his amazing book summing up the new knowledge of the world, says that in his opinion "the ultimate realities of the universe are at present quite beyond the reach of science, and may be—and probably are—for ever beyond the comprehension of the human mind."

If that is true about the physical universe, how much more true about our human life! It is a queer business, this human adventure of ours, and the older a man grows the queerer it seems. Everything about it is strange, from birth, where a single cell has carried over on its slender bridge what an amazing weight of inherited possibility from the race behind!—that is queer—until death, when this mysteriously compounded organism dissolves into its elements—which is queerer yet! And in between birth and death, how the loveliness of life snuggles close to its tragedy! A little child, beautiful today, crippled tomorrow; great nations rising to world power and then falling like houses of sand built by children on the shore, when the tides of destiny flow in; great servants of the public good blotted out while some old roué drags on his worse-than-useless life; righteousness and rottenness; beautiful homes and insane asylums; glorious creative work and unemployment; the laughter of little children and three hundred burned to death in a prison—it is a queer business! And all around this human queerness on the earth that unfathomable ocean of universal mystery in which we are enisled and to which there is no end:

> And though thy soul sail leagues and leagues beyond,—
> Still, leagues beyond those leagues, there is more sea.

We succeed in getting on happily most of the time without bothering about this too much. We absorb ourselves in immediate tasks. We get our academic degrees; we succeed in business; we fall in love; we take care of our children; we improve our golf score; we take life as it comes and make the best of it. We are not always vividly conscious of the abysmal mystery of life, but it is always there. It is the abiding background of life, and ever and again something happens—great love, great tragedy, a child's birth, a friend's death, a blind alley where a man has to stop and think, a meditative day in the country even, when imagination spreads its wings and flies—something happens and we lift our eyes to see the mystery of life.

Now, mystery is dangerous; it can do things to us. Remember the old maps of the sea before Columbus and Magellan! Those unsailed seas were unknown and so were peopled with nameless horrors, monstrous sea creatures. Like children frightened in the dark, man has always been afraid of the unknown. Even in a mystery play today, let the stage be darkened and out of it some weird sound come, and the hair of even the intelligent will fairly stand on end. Mystery can do things to us, and mystery is doing things to many folk today. Cynicism, disillusionment, anxiety, fear—how often the thousand and one maladies of haunted lives come from emotional reaction to the mystery of life!

If some one protests that science has illumined many areas and driven off specters of the imagination that once frightened man, I agree. Many an ancient superstition that used to terrify men has retreated before the face of light, but, for all that science has done or can do, we still face mystery. Indeed, it was a scientist who said that all our modern knowledge is like a bonfire at night; we pile on the fuel and let the flames leap high, thereby increasing the area of illumination, to be sure, but increasing also the area of darkness that the light impinges on. More light makes more mystery visible.

What is out there in the unknown, and what should be our attitude toward it?

Obviously, the first lesson to be drawn from the mysteriousness of life is distrust of dogmatism. Whenever you see any one standing over against the mystery of life, whipping off finalities as though he could settle it, distrust that man. Indeed, let us make our distrust of dogmatism comprehensive so that it includes both dogmatic religionist and dogmatic irreligionist. Today in intelligent circles, the dogmatic religionist is fairly well outlawed. He is laughed at for his pains. Listen, for example, to a recent exhibition of an obsolete attitude and see how ridiculous it is. Let us take it from our own church family, lest we be suspected of laughing at some one else. Says a narrowly sectarian paper: "Baptists have the whole truth. Nobody else has. West Kentucky Baptists come nearer standing for the whole truth and all the truth than any other set of Baptists in this round world." Ah, you West Kentucky Baptists, how the world has waited for you! Even East Kentucky Baptists, marvelous as they are, have never discovered the truth of life as you have! No, in all intelligent circles, the day of that kind of thing in religion is going.

But, strangely enough, the day of that kind of thing in irreligion seems to be coming. Visiting a college campus sometime ago, I found the students in reaction against dogmatism in matters of religion. Ah! you say, just so; you cannot force religion dogmatically upon this younger generation. But, my friend, on that campus the shoe was on the other foot altogether. Those students were not reacting against a dogmatism that favored religion; they were reacting against a dogmatism that scorned religion. On that campus, long since, the department of religion had learned its lesson. It was intelligent; it was not dogmatic. There were, however, other chairs where little men were whipping out final solutions of the eternal mystery. No God—by no possibility anything like God! Mechanism—that was the magic secret which unsnarled all tangles and solved all mysteries. Human life upon this planet was an affair of chance! The heat happened to be just right at one stage of the planet's cooling and so life came, and out of life personality, and out of personality some amazing things, to be sure, but no God, nothing like God!

My friends, when we say today, Distrust dogmatism, we must mean in particular that kind of dogmatism, for in so-called intelligent circles it is much more common than religious dogmatism is. The spirit of the West Kentucky Baptists is not confined to West Kentucky. And, strangely enough, it particularly emerges in the field of irreligion.

There is one motto, on which great men of science and great men of faith would agree, that might well be hung upon the wall of every church and of every college classroom: "The more we know about the universe, the more mysterious it is."

This acknowledgment that our life is surrounded by mystery disturbs some religious people. Indeed, some one here this morning may be saying: This does not sound like the Bible; the Bible speaks with confidence, certainty, finality; give us the Bible! Very well, listen:

> Canst thou by searching find out God?
> Canst thou find out the Almighty unto perfection?
> It is high as heaven; what canst thou do?
> Deeper than Sheol; what canst thou know?

That is the Bible. "Righteous art thou, O Jehovah, when I contend with thee; yet would I reason the cause with thee; wherefore doth the way of the wicked prosper? wherefore are all they at ease that deal very treacherously?" That is the Bible. "My God, my God, why hast thou forsaken me?" That is the Bible. "How unsearchable are his judgments, and his ways past tracing out!" That is the Bible. "At present we only see the baffling reflections in a mirror." That is the Bible.

Indeed, we may well take that last for our text. It comes from Dr. Moffatt's translation of the thirteenth chapter of First Corinthians. The old version said, "Now we see through a glass, darkly," but this is much nearer to the original: "At present we only see the baffling reflections in a mirror."

That is true; life is full of mystery. Yet we should be thankful for that very fact. Suppose there were no mystery. That would mean that you and I can comprehend the universe completely: but that, in turn, would mean that the universe is so thin and small that it can be comprehended by little minds like ours. The universe is far too marvelous for that. It is high; it is deep, our minds, developing for a few millennia upon this planet, cannot grasp it. It is not so pitifully small that we can understand it—let us be grateful for that! I would rather live in a world where my life is surrounded by mystery than live in a world so small that my mind could comprehend it.

That is the first thing so say: Distrust dogmatism and be grateful that this universe is not so shallow that our little plummets can touch bottom.

The second thing to say is this: Wherever a mystery has been cleared up, the truth has turned out to be more marvelous than anybody had dared to dream—mark it!—*more* marvelous, not less. The flat and stationary earth on which our ancestors thought they lived presented a mystery: what did it rest on? Some people said that it rested on an elephant and that the elephant stood on a turtle. One old Hebrew poet, who wrote the Book of Job, said: "He . . . hangeth the earth upon nothing." That was a leap of insight, and yet a flat and stationary earth that rests on nothing is a mystery. Now, that mystery has been cleared up and the truth that cleared it up turned out to be so marvelous, beyond anything that man had dared to dream, that it took many a year before mankind could believe it—the earth not flat, round; not stationary, traveling six hundred million miles a year around the sun, and the whole solar system but an item in an immeasurable cosmos held together by gravitation. You see, wherever a mystery has been cleared up, the truth has proved to be more marvelous than folk had dared to think.

Fossils used to be a mystery. Those strange stone bugs and things in the strata of the earth—how did they get there? Some even said that God had deliberately put them there to perplex man's mind and test his faith. Well, the mystery of fossils has been cleared up and the truth that cleared it up, the long leisureliness of creation, slowly laying the foundations of the earth, and the eonic story of life's evolution, is so marvelous that some folk yet cannot believe it. This has always been so: whenever a mystery has been cleared up, the truth lay, not on this side of our imaginations but far beyond. This world always turns out to be more wonderful than any one had thought.

That is one basic reason why some of us approach the mystery of life with positiveness and triumph. To take a negative and timid attitude toward the unknown in a world where the unknown, when it is cleared up, has always turned out to be more marvelous than we had dreamed—that is irrational.

In my youth I studied the old physics. Now we have Einstein and Eddington. This world *is* more marvelous than we had thought. Some of our children come home talking familiarly about the fourth dimension. Undoubtedly it is here. We live in three dimensions only, but there is a fourth. Our ears tune in on a narrow scale of sound, but endless soundwaves must be above and below. Our eyes tune in on a small spectrum of color, but wide ranges of vision must be unguessed by us. Always the mystery has turned out to be filled, not by ghosts and hobgoblins, but by marvels.

Can we really think of the spiritual life of man as the solitary exception to this rule? My friends, this universe is more spiritually significant than any of us have ever dared to think—*I* stake my faith on that!

Indeed, it is not even a matter of what we ordinarily call faith.

For consider: whenever a mystery has been cleared up, there always has been an adequate explanation. Facts are never left high and dry in the air without an adequate explanation when any mystery is cleared up. When perturbations appeared in the orbit of the planet Uranus, astronomers said there must be an explanation for these perturbations. No explanation was in sight. They said there must be an explanation and they guessed another planet whose location they figured out. But no such planet was yet known. Then they searched both the sky and their star maps more carefully and discovered it—the planet Neptune. Whenever a mystery is cleared up there is always an adequate explanation. That is the kind of universe we live in.

Do you really mean that man's spiritual life is the only exception, that personality with all its possibilities and its achievements is but a fortuitous result of the heat's happening to be right at one stage of the planet's cooling? Nonsense, my friends! That is not dealing seriously with the law of adequate causation. There are facts here, prodigious facts which cannot be brushed aside like that: personality, the most amazing fact in the universe, self-conscious being with powers of memory and reflection, intelligence, purposefulness, and love; spiritual life, glorious life in Christlike souls, where beauty and truth have flowered out into bloom and fragrance; progress from some stone age to hopes of international goodwill and brotherhood; creative power to produce beauty, discover truth, achieve goodness—prodigious facts. And there is an explanation. Unless this universe is crazy, and it never yet has turned out to be crazy, there is an explanation. Moreover, there is an *adequate* explanation.

For one, therefore, I go out into this mysterious life with a song. There is an explanation. The mystery is one of light and not of darkness. I know the explanation only in bits. "At present we only see the baffling reflections in a mirror," but there is an explanation. For this strange human life with its hopes and tragedies, for this vast cosmos, the queer home of our adventure, there is an explanation.

If you say our ideas of God, as the explanation, are inadequate, we know that. "Canst thou by searching find out God?" The trouble is that our ideas are so far short of the reality. The truth is much more marvelous than we have dared to think. That is the second thing to say: that the mystery of life is not full of fear but of marvel, and that this universe is more spiritually significant than we have yet imagined.

The third thing to say is that in the meantime there is light enough to live by. Though we are often baffled and perplexed so that like Wordsworth we go off to some Tintern Abbey, feeling the "burthen of the mystery" and

> . . . the heavy and the weary weight
> Of all this unintelligible world,

when we come to our best hours and pull ourselves together, there is light enough to live by—decently with ourselves, kindly with our neighbors, courageously in our troubles—light enough to be at least a little radiant within and, without, to help build a fairer social order where personality may flourish.

Indeed, remember that our text comes from the thirteenth chapter of First Corinthians. Has it ever occurred to anybody that that chapter sounds baffled and perplexed? Upon the contrary, it is a triumphant song about those abiding values that a man can depend on and live by gloriously: faith, and hope, and love. Yet at the heart of that chapter you will find everything we have been talking about this morning. Paul says that our vaunted knowledge will disappear, that now we know in part and prophesy in part, and that when full knowledge comes our knowledge will vanish away. Paul says that sometime we shall see face to face but now we see only the baffling reflections in a mirror. Like all large minds, Paul felt the mystery of life, but he found something else here too: light, glorious light to live by—"Now abideth faith, hope, love."

Our morning's thought would be alike incomplete and unchristian without this truth. What is it that our religion does for us, anyway? Does it clear up the mysteries? Of course not. More harm has been done than wise work will undo for many a year by preachers who have pretended to clear up the mystery of life. Think of a preacher proposing to clear up the intellectual and moral perplexities of a cosmos like this! Think of a preacher tackling the problem of a world where little children are born defective, where whole races, like the Aztecs, rise and fall and pass away, and leave hardly a memory behind, where human life is battered by unequal and cruel circumstance, where today if you are born in India you have an average chance of living twenty-two years and if you are born in the United States you have an average chance of living sixty eight years—tackling a cosmos where the loveliest life was crucified, to clear up the mystery! No, our religion does not clear up the mystery or give us a formula to answer all questions. Upon the contrary, at the heart of our religion is the deepest mystery of all, the cross, where love was nailed to a tree by hate. But what our religion does do is to give us a kind of life, and power withal to sustain it, that can be lived joyously, triumphantly, in the midst of the mystery. It gives us light enough to walk by: faith, and hope, and love.

That is why we Christians so rejoice that the center of our religious life is not a proposition but a person. Propositions to clear up the mystery are of all things most temporary. But a person who faced all the bafflements that you and I face, hated, deserted, crucified even, and yet who, through it all and above it all, lived victoriously and when the final mystery was closing in upon him said, "These things have I spoken unto you, that my joy may be in you, and that your joy may be made full"—a triumphant character like that throws such illumination on our path that we have done well to call him "the light of the world."

You and I are going out from this church to our work again. Somehow or other, mystery or no mystery, we must manage to carry on with this business of living. How many of us here have been depleting our energies for that high task by negative reactions to the mystery of life? It is easy for a man to think himself into the depths by saying habitually to himself, Life is so puzzling, so bewildering, has so many baffling problems, unsolved riddles, unanswered questions; why? . . . why? . . . why? My friends, there are other souls, triumphant souls, who find life just as mysterious as you do but who have found something else. Remember Pompilia in Browning's "Ring and the Book." She faced a mystery dark and cruel enough. But you will recall her saying about a beautiful life that had singularly blessed hers,

> . . . Through such souls alone
> God stooping shows sufficient of his light
> For us i' the dark to rise by. And I rise.

That is the essence of the gospel. We say it about Christ:

> God stooping shows sufficient of his light
> For us i' the dark to rise by.

The Power to See It Through*

THERE is one character in the New Testament, mentioned only three times, concerning whom one suspects that many Christians have not even heard. His name was Demas and, alas, some of us are much more like him than like the great New Testament figures we know so well. First, in Paul's letter to Philemon, we read, "Demas, Luke, my fellow-workers." So Demas, along with Luke, and named first at that, was standing by Paul in his Roman imprisonment, a devoted and promising disciple. Second, in Paul's letter to the Colossians, we read, "Luke, the beloved physician, and Demas." Reading that, one wonders why Demas and Luke, who were praised together at the first, were separated in this passage as though Luke indeed retained Paul's confidence as "the beloved physician" but Demas had become merely "Demas." Third, in the Second letter to Timothy, incorporating, we suppose, one of the last messages Paul ever wrote, we read, "Demas forsook me, having loved this present age." Three points on a curve, that enable us to plot its graph! For here is the story of a man who made a fine beginning and a poor ending: Demas, my fellow-worker; Demas; Demas forsook me.

One's imagination plays about this condensed biography, especially the relationships between Demas and Luke. Intimate companions of Paul in the Roman circle, they must have known each other very well. Now, Luke is the only narrator of Jesus' life whose gospel records the parable about the man who started to build a tower and was not able to finish. Matthew did not remember that, nor Mark, nor John; only Luke recalled it. One wonders if he remembered it because of Demas. Demas was slipping, let us say. Through Paul's little group in the Roman prison anxious apprehension ran that Demas was not holding

* A New Year's Sermon.

out, and one imagines Luke pleading with his friend. The Master himself, he might have said, warned his first disciples about the peril which is besetting you. For once he said, "Which of you, desiring to build a tower, doth not first sit down and count the cost, whether he hath wherewith to complete it? Lest haply, when he hath laid a foundation, and is not able to finish, all that behold begin to mock him, saying, This man began to build, and was not able to finish." So one thinks of Luke pleading with his friend, and at least Luke, alone among the evangelists, put the parable into his gospel. He had seen its truth too vividly illustrated in the life of a friend ever to forget it. Demas, my fellow-worker; Demas; Demas forsook me.

As one considers this familiar experience of a fine beginning and a poor ending, it is obvious, for one thing, that the qualities which make a good start possible are not identical with the qualities that see life through to the end. Starting power and staying power are not the same thing in any realm. A ship can make a grand getaway at the launching only to make a poor stand later against the fury of the waves and winds when the northeasters are unleashed. So one sees in Demas a character—how familiar!—capable of fine impulses, generous responses, idealistic loyalties, and eager loves; only he lacked staying power.

One thinks of this not simply because of the New Year season, which is naturally a festival of fresh beginnings, but because our generation, above every other generation in history, has stressed the gospel of a good start. How we have emphasized the importance of childhood and of the influences that play on childhood! To give a child a good start, we have said, is the most essential benediction that can be bestowed upon a human life. So we have thought and accordingly have labored. Now, that gospel of a good start is profoundly important and it tells the truth; only, not the whole truth. For many of us here had a good start. We have no complaints about that. In family and church, in school and early Christian training, we had a fine beginning. But for all that, some of us are Demas and all of us know we could have been. Over what thin ice have we skated! How easily we could have broken through! How many of us here have already fallen far from a faith that once was strong and a character that once was clean. We know Demas. The mirror shows him to us. Introspection reveals the process of his downfall. Nearly two thousand years ago he lived and died, his very name barely preserved, as though by accident, and yet how vivid he is in our imaginations! Demas, my fellow-worker; Demas; Demas forsook me, having loved this present age.

Another general truth concerns our thought: namely, that however beautiful one's start, nothing matters much in human life without a good ending. Of course one does not mean that we may demand an outwardly successful and fortunate conclusion, as in old sentimental novels where everything had to come out all right. But without a *good* end, without morale and staying power and steady character to see a man through to a worthy conclusion what else in human life can be much worth while? Jesus could have spoiled everything in the Garden of Gethsemane and, had he done that, all for nothing would have gone his unremembered Sermon on the Mount and his unselfish months of ministry. The career of Jesus was like splitting a log. Every previous blow of the ax is indispensable but it is the last blow that splits it. So we know there was a Christ, and the rich meanings of his ministry have come to us because he had staying power to go through to the end, where he could say, "It is finished."

What would you consider the most lamentable tragedy in human life? To face suffering, to be cruelly handicapped? Surely not! For we have seen some terribly handicapped people who had moral staying power so that they came through to a great conclusion, all their flags flying when they came into port. But there is a tragedy so appalling that when one has seen it in the circle of one's friends the very reminiscence of it makes one's blood run cold—to be so fortunately born, to have so glorious a boyhood, to rise to such responsible position, to be so loved, so trusted, and then to crack as though all the time the shining metal had had a flaw in it, to betray one's trust, deceive one's friends, blow out one's brains! You see, whether it be in dramatic fashion like that or in homelier wise, where a fine beginning lapses by slow degrees into a disheveled ending, Demas is the tragedy.

In this regard life is like marriage. How beautifully love begins!

With what romantic launchings can it get its start! But we elders, who watch the young folks at their lovemaking and their weddings, habitually ask a deeper question. They have qualities that can start a home; have they the qualities that can keep one—the deep fidelity, the long-term loyalty, the steady and abiding love that can keep a home? For in marriage, as in all life, a good beginning only makes more tragic an unhappy end.

On this first Sunday of the New Year, therefore, let us talk together not about starting power—there is no soul here that has not more than once made a fine beginning—but about staying power. I celebrate the qualities of faith and character that enable a man to see life through.

For one thing, staying power is always associated with a certain central integrity of conscience. Whatever else life may give or may deny, one thing is absolutely indispensable to a man—that he should not break faith with himself, that he should not inwardly be a failure. Such quality of conscience, making it indispensable that a man live on high terms with himself, whatever happens, is of the essence of staying power, and it is the glory of great artists that so commonly in their art they have exhibited it. Elsner was a teacher of music in Warsaw to whom came, one day, a young man for music lessons, and at the end of the first term one finds this in Elsner's record: "Lessons in musical composition: Chopin, Fryderyk, third year student—amazing capabilities, musical genius." That was a fine start. But to finish that career was costly. It cost hard work—one would take that for granted. It cost discouraged hours—one would expect that. Once Chopin was so disheartened he talked of turning to interior decorating instead of music. But, deeper yet, Chopin's career cost conscience. He would not, for popularity's sake, write music that violated his own interior standards. One thing was absolutely indispensable, no matter what happened: he must not break faith musically with himself. So Chopin became "Chopin." As another put it, "the artist's conscience is a fearful thing."

Now, as we see Paul and Demas in Rome, it is obvious Paul had *that*. He would have liked outward good fortune and success could he have had them on honorable terms—of course he would! But whether fortune or misfortune befell, one thing was absolutely indispensable—he must not break faith with himself and the Christ within him. Not simply as a matter of duty but as a matter of happiness, that was indispensable. Demas, however, was of another sort. He soon found something else that was indispensable. "Demas forsook me," wrote Paul, "having loved this present age." So that was it! Roman civilization was brilliant like our own. It had ugly aspects, but for agile minds and grasping hands there were prizes to be gained. All around Paul's poor prison house was Rome. So Demas, no Chopin in his character, wrote his music down. He did not have an artist's conscience, Christ had never dug so deep as that into Demas. To be loyal to the royal in himself was not absolutely indispensable. He loved this present age.

You see, I am not really talking about Demas now, but about us. One would not minimize the sacrifices that such a conscience as we are speaking of often costs in a world like this, but the great souls who have most possessed such conscience have commonly thought of it not as a burden of duty but as a gospel of liberty. Listen! No man ever needs to be a failure. Trouble, outward breakdown of hopes, may come, but a man who cares most that he should not be a failure can capitalize trouble. "All sunshine," say the Arabs, "makes Sahara." Men may give the hemlock to Socrates, nail Jesus to the cross, behead Paul outside the gates of Rome. Livingstone may die in the heart of Africa, his work unfinished, and Lincoln may be shot by a crazy man. All such souls have known an inner liberty. Whatever happened, they did not need to *be* failures. That was within their control. Still they could be loyal to the royal in themselves and come to their last port with their flags a flying.

That is the final difference between people. Paul faced many kinds of failure but he himself was no failure. If, however, the old legend is correct, Demas went back to Thessalonica and became a priest of idols in a pagan temple. He himself was a failure.

In the second place, staying power is always associated with the experience of being captured by a cause, laid hold on by something greater than oneself to which one gives one's loyalty—an art, a science, a vocation, a social reform, an object of devotion which one conceives to be more important than oneself. This was the common property of those to whom we have turned as illustrations of persistent character—Chopin in music, Socrates in philosophy, Livingstone as a missionary, Lincoln as a statesman with a cause. They all cared for something so much superior to themselves, to which they gave their long-term loyalty, that they stood the gaff, as we say, so far as their individual fortunes were concerned, and followed through to a strong conclusion for their cause's sake. All staying power in character is associated with that.

Christ had never gotten so deep as that into Demas. Demas had laid hold on some of the more comfortable aspects of the Christian gospel, but the Christian gospel had never laid hold on Demas. Demas had possessed himself of this or that detail of Christ's message, but Christ had not possessed himself of Demas. So the man's Christianity was a superstructure easily put up, easily taken down—jerry-building on slim foundations. For the foundation of enduring character is always laid in something greater than oneself which one will serve through life and death.

There is a fascinating contrast between two phrases in the New Testament: the first, Paul's description of Demas—"having loved this present age"; the second, the description of a true Christian in the Epistle to the Hebrews as one who has "tasted the . . . powers of the age to come." So, *that* is the difference, as the New Testament sees it. An apostate is a man who loves the *status quo*, this present age; a Christian is a man who has tasted the powers, been laid hold on by the hopes, of the age to come.

When some one tries to tell you that the Christian social gospel is a modern innovation not in the New Testament, face him with that. The Christian social gospel is in the very heart of the New Testament—set, to be sure, in mental frameworks appropriate to the first century and different from ours but indubitably there. The primary emphasis on the Kingdom of God in Jesus' teaching and in the first church was so dominant that they tested Christian discipleship by it. A man who loved this present age was an apostate; a man who had tasted the powers of the age to come was a Christian. Whenever we see a New Testament Christian carrying through to the finish, one fact is always apparent: he had set his devotion on a coming Kingdom of God on earth for which he was willing to live or die.

The upshot is that one often sees today outside the church men who seem closer of kin to New Testament Christianity than many inside the churches. Sometimes a downright unbelieving scientist who gives himself to his science and for the sake of humanity stands by it, serving it through thick and thin to the end, seems closer to a New Testament Christian than many of us in the churches. At any rate, he has tasted the powers of the age to come.

Or here is a man who puts his conscience above narrow nationalism, who not simply on Sunday, as in the Navy, but every day runs the white flag of the gospel to the top of the mast with the Stars and Stripes under it. He will no longer subjugate his conscience before God to the mad paganism of nationalistic policies that even now, by old familiar steps, are leading mankind to another holocaust. Such a man may be, and often is, very disturbing but he is closer akin to a New Testament Christian than many in our churches. At least he has tasted the powers of the age to come.

Or here is a man who will not surrender to the abominable and often savage pressures of racial prejudice. He knows that in God's eyes the sons and daughters of mankind are not seen in terms of their skin's color or their ethnic origin. He cannot deny what both his conscience and his intelligence affirm, that despite our outdated discrimination and segregation the future belongs to mankind conceived as one family under the fatherhood of God. This difficult and disturbing conviction he holds to and, what is more, he puts into practice. He may be an irritating neighbor in our bitterly prejudiced world, but he is much nearer New Testament Christianity than many of us are. He has tasted the powers of the age to come.

I suspect that this is the outstanding challenge to us in the churches—our attitude not on theological questions but on practical, ethical, social questions. We find it easy to love this present age. We make fine beginnings, especially at New Year's time, but then some comfortable corner of this present age invites us and we nestle down. So our Christian profession lapses, our faith grows formal, and we do not amount to much in the end as Christians. If I should accuse some of you of being Judas Iscariot you would be indignant. You would never deliberately sell anybody out. But Demas—ah, my soul, how many of us have been that!

Finally, staying power is commonly associated with profound resources of interior strength replenished by great faiths. There is a phrase in the Bible on which a colleague of mine once preached a sermon entitled "An Appalling Alternative"—"I had fainted, unless I had believed." That is true of life. We do faint, peter out, go flat, lose our morale unless our interior resources are replenished by faith in something. We may be sure that Demas, before he left Paul, had lost some of his first convictions about Christ and the God whom Christ revealed.

Suppose that some one should ask you what your faith in the Christian God really does for you. What would you say? For one thing, I should say that when a man believes in God he does not need to worry about the universe any more. That is off our hands if God has it on his. If I imagined the universe as without any God, aimless, purposeless, an accidental dance of atoms, spiritually meaningless, then I would worry about it. As Carlyle said, a cosmos like that is "one huge, dead, immeasurable Steam-engine, rolling on, in its dead indifference to grind me from limb from limb." But if a man believes in God, that is off his mind. He can concentrate upon the task in hand, get on with his moral business here on earth with some high hopes about its outcome, and not be haunted by a huge, cosmic apprehension.

Deeper yet, a vital faith in God means a faith in an eternal moral purpose in the light of which a thousand years are as yesterday when it is past and as a watch in the night. That gives a man wide horizons, long outlooks, steady hopes, so that when people lose heart over the disappointment of some immediate expectation, such faith still has standing ground and carries on. Of all mad things in history can you think of anything madder, with Nero upon his throne and Paul in his prison, than to have believed that the gospel for which Paul stood would outlast and wear down the empire? That is, of course, what "got" Demas: the tremendous power of Rome on its eternal hills, with its inveterate and triumphant evils, against the seeming weakness of Christ's gospel. Who in a sober and realistic hour could have supposed that Paul would outwear Nero? But that, you see, is exactly what happened. A man who has faith in God always expects that to happen, though it take a thousand years. So, of course, he carries on.

Deeper yet, a vital faith in God gives a man available resources of interior power. We never produce power. We always appropriate it. That is true from the harnessing of Niagara to eating a dinner or taking a walk in the fresh air. We never create power; we assimilate it. So, a man with a real faith in God senses around his spiritual life a spiritual presence as truly as the physical world is around his body, and as truly from that divine companionship he draws replenished strength. He knows the deep wells of staying power.

I celebrate the resources of a Christian faith to see a man through.

If faith in God means such things, how do men live life through without it? How do they meet the shocks of fate, the ugliness of evil, the shame of man's inhumanity to man, the disheartenment of moral failure, the impact of personal sorrow, and still keep their morale? I celebrate the resources of Christian faith.

Technically I know little or nothing about music. I venture this comment, however, about the difference between the best of the old music and the ordinary run of the new. The trouble with so much of the new music, as an older man at least sees it, is not its noisy cacophony but something deeper; it never seems to believe in anything enough so that it thinks it worth while to say it over and over again. It picks up a trivial theme and drops it. It never goes through with anything. It lacks sustained convictions. It is fulfilled with unimportant discontinuities. But when one hears a great symphony by Tschaikowsky, let us say, or Beethoven, *there* are convictions so profoundly believed that the music goes through with them to the very end. One says to himself, Surely that theme has been said as beautifully as ever it can be said. Yet that theme returns again and again, elevated and resplendent beyond our dream. A man says to himself. Now, surely, all the possibilities have been exhausted and, lo, at last the theme marches back once more into the music glorious like an army with banners. Whatever may be your judgment about music, great living is like that. Is there anything a man could wish for his friends at New Year's time better than a life like that—great convictions which life develops, expands, elevates, and glorifies, fine at the beginning, loveliest of all at the last? And is there anything that a man could better pray against for himself or his friends than the opposite?—Demas, my fellow-worker; Demas; Demas forsook me.

On Catching the Wrong Bus

RECENTLY the newspapers carried the story of a man who boarded a bus with the full intention and desire of going to Detroit, but when at the end of a long trip he alighted at the destination, he found himself, not in Detroit, but in Kansas City. He had caught the wrong bus. Something like that goes on habitually in human life. People on the whole desire good things—happiness, fine family life, competence in their work, the respect of their friends, an honorable old age. Nothing is more common in our consciously held desires and intentions than such good goals, but after a long trip, how many, alighting at the destination, find themselves somewhere else altogether!

That man who started for Detroit and landed in Kansas City would not at first believe it. Stepping from the bus, he asked for Woodward Avenue, and, told there was no Woodward Avenue, he was indignant. He knew his Detroit; there was a Woodward Avenue; and protesting against inhospitable failure to direct him, it was some time before he could face the fact that despite the clarity of his desire and his intention, it was not Detroit. He had caught the wrong bus.

The Prodigal Son did not start out for a swine pasture. His desire was centered on happiness, freedom, independence, adventure —good goals, that he could justify to himself, his family and friends. Such was the admirable destination he proposed for himself and started out for, but alas! the means he chose landed him somewhere else altogether.

Life is full of this experience. These charming young couples one marries week after week all desire lovely families, and, reading their hearts in their eyes, one sees the fair dreams they cherish of the homes they plan, and of the children they hope for. But as the decades pass the minister sees so many marriages he celebrates start for Utopia, and end in Reno, that he finds himself at the marriage service offering a homely prayer that no one hears: God grant they may catch the right bus!

This truth that the destination we reach depends not on our ideals alone but on the bus we catch, is personally critical. For the most part we do desire good things: happy homes, respectable characters, an honorable standing in our fellows' eyes, useful lives not untouched by the spirit of Christ's unselfishness, and, if God wills, an old age unashamed. Say your worst about us, we have fine desires for good destinations. But often we let it go at that, contenting ourselves with these unimpeachable ideals that we think represent our real selves, whereas the critical question rises: Are we on the road that leads where we want to go, now, this morning, in our immediate, practical habits and choices? Are we on the right bus?

Never before in history, for example, did more people than now desire a great good thing, a world organized for peace and free from the curse of war. That destination we all want to reach, but multitudes, sharing that desire, are not facing the other issue—the road that leads to it, the cost of it in the surrender of old ideas of national sovereignty and old practices of imperialistic exploitation, the new outlooks required, the rethinking of our economic life, the profound moral regeneration which alone can make it possible. More than anything else I dread living to see this generation, so desperately wanting a world brotherhood of peoples, landing somewhere else altogether because it took the wrong bus.

In one of his most familiar sayings Jesus summed this matter up. We commonly think of Jesus as presenting us with the high ideals we ought to set our hearts upon, but he did not forget this other matter. "Narrow is the gate, and straitened the way, that leadeth unto life, and few are they that find it." That's it! To desire life, full, abundant, happy, free—when Jesus talks about that goal, saying, "I came that they may have life, and may have it abundantly," we find it easy to desire, but are we willing to face the road that leads to it? "Narrow is the gate, and straitened the way, that leadeth unto life."

For one thing, in this saying of Jesus we confront the serious implications of a law-abiding universe. It is one thing to desire a great goal; it is another thing to fulfill the conditions of reaching it, and the conditions must be fulfilled. By no trick or magic can we reach the right place on the wrong bus—not in God's world!

Despite our boasted science multitudes still believe in magic, something for nothing, great ends reached without meeting the conditions. They know that is not true in the physical world, but in the spiritual realm they still think they can get away with it. At this point the Christian preacher faces a baffling problem. What can the preacher do on Sunday except present great ideas about life, high ideals for life, deep resources in life, Christ exalted as the one toward whose perfection we should strive? And if the preacher does it well there is response; we do consent to the grandeur and nobility of such ideals. But then look at the buses we get on that do not lead that way at all!

Forgive me, then, for speaking about this simple, practical, close-at-home matter today. I am tired of saying in general that as Christians our high ideal is to be Christlike, and having everyone agree, but then seeing what often comes of it, that while folk may choose that ideal as the end they seek, the means which alone can lead to it they do not choose; the disciplines, the spiritual companionships, the daily habits, the practical methods of life that alone make Christlikeness possible they do not make their own. What is the use of their idealism therefore? It is not the ideal of getting to Detroit that gets you there, but the right bus. I shall be content to preach this sermon if just one person here, checking the bus he is on, discovers that it is not going to the place he wants to land in, and changes to another.

From its first founding I have been interested in Alcoholics Anonymous, an amazing organization of men and women, all of whom were once hopeless slaves of drink and who now, recovered to sobriety and self-control, are banded together to help their fellow victims. As one sees them, splendid, admirable people, one knows that they never set out for that dreadful place they landed in. They had fine ideals, good intentions for happy, respected, useful lives and families, and one often wonders how they ever expected to get to the place they wanted to be, on the bus they chose to travel on.

Do not misunderstand me to be belittling the importance of fine ideals. They are important. A lecturer recently, with an engagement to speak in a certain city arrived on a train that was late. He jumped from the train into a taxi and said to the chauffeur, "Drive fast, step on it!" And the taxi driver did. He stepped on it. And when after some fifteen minutes, speeding through the streets and skidding around corners, the lecturer said, "Well, aren't we about there?" the taxi driver said, "I don't know, sir. You never told me where we were to go." Some people are like that, busy, hectic, with no determining aim to guide their hurried lives. Many, however—and one suspects that more of them are here today—are of another sort altogether. They do have fine ideals, grand intentions in general for their lives and families, but alas! they have never faced up to the basic meaning of a law-abiding universe where no idealistic desire alone ever yet carried anyone to any good destination on the wrong bus. Such folk need to confront, not so much the question of fine aims and high ideals, as the question concerning the road they are practically traveling today. Ask any scientist in his laboratory about this. He wants something; above all else he wants to discover something and get somewhere; there are thousands of ways of missing it, just one way of finding it, one set of conditions to be fulfilled if he is ever to achieve it. Do we suppose that that fact applies in the physical realm and not in the spiritual? In this regard Jesus was a scientist before science came, laying down the laws of the spiritual realm and insisting that the conditions must be fulfilled. "Narrow is the gate, and straitened the way, that leadeth unto life."

Consider further that we face here not only the profound implication of a law-abiding universe but one of the most searching tests of our own personal sincerity. It is one thing, and comparatively easy too, to desire something ideal and right; it is another thing to be willing to pay the price. At that point hypocrisy flourishes. Many people who weigh two hundred and fifty pounds desire in general to weigh one hundred and fifty, but the price! One look at them reveals that they do not really desire to weigh one hundred and fifty pounds. Narrow is the gate, and straitened the way.

When from such homely matters one carries this truth up into life's most exalted realms the same fact holds. Professor Mortimer Adler of the University of Chicago says that ultimately mankind will achieve a world permanently at peace, but that it will take five hundred years to do it. That is just the time Thomas Jefferson said it would take American civilization to reach the Pacific coast. In his *Notes on Virginia* Jefferson said it would take two hundred years before we reached the Mississippi and between two and three hundred years more before the conquest of the continent reached the Pacific. It was less than a hundred and fifty years ago he said that, and we have been on the Pacific a long time now. Perhaps we can beat the timetable again in building a world order that will assure peace, but it is going to cost a kind of wise and sacrificial devotion the nations now are not exhibiting. "My friend," Du Pont de Nemours once wrote to Thomas Jefferson, "we are but snails, and we have to climb the Cordillera!" And then he added five words like the crack of a whip: "By God! We must climb!"

In every realm the truth holds: "Wide is the gate, and broad is the way, that leadeth to destruction, and many are they that enter in thereby. For narrow is the gate, and straitened the way, that leadeth unto life, and few are they that find it." All great achievement—intellectual, artistic, spiritual, ethical—is reached in Jesus' meaning of the word, not by a broad, loose meandering road, but by a narrow way.

Concentration is narrow. Gladstone, asked the secret of his successful career, answered with one word: "Concentration!" *Decision* is narrow. When one decides, one gives up vagueness and generalities, and becomes particular and concrete. *Self-discipline* is narrow. Ask a man like Toscanini what it means! No broad road for a loose, meandering gypsy to travel on ever led to such artistry as his. *Loyalty* is narrow. It binds us to definite devotions. The man who swears allegiance to a cause has limitations stronger than a slave's because his heart is given. When I love my friend I am not loosely free; I do not want to be loosely free; my limitation is my glory, I love my friend. But the unloyal man travels a broad road; he has no attachments; he is devoted to no friend; he is a man without a country. "Wide is the gate, and broad is the way."

Here, then, is a central test of our personal sincerity—we who so easily profess Christian ideals for ourselves, our families and our world—are we willing to pay the price?

This test is going to come sternly home to us as a nation, desiring as we do a world organized for peace. Granted, that that desire in general is widespread, deep-seated, strong. It had better be, for many reasons, and for one reason in particular that I have never heard anybody mention. In ancient Greek times the average age of death in the population was about twenty-nine. In Massachusetts, in 1800, the average age of death was about thirty-five. As late as 1890 in the United States the average age of death was forty-three. So in that old world of our fathers, the men who planned wars fought them. The same age group that said, We must go to war, shouldered the guns and went. But now with the average age of death away up in the sixties, we—millions upon millions of older folk—may say war, but then not we but our sons and daughters go out to fight it. We, the elders, pick out our finest, bravest, most promising youths and send them out to fight while we stay home. It is an intolerable situation, the older age group more and more controlling the policies of nations, and the younger age group bearing the terrific burden of the consequence. Who of us elders would not gladly lay down his life to save from death some promising youth, his valuable life still ahead of him, whom we have sent out to fight? But we cannot do it. Modern war presents the older generation with a heartbreaking situation. Of course we desire a world organized for peace! Never was that desire stronger or more universal. But the test of our sincerity in desiring it still lies ahead of us. Are we as a nation going to be willing to pay the price?

As for personal life, God grant that each one here may apply this to himself! Fine ideals, good desires in general—we are taking that for granted. But at that point the question of sincerity rises.

Which bus are we on, now, this morning, in our practical, immediate habits and ways of living? Are some of us on the wrong bus?

Obviously we are dealing here with one of the commonest causes of brokenhearted regret and penitence. It is so easy to catch the wrong bus. We do it when we do not mean to. We get on it without realizing we are there, not at all surrendering our fine dreams and aims but all the time thinking, like that man going to Detroit, that we are headed where we want to go, whereas we are really going somewhere else. How many such cases a personal counselor sees!

A family comes to New York, a fine family with high ideals for themselves and their children. Make a direct attack on their ideals and one would be met with stout resistance. They do desire a happy, united, loyal, respected, Christian home, fully intending to ally themselves with the best in the community, the church and social service, fine friends and great opportunities. But in New York there are a lot of buses running. I almost hesitate to describe one of them lest some should think that I am turning Puritan. I am not. I am just describing what I see—that night club, cocktail hour, drink-because-others-do, and don't-be-prudish-because-it-makes-you-seem-queer way of living. So this family, not consciously surrendering a single one of its high ideals, boards that bus—not so bad at first, but not so good either—and travels without recognizing it far away from the decent moral standards that are the underpinning of any strong and lovely home. And then some day that bus reaches its destination. Alas! that was not where they had intended to land. "There is a way," says the Scripture, "which seemeth right unto a man, but the end thereof are the ways of death."

This kind of experience in family and personal life more than any other makes a man call himself a fool. A sinner? Yes. But sometimes I think a man can face having been a sinner and still retain some self-respect. To have had fine aims, however, good intentions, high ideals, and then like an idiot to have caught the wrong bus—the most ashamed people I ever see are those who thus blame themselves for being fools.

Do you young people still read De Maupassant's stories? Brilliant, clever, gay, often ribald and indecent, no one can read them without seeing behind them a young man, his heart set on a free, full, happy life. But no one can read them either without guessing what bus he himself had boarded and wondering where it landed him in the end. I never knew what happened to De Maupassant until the other day. It was all over for him by the time he was forty-three. His biographer says: "By 1891 he was a wreck . . . The story of his last years makes painful reading. In 1892 he was committed to a private asylum. On July 6 of the following year the end came." So, he headed for a full, free, happy life, but he caught the wrong bus.

Thus we come to the consequence of the matter. One of the most crucial needs of the world today, personal, domestic, national, international, is the re-establishment of Christian moral standards. They have been dreadfully shaken. The whole Nazi movement was built upon the proposition that there were no such standards, things everlastingly right and everlastingly wrong, with God himself pledged to see to it that nothing traveling a wrong road ever comes to a right end. Beneath the urgent political needs of the time for international organization and all the rest is this fundamental need, the re-establishment of moral standards, and moral standards have their inception, their development and their confirmation, inside the lives of individuals. Take it for granted that we desire good goals—happiness, prosperity, peace. But our immediate volition cannot deal directly with goals; our immediate volition has to deal, here and now, with the choice of means, with the road we start on, with the bus we board. In God's name, let us look to it, lest having desired great things we discover again that hell can be paved with good intentions! For the gospel is that there is a right way, offered us in Christ. It does cost concentration, decison, self-discipline, loyalty, as everything most worth while in man's experience does, but it leads to life. I want some choices made here this morning, that years from now, when the trip is done, will land us where we really want to go, knowing for ourselves the meaning of the Master's word, "I am the way."

When Life Reaches Its Depths

THESE are days when our lives do go down into the depths. To be sure, life happily has not only depths but shallows, not only profundities but gaieties. We could not endure life without that. Our thought this morning concerns our most serious moods, but this other side of our nature is important, too—the superficial, if you will, the light-hearted, cheerful and merry.

Obviously this side of our nature finds response from the world without. The gay asks for gaiety and it is answered; the merry mood asks for trivialities and they are there; the shallows call to the shallows and there is response. But surely that alone does not exhaust the meaning of anybody's life. Sometimes life does run out into its depths, and then, when the deep in us calls for something deep to answer it, we face one of life's great hours.

That very phrase comes from the forty-second Psalm. The psalmist's experience had run out into the depths in trouble, and, remembering the thundering cataracts that pour down in springtime from the melting snows of Mount Hermon, and roar, and echo, and answer one another in the gorges beneath, he used that similitude to describe his experience. "Deep," he said, "calleth unto deep at the noise of thy waterfalls." Every serious life has that experience, where the profundities within ask for an answering profundity. No longer do the shallows suffice. Life within faces some profound abyss of experience, and the deep asks for an answering deep. So when deep calls unto deep and the deep replies, we face the essential experience of religion.

This explains the deathless hold that religious faith has upon the human spirit. Irreligion reduces the world to a fortuitous, self-arrangement of physical elements, and thereby empties the world of the meaning that religious faith finds in God. There is no God, says irreligion, no Divine purpose in life, no goodness beyond our human goodness, no high source for our existence, and no destiny at last except a universal ash heap. Nevertheless, while irreligion thus takes all depth of meaning out of the universe, it leaves man still with the deep in him—depths of trouble, of love, of moral need, of ethical devotion, of spiritual insight—the same old profound experiences that man's nature has known throughout its history. But in irreligion when these deeps within call for a responsive depth, only the shallows are there to answer.

This is the ultimate tragedy of irreligion. I am not saying that all irreligious people must be unhappy. There is much in the world that responds to much that is in them. Their gay moods can be answered by gaieties, their esthetic moods by beauties, their truth-loving moods by science, their affectionate moods by human love—there is much in the world, religion or no religion, to make it interesting and valuable. Yet, when all this is granted, for the thoroughgoing irreligionist a tragedy lies in wait. Some day his life will go out into the depths—profound trouble, profound love, profound moral need, profound ethical devotion, profound spiritual insight—and then the deep will call out for a depth at the heart of life to answer it. And what if there is no deep there!

If this is true in ordinary times, how much more true it is in this, one of the most serious days in man's history! To see how true it is, and how indispensable a matter Christian faith is standing for, consider those hours when life does move out into its depths. For example, in trouble. A man, let us say, has had a smooth and easy life where tragedy has been like a rumor from a far country, but one day a knock comes on his door and tragedy steps in. That experience always adds a new dimension to life, and it is the dimension of depth. "Deep trouble," we say, not broad, long, high—those adjectives would not apply—but "deep trouble." When the psalmist says, "Out of the depths have I cried unto thee, O Lord," we know what he means. He is in trouble. We all enjoy comedy. It is a benediction in a weary hour. The shallow calls to the shallow, and we delight in it. But everyone knows that a tragedy like *Hamlet* goes deeper than comedy.

Each of us has a date with this experience, and when it arrives the psalmist's words come true: "Deep calleth unto deep." For when tragedy faces life one does cry out for something deep to answer it—a faith profound enough to give trouble meaning, and strong enough to sustain one in its endurance. When death takes those we love, when children slip through our arms, when war breaks and catastrophe crashes down and life tumbles in, or when one writes in one's diary what Katherine Mansfield, a brilliant young English author, stricken with tuberculosis, wrote, "There is no limit to human suffering. When one thinks: 'Now I have touched the bottom of the sea—now I can go no deeper,' one goes deeper," then out of the depths the soul cries for answering depths. In such an hour how shallow irreligion is!

One of our contemporary irreligionists says that man has "no reason to suppose that his own life has any more meaning than the life of the humblest insect that crawls from one annihilation to another." So, out of the depths I cry and only the shallows answer—no meaning in life, life coming from nowhere, going nowhither, signifying nothing! As one of our modern poets puts it,

If after all that we have lived and thought,
All comes to Nought—
If there be nothing after Now,
And we be nothing anyhow,
And we know that—why live?

In Christian faith, however, the deep in us is not thus answered by the shallows. For when our profundities call out for an answering profundity, Christian faith says, God is there; his eternal purpose comprehends all life; this world is a place for the growing of souls, and in that process adversity is as indispensable as joy; all supreme spirits have come up out of great tribulation; there is power available to enable one to win that victory. So, deep calleth unto deep!

Carry our thought further now and see that in another area life runs out into its depths—not only in trouble but in love. How naturally we say, He is deeply in love! Wherever love is strong and beautiful life reaches its depths. Anyone, for example, who has had a great mother has had one of the unfathomable experiences. Strange how powerfully it keeps its hold long after the mother herself has passed into the invisible! Strange how a man fights his battles out and wins such victories as he is able, and grows old, older far than his mother was when she died, but still feels that to her he owes the major part of everything that he has done. Others might fail him, but she never; others might doubt his possibilities, but she rose on them like the sun and fell on them like the rain, in her encouragement.

Say our worst about human nature, there is in it this depth, the love of fathers and mothers, the love of true friends, the love of true marriage, causing Robert Browning to say to his wife,

> Oh I must feel your brain prompt mine,
> Your heart anticipate my heart,
> You must be just before, in fine,
> See and make me see, for your part,
> New depths of the divine!

Say our worst about us humans, we do, like Christ himself, having loved his own, love them unto the end. There is this depth in man!

Now, over against this deep of true love put a summary statement of irreligion by one of its brilliant contemporary devotees: "Living," he says, "is merely a physiological process with only a physiological meaning." How can one believe that? Then the deep of love in man is solitary—nothing at the heart of reality to answer it; it came from nowhere and is going nowhither; it is an accident; when it cries out for the deep there is no deep to respond. That is the tragedy of irreligion.

Indeed, irreligion cannot permanently stand this bafflement, that the profundity in man should be unanswered by a profundity beyond, and so irreligion is irresistibly tempted to depreciate, defame, and at last deny, the profundities in man. If you doubt it, read our irreligious literature, our pagan novelists and essayists. So Professor Edman of Columbia University sums it up: "Love," he says, in much of our current, cynical literature, is represented as "simply lust on parade," and friendship as only "the desire for attention or for praise." Thus the deeps in man are smeared. Love is reduced to sublimated lust; motherhood is reduced to an accidental, biological phenomenon; friendship is reduced to camouflaged homosexuality; and life itself is reduced to merely a physiological process with only a physiological meaning. I am not saying, of course, that every irreligionist explicitly does that, but I am saying that our modern world is shot through and through with a gross, debasing paganism that springs from, and is supported by, such irreligion.

Christian faith does fight an indispensable battle for man's depths. For Christian faith says, Love is real, the divinest reality in the universe; "God is love," "Now abideth faith, hope, love, . . . and the greatest of these is love." That, I am sure, is the only philosophy that can ultimately sustain man's greatness. Alas for souls in whom this deep goes unanswered by any corresponding deep, until at the last they are tempted even to deny the deep within themselves!

Carry our thought further now by noting that life runs out into its depth not simply in trouble and in love but in moral need. Sometime since in a New York hotel a chambermaid one morning found the body of a young man, dead with a bullet hole through his head, and on the dresser his last will and testament lay, written on a sheet of hotel paper: "I leave to society a bad example. I leave to my friends the memory of a misspent life. I leave to my father and mother all the sorrow they can bear in their old age. I leave to my wife a broken heart, and to my children the name of a drunkard and a suicide. I leave to God a lost soul, who has insulted his mercy." That young man had gone into the depths of moral need. Even when it is not so tragic, that experience still is deep. You read detective stories? You are interested in the application of modern science to criminology? It has gotten so now that a man can hardly go into a room without leaving traces of himself. He leaves fingerprints all over. He leaves fibers from his clothes and hairs from his head. Always where he goes he leaves something of himself behind. Man discovers that he does that morally. He leaves his moral fingerprints on everything he touches. He cannot go into a room without leaving his traces. And in hours of penitence he understands what the converted sinner in Masefield's poem meant when he said, "The harm I done by being me."

In such hours of penitence and moral need how utterly shallow irreligion is! Says one of our contemporary irreligionists, "We don't matter. Man matters only to himself. He is fighting a lone fight against a vast indifference." Picture a man in real moral need, the deep crying out for the deep, and nothing there to answer him except a vast indifference! Christian faith is fighting a battle for man's profound experiences, and to everyone here today in moral need it offers no vast indifference as an answer, but forgiveness, a second chance, the possibility of a fresh beginning, reinstatement, an inner spiritual power potent enough to enable you to win the victory. So, when in the Far Country the Prodigal comes to himself and says, "I will arise and go to my father," there is not a vast indifference at the other end of the journey, but a father where deep can call unto deep.

Take a further step and note that life runs out into its depths not only in trouble, love, and moral need, but in the very opposite of moral need—profound sacrificial ethical devotion. Once Abraham Lincoln was taken to task by his friends for some criticism that his policies were evoking, and he said this to them: "I do the very best I know how—the very best I can; and I mean to keep doing so until the end. If the end brings me out all right, what is said against me won't amount to anything. If the end brings me out wrong, ten angels swearing I was right would make no difference." When a man thus honestly cares about doing right, when he is profoundly in earnest about setting his compass to the true pole, he wants to know that there is a true pole there to be true to. He cannot be content with subjective feeling only; he wants an objective right to be dedicated to. As Lincoln himself said on another occasion, "The question is not first of all whether God is on our side, but whether we are on God's side." When a man has sacrificial devotion to give, he wants a real God to give it to.

When Jesus in Gethsemane said, "Not my will, but thine, be done," that was a deep experience. But picture Jesus going into Gethsemane and finding there awaiting him nothing but what irreligion can offer—a vast indifference! How different his story would have been! When one has a great ethical devotion to give, he wants a great God to give it to.

Well, trouble, love, moral need, ethical devotion—such deeps are in us, and one other too, spiritual insight. As Browning said,

> Oh, we're sunk enough here, God knows!
> But not quite so sunk that moments,
> Sure tho' seldom, are denied us,
> When the spirit's true endowments
> Stand out plainly from its false ones.

We do have hours of insight like that, when the ground rises under our feet and the horizons expand and the vision grows clear. Who here does not understand such hours—under the spell of great music, under the stars at night, in the presence of high mountains, in quiet hours of receptive meditation, in crises when the soul rises up to make momentous choices—and how could one better sum up the witness of hours like that than by saying that when insight thus is clarified we see and feel the deep in us answered by a corresponding depth, and the best in us finding response in the Eternal Spirit?

So the Christian faith is fighting a battle for what we see and feel in our hours of deep trouble, deep love, deep moral need, deep ethical devotion, and profound spiritual insight. And if someone says, But life is not all such serious business, I say, No, but it is the deep sea that supports the dancing waves upon the surface; it is the profundities that sustain the superficialities and make them lovely; and if a man tries to live only in the shallows, with no deeps answering his deep, then the Nemesis is that some day his shallows will grow intolerably wearisome.

Note, now, the conclusion of the matter. Throughout this sermon we have been starting with the profundities in ourselves, and saying that they are answered by profundities in God. Suppose, however, that someone asks, What makes you think that these profundities in God that Christian faith believes in are really there? I would say in answer, Where did the profundities in ourselves come from? How did they get here? If fish have fins, it is because the water was there first. If birds have wings, it is because air was there first. If we have eyes, it is because the sun was there first. All the functions of living beings are but responses to something objective in the universe. Always the universe was there first, and our powers and capacities are but our answer to it. How can one suppose that the deeps in the human spirit are the only exceptions to this universal law? In a world where lungs argue the priority of air, where eyes argue the priority of light, where the esthetic instincts in man argue the priority of beauty, where scientific curiosity in man argues the priority of truth, how can it be that the deepest things in man—great fortitude, great love, great moral want, great devotion, deep insight—argue the priority of *nothing?* It is preposterous.

So, in a sense, our whole sermon has been wrong side up. We started with profundity in man and saw it answered by profundity in God, but the deeper truth is that God came first, and all that is fine, true and beautiful in us is but our partial response to him. As the New Testament says, "We love him, because he first loved us." So today may the deep in the Eternal call unto the deep in us, and may there be indeed in our spirit a depth to answer it.

Handling Life's Second Bests

WE ARE concerned today about a factual personal problem so nearly universal in its application that we need not be bothered by its exceptions: namely, that very few persons have a chance to live their lives on the basis of their first choice. We all have to live upon the basis of our second and third choices. To one who reads biography this comes to be so much a matter of course that he takes it for granted.

Whistler, the artist, for example, started out to be a soldier and failed at West Point because he could not pass in chemistry. "If silicon had been a gas," he used to say, "I should have been a major-general." Instead, he failed in soldiering, half-heartedly tried engineering, and then tried painting—with such remarkable results as one sees in the portraits of his own mother, Miss Alexander, and Carlyle.

Let us approach this inescapable human problem of handling life's second-bests by way of one of the most impressive exhibitions of it in history. In the sixteenth chapter of the book of The Acts, in the record of Paul's journeys, we read this: "When they were come over against Mysia, they assayed to go into Bithynia; and the Spirit of Jesus suffered them not; and passing by Mysia, they came down to Troas. And a vision appeared to Paul in the night: There was a man of Macedonia standing, beseeching him, and saying, Come over into Macedonia, and help us. And when he had seen the vision, straightway we sought to go forth into Macedonia, concluding that God had called us to preach the gospel unto them."

So simple and succinct is this narrative that one would little suspect that we are dealing with one of the most significant events in human history. Here Chistianity passed over from Asia into Europe.

It was a momentous day when Columbus set sail from the shores of Spain or Vasco da Gama discovered the sea route to the Indies, but could even such events be more pregnant with consequence than the day when Paul carried Christianity out of Asia, in a few centuries to be overrun by Mohammedanism, through Troas into Macedonia and so to Europe, where Christianity was going to have its chance? But Paul had not planned to go to Europe. That was a second choice. Paul had planned to go to Bithynia. "They assayed," it reads, "to go into Bithynia." And no wonder, for Bithynia was one of the richest povinces of Asia Minor, and to have carried Christianity there would have been a triumph indeed.

Moreover, we may be sure that if Paul wanted to go into Bithynia he wanted to go very much and tried to go very hard, for Paul was never a half-way man. And he could not go; the way was blocked; his plan was broken. We read, "The Spirit of Jesus suffered them not," but that is only another way of saying that some circumstance blocked their course. It must have seemed to Paul lamentable at first. I picture him arriving on the shores of the Aegean, saying, I wanted to go to Bithynia and here I am in Troas! And lo! through Troas a way opened to the preëminent ministry of his career. Paul rendered his most significant service wth the left-overs of a broken plan.

Wanting Bithynia and getting Troas, how familiar an experience that is! But to take Troas, the second-best, the broken plan, the left-over of a disappointed expectation, and make of it the greatest opportunity we ever had, how much less familiar that is! Yet, as one reads the story of human life, one sees that powerful living has always involved such a victory as Paul won in Troas over his own soul and his situation.

When a career has at last been finished and the halo of well-deserved reputation now hangs over it so that one cannot think the name without thinking of some high enterprise with which the name is indissolubly associated, then in the glamour of that retrospect we are tempted to forget that almost always the turning point of the career is the experience that Paul had—getting Troas when he wanted Bithynia.

When, for example, we think of Phillips Brooks, we think of

spiritual ministry, a great personality pouring his soul out with abundant power upon the people. Of all the letters that Phillips Brooks received, it is said that he cherished most this one from a small tailor shop near Copley Square in Boston: "Dear Mr. Brooks: I am a tailor in a little shop near your Church. Whenever I have the opportunity I always go to hear you preach. Each time I hear you preach I seem to forget all about you, for you make me think of God." Nevertheless, remember that Phillips Brooks did not plan to be a preacher. He planned to be a teacher. That was his Bithynia. As soon as he graduated from college he plunged into his chosen profession of teaching and he failed. He failed completely. Listen to young Brooks writing about his scholars as he is failing: "They are the most disagreeable set of creatures without exception that I have ever met with. . . . I really am ashamed of it but I am tired, cross and almost dead, so good night." Listen to Phillips Brooks after he had failed and been dropped from his position: "I don't know what will become of me and I don't care much"; "I shall not study a profession"; "I wish I were fifteen years old again. I believe I might make a stunning man: but somehow or other I don't seem in the way to come to much now." Listen to Phillips Brooks' father, concerned about his son, so humiliated that he will not talk even with his friends: "Phillips will not see anyone now, but after he is over the feeling of mortification, he will come and see you."

There is a sense in which Brooks never recovered from the disappointment. At the flower of his career he came down once from the office of President Eliot of Harvard white as a sheet and fairly trembling because he had declined what he knew to be his last opportunity to become a teacher. He wanted Bithynia and he got Troas but through Troas he found the door into a service that if he had lived a hundred lives he might never have found again.

Or consider Sir Walter Scott. We think of him as the novelwriter whose stories charmed our youth so that for many years some of us would have voted Ivanhoe the best tale ever told. Sir Walter, however, did not want to be a novelist; he planned to be a poet, but Byron's sun rose and dimmed his lesser light. "Byron hits the mark," he said, "where I don't even pretend to fledge my arrow." Then he turned to writing novels, so ashamed that, as you know, he published the first of them anonymously. He did not want any one to know that he was writing novels. He wanted Bithynia; he got Troas and through Troas an open door to the best work he ever did.

Is there anybody here who has not wanted Bithynia and gotten Troas? We older people watch the youths come up, as we did, with their ambitions and plans for Bithynia and we wonder what they will do when they face the inescapable experience. When they are shut out from some Bithynia and land in Troas, will they know how to handle that? Will they have the spirit and attitude and the technique to make of it their finest chance? And since it is so inescapable a problem, we well may ask what it was in Paul that enabled him to turn his defeat into victory.

For one thing, his religion entered in. Whatever else was shaken when he got to Troas, his conviction still was there that God had a purpose for his life, that if God had led him to Troas there must be something in Troas worth discovering, that God's purposes included Troas just as much as Bithynia, that God never leads any man into any place where all the doors are shut. Paul's religion entered in.

It is in just such situations as this that one can tell how much real religion a man has. We hear a man reciting a familiar creed: "I believe in God the Father Almighty, Maker of heaven and earth," but no matter how serious he may seem about it you cannot tell from that alone how real it is to him. You hear a man singing,

> He leadeth me: O blessed thought!
> O words with heavenly comfort fraught!
> Whate'er I do, where'er I be,
> Still 'tis God's hand that leadeth me.

But however much in earnest he may seem you cannot tell from that alone how deep it goes with him. When, however, you see a man who, wanting Bithynia, gets Troas and, still certain that there is a purpose for his life, takes a positive attitude toward Troas as if to say, If God has led me here there is something worth while here to do, you know that that man's religion is practically operative. If, therefore, Paul had merely said what he did say, "To them that love God all things work together for good," we might have cocked suspicious eyebrows at him, thinking that that proposition is extraordinarily difficult to prove. What is impressive about Paul is that whenever he did land in a disappointing Troas, and he landed in a good many of them, he did so effectually love God that he *made* all things work together for good. Paul's religion meant to him a positive faith about life and a positive attitude toward life so effective that watching his career is again and again like watching the Battle of Marengo—in the morning an obvious defeat, in the afternoon a resounding victory.

Consider a modern counterpart of Paul, Adoniram Judson. When Judson was a young man he gave himself to missionary service and his ambition centered on India. That was his Bithynia. When at last he reached India they would not let him in. The East India Company would not allow him to stay and the governor told him to take the first ship back to America. For a year he labored to open the doors of India and they were bolted shut. So he turned to Burma. That was his Troas, unknown, untouched Burma. Can one suppose that through all that humiliation and disappointment Judson could always see the leadership of God? Of course he could not; he was human. Can one suppose during those months that he lay in the prison of the Emperor at Ava and Oung-Pen-La he could always see evidences of the divine purpose? Of course he could not; he was human. But he did so handle the affair in Burma that the doors began to open until no well-instructed man today can think of Burma without thinking of Adoniram Judson, or think of Adoniram Judson without thinking of Burma; and when the consequence began to appear he could look upon his life in retrospect as though it had been planned of God. To live your life through—not argue it through; that never is sufficient—to *live* your life through into the conviction that there is an eternal Purpose with which a man can ally himself is one of the finest achievements of the human spirit.

Altogether the most thrilling story of the Old Testament is on this theme. One day in Palestine we stopped our automobile by the roadside and ate our lunch at Dotham where long ago Joseph had been sold by his brethren. Still the camel trail goes up from across Jordan, and then runs down to the coast cities and so to Egypt. Now Joseph, stolen from his home, betrayed by his brethren, dropped into a pit, sold to Midianite slave-dealers, made a man-servant in a household in Egypt, lied about by his master's wife and put in prison—can one suppose that during all that humiliation and disgrace he could see where God was taking him? Of course not. But he so kept his faith and handled his life that the doors opened into the biggest business of his career, and when at last those penitent and frightened brethren stood before him, you remember what he said: "I am Joseph your brother, whom ye sold into Egypt. And now be not grieved, nor angry with yourselves, that ye sold me hither: for God did send me before you to preserve life. . . . So now it was not you that sent me hither, but God."

Such was Paul's feeling as he looked back on the day he missed Bithynia and found Troas, and such will be ours if in Troas we will let our religion enter in.

In the second place it was not simply Paul's religion that enabled him to win this victory but the fine fruit of his religion, his care about people.

The trouble with so many of us when we land in Troas is that we begin to pity ourselves. Paul could have done that. He could have started the process we indulge in—"ifing."

> If I had not missed Bithynia; if my plans had not been broken, if, if! I have given up everything for Jesus Christ. I could today be one of the great rabbis of Jerusalem saluted in the market place. I have given it all up for Christ. I spent a long time in Arabia thinking through the gospel. I have been fourteen years in a trying, difficult, unrecognized ministry in Cilicia, at odds even with my Christian brethren because once I persecuted them. And now, when I am beginning to get on a good footing with my fellow Christians, with Barnabas and a few others trusting me, I have come up through Asia Minor on a preaching mission. See what they have done to me. They stoned me and left me for dead in Lystra. Even after that, all I asked was that I might have a chance to get into Bithynia and do some good work, and now I cannot; I am foiled; my plan is broken.

How easy it would have been for Paul in Troas to feel sorry for himself!

Upon the contrary, he at once began thinking about other people.

He wondered if there was not some one who might be better off because he had landed in Troas. He had not been there a night before he saw a man from Macedonia saying, Come over and help us. It was Paul's unselfishness, his generosity, his magnanimity that opened the doors for him in Troas.

Once there was a man named William Duncan who gave himself to the missionary cause and in time was sent by his board to a little Indian island off Alaska called Metlakatla. It was an unlikely Troas for a young man to land in who had doubtless dreamed of some Bithynia, for those Indians were a poor, ignorant, miserable tribe, and their morals were vile beyond description. Dean Brown of Yale, however, who visited Metlakatla after William Duncan had been there about forty years, made this report, that you will find every Indian family in a separate house with all the decent appointments of home life, that you will find a bank, a coöperative store, a sawmill, a box factory, and a salmon cannery run by Indians in profitable industry, that you will find a school where Indian boys and girls learn to read and write and think and live, and a church where an Indian minister preaches the gospel of eternal life and an Indian musician, who once was a medicine man playing a tom-tom, now plays a pipe organ, and a congregation of Indians sing the great hymns of the church to the praise of Almighty God—and all because a man named William Duncan, landing in Troas, cared enough about people to find there the chance of his life!

My friends, there is nothing in that spirit or consequence that cannot be transferred to our lives. We are all in Troas. Just as at Sebastapol each heart thought a different name while they all sang Annie Laurie, so when today we say "Troas" each one of us thinks of some situation we would not have planned to be in. There is only one way—love. Was it not George Macdonald who said: "Nothing makes a man strong like a cry for help"? You walk down the street utterly fatigued, so tired that you would like to lie down on the curb and go to sleep, and suddenly there is a cry; there has been an accident; a child is hurt; and you never will remember how tired you are until it is all over. Nothing makes a man so strong as a call for help.

A mother is completely fatigued. She has been telling her friends for weeks that there is nothing left of her, and then a child falls ill and needs her. Week after week, by night and day, she stands by and never thinks of being tired. Nothing makes a man strong like a call for help.

It would be strange indeed if there were not some young men and women here not altogether dull to the dangers of our civilization, not altogether blind to the possibility of losing it, thinking that perhaps there is something in them that might help build a more decent world for human children to be born in. That is their strength. Nothing makes a man so strong as a call for help. And the trouble is that when we get into Troas we pity ourselves; we miss that man from Macedonia, saying, Come over and help us.

Indeed, so true is this principle of life that it holds good of even small excursions into Troas. When annoyances and irritations come, when one is lied about and hated and denounced, there is only one way out—goodwill. You remember Edwin Markham's lines:

> He drew a circle that shut me out—
> Heretic, rebel, a thing to flout.
> But Love and I had the wit to win:
> We drew a circle that took him in!

If in the midst of life's harassments and irritations one has grace enough to do that, he sometimes will find in that very difficulty his choicest opportunity for usefulness.

This, then, is the conclusion of the matter: that because Paul had these two elements in his life, as soon as he landed in Troas his imagination was filled, not with defeat but with victory. Coué was right that it is the imagination which makes or unmakes us. If you put a thirty-foot plank as high as a cathedral tower hardly anybody can walk it, and it is not because the physical difficulties are greater than they would be on the ground but because one's imagination keeps picturing him falling off. So when we get into Troas we think we are defeated. I wanted Bithynia, we say; I have got Troas. So we think defeat, we say defeat, we imagine defeat, and we are defeated. But as soon as Paul landed in Troas he saw an open door, a beckoning man, a new chance, and a successful issue.

What helped him most, I suspect, was that his thought went back, as it so habitually did, to the cross of his Master. That was a Troas to land on! What a Bithynia it would have been if his people had accepted Jesus as Messiah! And now, shut out from that Bithynia, he came to his Troas, his Calvary, and he so clothed it with the purpose of God and the love of man that

> All the light of sacred story
> Gathers round its head sublime.

He took a very hard thing and he made of it a triumph.

Handicapped Lives

OUR subject probably takes us all in. There may be some young, shining Apollo here who never has been aware of limitation, but one suspects not. At least, I never yet knew a man who on intimate acquaintance did not turn out to be dealing with handicaps.

Reading biography confirms the impression that all human beings are handicapped somewhere and that in no small degree the secret of the quality of any one's spiritual life depends on the way he is dealing with these limitations. In some ways, reading biography is disillusioning; we find our heroes far too human, with frailties and foibles like our own; but this compensating service biography does for us, constituting our heroes heroic still—it makes them all our companions in the handling of handicaps.

We thought, perhaps, that a scientist like Pasteur, upon whose titanic work modern medicine rests, must have had lusty health to labor with. We discover that he had a paralytic stroke at forty-six and was handicapped for life. We thought, perhaps, that a man like Henry M. Stanley, acclaimed of the whole world and buried from Westminster Abbey, must have had a grand heritage. We find he was brought up in an almshouse, and that his real name was not Stanley at all. We find Beethoven writing music although deaf and Milton writing poetry although blind, and we discover that in general the great work of the world has been done by handicapped people. They may have had faults and foibles like the rest of us but they had handicaps also, often far more severe than we have faced, and they dealt with them superbly.

How did they do it? What was the inward technique with which they handled limitations? Is there any one of us who does not need to learn that?

Biography in the Bible in no way differs from life stories outside. It confirms the universality of our problem. Take Paul's "thorn in the flesh," for example—"a messenger of Satan to buffet me." "I besought the Lord thrice," he wrote, "that it might depart from me. And he hath said unto me, My grace is sufficient for thee: for my power is made perfect in weakness."

No one knows what Paul's thorn in the flesh was. Epilepsy, eye trouble—many have been the guesses but no one knows. If Paul had been like some of us, some one would know. Think of writing all those letters and telling nobody the symptoms of his trouble! Ephesus, Colossæ, Thessalonica, Corinth, and Rome would have been informed about it had Paul been like some of us. We know nothing, however, about Paul's trouble except that behind the scenes, like the rest of us, Paul had to handle a limitation that he prayed to escape, that he could not evade, that he had to settle down and live with somehow or other. Ah, Paul, handicapped man yet radiant in personality and successful in work, how did you handle it? What was the grace that was sufficient for you?

Often in churches we hear theological, ecclesiastical, and liturgical matters discussed as though the central problem of man's spiritual life somehow lay there. How far that is from the truth! How many of us really have the crux of our spiritual problem in details of theology or theories of church and liturgy? But we may be sure of one place where many of us do have the central problem of our spiritual life, the watershed from which the streams of life may flow to far-dissevered destinies, and that is in the region of our handicaps.

Here is a boy born a cripple or crippled in early infancy; he has grown up through his first years with no idea of what has happened to him, but sometime in childhood it will dawn on him that he is not like other children, that he has a handicap. His spiritual problem will center in the way he deals with that. Or here is a man whose parents did not understand the critical importance of the emotional experiences of childhood, who now wakes up to discover that something is wrong inside, that all his basic, habitual emotional reactions flow in channels of suspicion, distrust, fear, anxiety, and vindictiveness, so that like a stream in endless agitation he looks in envy at smoothly-flowing personalities that can maintain a tranquil, deep, and even course. That man's spiritual problem will center in the vicinity of his handicap. Or here is a man who in youth had all the natural ambitions of young manhood for success but who now recognizes that he never will arrive at his desired goal. He will never write the poetry or compose the music or preach the sermons or hold the business positions that he dreamed. Again and again he has stepped on the gas but the speed is not in him. Nature did not equip him with eight cylinders or with six—only four, and those none too good. It is a crucial hour in that man's life when he stands open-eyed before his handicap. Or here is a man who was highly endowed and whose promising youth wakened in his friends capacious expectations, but upon whom, like a beast from ambush, an accident leaped, and now he must work with crippled machinery. Again and again he has tried to throw on the old power in the old way but it only burns out the fuse. Somehow or other he must face his handicap.

Moreover, there are some whose limitations lie in personal relationships—a life that wanted love and missed it, a home where marriage might have been a thing of beauty but was a tragedy, a family where a child was greeted as a blessing and became an inward agony, a household where death has severed a tie that was the support and glory of the home. Among the few things that are true of all of us is the fact that each one has a handicap.

How, then, shall we deal with it? What is the technique? Where is the grace that is sufficient for us?

In the first place, if we are to deal handsomely with our handicaps we must at least have the grace to take, not a negative, but a positive attitude toward them. The first instinctive reaction toward a handicap is a negative attitude—rebellion or self-pity. How we rebel against our limitations! Why, we say, why, wanting to do some hard and honest work in the world and to contribute something worth while to life, should I be thwarted by this extraneous thorn in the flesh? It was a common human failing that caused Job's wife, when the crippling calamities fell on her husband, to advise him to curse God and die. Many a handicapped man has cursed God.

James Thomson, who wrote "The City of Dreadful Night," for example, as a culmination to bereavement and lost health had insomnia. His life was so clouded in gloom that he, doubtless, was speaking in the words of one of his characters:

> Who is most wretched in this dolorous place?
> I think myself; yet I would rather be
> My miserable self than He, than He
> Who formed such creatures to His own disgrace.
>
> The vilest thing must be less vile than Thou
> From whom it had its being, God and Lord!
> Creator of all woe and sin! abhorred,
> Malignant and implacable! I vow
>
> That not for all Thy power furled and unfurled,
> For all the temples to Thy glory built,
> Would I assume the ignominious guilt
> Of having made such men in such a world.

Well, such an attitude is natural if you have insomnia. But it is a poor technique for dealing with handicaps.

Many people, therefore, less vehement and tumultuous, try self-pity. They stroke their wounded spirits. If, they cry, I had not had this handicap, what a person I would have been! And so, drifting into imaginings of all they would have been and achieved, had not that handicap been there, they become very sorry for themselves that such a miserable thorn in the flesh should have kept them from so glorious a paradise. That is natural but it is not an efficient technique for dealing with limitations. A man must talk to himself more intelligently and courageously than that if he is to secure the grace that is sufficient for him.

For example, let a man say this to himself: Do you suppose that you are peculiar in having to handle second-bests? Few people get their first choice. To take a second-best and make something out of it is life. Whoever yet had a chance to live his life out under the ideal conditions he would have chosen?

Once when Ole Bull, the great violinist, was giving a concert in Paris, his A string snapped and he transposed the composition and finished it on three strings. That is life—to have your A string snap and finish on three strings. How many here have had to test that out! Some of the finest things in human life have been done that way. Indeed, so much the most thrilling part of the human story on this planet lies in such capacity victoriously to handle handicaps that, much as I should have liked to hear Ole Bull with all the resources of a perfect instrument at his command, if I could have heard him only once I should have liked to hear him when the A string snapped and, without rebellion or self-pity or surrender, he finished on three strings.

As soon as a man begins to take this positive attitude toward his handicaps, they begin to present themselves to him as opportunities —always challenging, sometimes fascinating. It is a good cook who, after the dinner has been burned, knows how to make a fine meal out of the left-overs, and a good cook will be challenged to try. When a man begins to see a possible technique here for dealing with his limitations, he begins to say to himself this: There are two kinds of elements in every situation, first, the things you cannot help—if the dinner has been burnt it is burnt; if the A string has snapped it has snapped—but, second, the things you can help—your attitude. Rebellion gets you nowhere. Self-pity gets you nowhere. But insight to see that something can be done with the second-bests and adventurous daring to try might be a handle to take hold of.

Some great stories have been told of people who did use that handle. Joseph did not want to be sent to Egypt. Betrayed by his brothers, sold in slavery, lied about by his master's wife and put in prison—that was a bad second-best. But that old story, born beside Bedouin campfires, now is naturalized beside modern radiators, because thus to face a second-best and make something of it, as Joseph did, is life.

Robinson Crusoe did not want to land on a desert island. Who wants a desert island even when he is tired of multitudinous New York? But while many a story rises and falls and passes away, that old tale retains its endless fascination because to be handed thus a second-best and make something of it is life.

Francis Parkman did not want poor eyesight. Who wants that? But one who knows his story reads his superb writings with an added thrill, seeing behind the printed page the manuscript with the wire screen across it where Parkman guided his pencil that he might write legibly.

So Paul did not want a thorn in the flesh. Temperamentally vigorous, active, aggressive—how he must have rebelled against it! "I besought the Lord thrice," he said, "that it might depart from me," and something tells me he lost count after that. But I suspect there are qualities of understanding and sympathy in Paul and a deep and moving music in some of the great passages of his epistles that never would have been there if he had not had to finish on three strings.

In the second place, if we are thus to take a positive attitude toward our handicaps, some of us will have to throw off a false sense of responsibility. The reason why many of us fret so at our limitations is that we keep comparing ourselves with others and wishing to be what they are or do what they do. We habitually measure ourselves by other people and assume a responsibility for being as fortunate, as useful, and as happy as they. Limited as I am, we say, I cannot be like So-and-So. It is a great day in a handicapped man's life when he makes up his mind that he has only one responsibility, not to be like anybody else but to handle his special situation as well as he can.

A consulting psychologist said some time ago that of the many cases of emotional maladjustment with which he deals, a large proportion were due to the fact that people would not accept themselves. Just so! We will not accept ourselves. We will not say what I am confident Paul in effect said: I, Paul, hereby accept myself with a thorn in my flesh and do hereby throw off all responsibility for dealing with any other Paul than myself, and having thus accepted myself with my handicap, which I cannot help, I will now fall to and see what good thing can be gotten out of myself in my special situation.

There are people here the inner tone of whose spiritual life and the outer result of whose practical endeavors would be transformed, if in that sense they would accept themselves.

Upon the other hand, see what we do. Born to be berry bushes and produce good berries, we lift anxious, envious eyes to apple trees with their larger-sized fruit, or, born to be apple trees and produce good apples, we look with worried jealousy at maple trees with their more capacious shade, or, born to be maple trees, we are anxious because elm trees are taller and more graceful. We will not accept ourselves.

Roll off, I beg of you, all responsibility for handling any other self or any other situation than the one you face.

I am well aware that this is not the ordinary tone of the pulpit. The preacher is all for putting responsibility on people. He ordinarily assumes that people are indifferent to their responsibility and proceeds to present to their acceptance the obligations that he thinks they ought to assume. But any man who works in confessional conferences with individuals learns that there are many people who never will get anywhere with their own problem or any one else's until they accept themselves. John Smith, he says, stop feeling responsible for being as fortunate or successful or happy or useful as some other man! That is not your business. You have been given this special field to till. Accept it. If the soil is thinner and the rocks more numerous and the prospects less promising than another's, that is simply life's problem which, in some degree, we all face. Stop looking over the fence and daydreaming about what you would do with another man's field. Your limitations are also your opportunities. Remember what Emerson's squirrel said to the mountain:

> If I cannot carry forests on my back,
> Neither can you crack a nut.

That spirit has brought out of small chances some of the most priceless results in human history.

If a man says he does not like himself, that is easily understood. There are millions of people with inside information about themselves who do not like themselves. Thomas Gray did not like himself. He had a melancholic temperament and he wanted a sanguine one. He wrote once to a friend, "Low spirits are my true and faithful companions." But when you read his "Elegy Written in a Country Churchyard," you feel that a priceless thing has been done with those somber moods that a merely jocund and hilarious temperament could not have achieved.

Diminutive edition of a man, William Wilberforce probably did not like himself. Boswell went to hear him speak once and said afterward, "I saw what seemed a mere shrimp mount upon the table; but, as I listened, he grew, and grew, until the shrimp became a whale." That shrimp of a man never had good health. For twenty years on doctor's orders he took opium to keep body and soul together and had the courage never to increase the dose. But more than any other Englishman he stopped the British slave trade, and as one stands in Westminster Abbey beside the grave of "The Attorney-General of the unprotected and of the friendless," one feels that that sensitive, suffering life translated itself into a persistent, unconquerable sympathy with downtrodden people that a lusty hulk of a man in perfect health probably never would have felt.

Do not despise your limitations. They are your opportunities. God will never judge us in masses. Each one of us will have a private examination. What did we do with our special situation? That is all. If you say, I am just as good as So-and-So, you will have missed the point. Perhaps So-and-So had much more severe handicaps. You should have done better. If you say, I am a failure, So-and-So beat me, you will have missed the point. God may say, Well done, good and faithful servant; you had a desperately difficult situation and you handled it superbly.

In the third place, if we are thus to take a positive and hopeful attitude toward our limitations, many of us must clearly perceive that however severely our outward service may be limited, we can always make a spiritual contribution to the world.

Some one has defined influence as the effluence of affluence. The most powerful and permeating influence is the aroma of rich and fragrant spirits, the effluence of affluence.

Now, handicaps, far from preventing the development of this influential quality, are almost the indispensable setting of it. Bring on your strong and shining Apollo who never had a handicap, who with integrated personality, fortunate circumstance, and physical health has lived untroubled by limitations, and, however energetic may be his active service in the world, there are some things he cannot do for us that Helen Keller can. She is handicapped—blind, deaf, the doors shut on every side except the one door than even her handicaps can never shut, her chance to be a very radiant soul in a difficult situation. Being that, she does something to us which no shining Apollo can do.

The relationship, in this regard, between active and fortunate people on one side and handicapped spirits on the other is a fascinating study. Many of us may not be able to understand the argument or appreciate the antique beauty of "Paradise Lost" and "Paradise Regained," but one thing we all appreciate, the blind Milton sitting down to write them. That does something to us. Longfellow's translation of Dante may not by itself impress us. But when we learn that Mrs. Longfellow accidentally set her dress on fire, that Longfellow desperately but vainly tried to quench the flames, and that, after it all was over and Mrs. Longfellow had died, he sat down in his wifeless, motherless home to translate Dante to occupy his mind, and, what is more, did it beautifully, that does something to us.

How often we, with the shining sword of fortune and happiness still in our hands, tempted, for all that, to be laggard and cowardly, lift our eyes to see some man who has lost his sword, fighting with the scabbard, undaunted, high-spirited, unafraid—until we grasp our blades afresh and hew ahead! One cannot easily estimate the spiritual stimulus that comes into human life from handicapped people who have found grace sufficient for them.

My friend at a mid-western university tells me that in all his years there he never heard such cheering, not even at a football victory, as greeted a crippled boy carried in the arms of his companions across the platform on Commencement Day. Four years before, that boy had answered "Present" at the first roll call of his class. "Stand up!" said the professor. "I should like to, sir, but I have not been able to stand up since I was four years old." But, by being what he was in a difficult situation, that boy made such an impression on the university that, when his companions carried him up for his diploma, the great assemblage broke forth into such cheers as that college generation had not heard before.

Never despise your handicaps. They are an opportunity for a kind of spiritual service that lusty Apollos cannot render.

If you say that it takes great faith to live like this, you are right. You will not get this quality of life out of the atheistic cults some are trying to substitute for profound religion. If you say there are hours when you hate your handicaps, quite so! Even Christ prayed against the cross. *That* was a handicap. To die at thirty-three on a cross is a handicap. "If it be possible, let this cup pass away from me." He too prayed three times. But as it turned out in the end, no cross would have meant no Christ. That handicap was his most shining instrument. My friends, it was not the Greek Apollo, charioteer of the victorious sun, who won the world. It was the handicapped and crucified Christ.

No Man Need Stay the Way He Is

CONSCIENCE is one of the most appalling scourges of mankind. To be sure, conscience is indispensable and at its best may be called the voice of God within us but, for all that, it can be and in many lives is an appalling scourge.

Conscience can attach itself to the mint, anise, and cummin of conduct, until its wretched possessor is half insane with scrupulosity about things that do not matter. Or conscience can swing to the negative side of conduct and so inhibit and repress a man, who might have been creatively happy, that he is imprisoned in negative conscientiousness. Or conscience can sanction absurd or cruel customs. So Captain Kemble in old Boston, after a long sea-voyage, was put in the public stocks because on the front steps of their own house he kissed his wife on Sunday, and so still there are social conventions concerning which people become unreasonably conscientious. Or conscience can become hypersensitive until, instead of producing lovely and gracious character, its harried possessor worries about anything done or left undone, so that one would choose a kindly sinner for company rather than so distressing an exhibition of wretched conscientiousness. Indeed, conscience can get completely out of hand and, long after the sin in question has been repented of, turned from, and left behind, can make a man so needlessly remorseful that unless something can be done for his haunted soul he will land under psychiatric care. "Every physician," writes one medical man, "who has much to do with nervous troubles and emotional disorders soon comes to recognize that thousands of well-meaning individuals are suffering from mental torture and various nervous disorders as the result of overworking the conscience."

If some one here is underworking his conscience, this sermon is not for him. But I call to witness the experience of the rest of us, that conscience is a powerful and sometimes terrific fact. Having had the good fortune of a fine home in childhood, I am not bothered by obsessing fears but, having experienced one thing, I do fear it in solemn earnest: the inexorable movement of an unworthy deed from expectation through committal into memory, where it settles down, towers up, fills the sky, and begins its deadly reiterated accusation—Shame on you! A man says, But I will not let myself be so afflicted by my conscience; is it not *my* conscience? only to discover that no man's conscience is at the beck and call of his volition. A man says, But I will attend to other things and fill my days with fortunate preoccupation, only to discover that, waiting for every chink of opportunity, that voice haunts him, saying, Shame on you! Such remorse Victor Hugo compared with the tide which, though it ebb, comes ever back to the shore again.

To be sure, so intolerable is conscience when it thus swings into full action, that we all are inwardly equipped with devices to evade it. A consulting psychologist has recently written that in a mixed company of husbands and wives he first asked the husbands to answer a questionnaire about the queernesses of their wives and received, he says, enthusiastic coöperation. Then he asked the wives to fill out a questionnaire about the queernesses of their husbands and once more the response was heartfelt. Then he asked each individual to fill out a questionnaire about his or her own queernesses and received, he said, mostly a blank stare, not because in theory they doubted that they themselves were queer but because, to their own happiness, they had not thought much about it. So Jesus said long ago that men look for motes in others' eyes and forget the beams in their own. Nevertheless, while each of us is equipped with such devices to alleviate self-accusation, that is not the whole story. One sometimes wishes that it were. For conscience can be terrific, making a man feel, as Coleridge said,

Like one that on a lonesome road
Doth walk in fear and dread,
And having once turned round, walks on
And turns no more his head;
Because he knows a frightful fiend
Doth close behind him tread.

Even when conscience is not so strenuous, it is bad enough, saying to us, You there with your heritage, your opportunities, your home, your friends, look at yourself, no better than you are! Here is an inexorable fact with which we have to deal one way or another—an inner voice that keeps saying, *You ought not to be the way you are.*

In a world where every normal human being has to listen habitually to that voice, there surely can be no health, nervous, emotional, moral, or spiritual, unless mankind hears another message, *No man need stay the way he is.* It is because every normal human being hears the first voice, demanding moral change, and millions are trying to live without the second voice, promising moral change, that life is so devastated by conscience. If ever we dealt with a real problem, this is one.

Certainly in the New Testament it is real. It was vivid to Paul. "The good which I would I do not: but the evil which I would not, that I practice. . . . I delight in the law of God after the inward man: but I see a different law in my members, warring against the law of my mind, and bringing me into captivity under the law of sin which is in my members. Wretched man that I am!" A truer description of a universal human problem it would be hard to imagine. The great seers have consistently said the same, from Plato describing the problem as driving a chariot with two horses, one white and eager, the other dark and obstinate, to Goethe's Faust, saying, "Two souls, alas, are lodg'd within my breast." If Paul stepped out of his seventh chapter of Romans into the triumph of his eighth—"There is therefore now no condemnation to them that are in Christ Jesus"—it is because his Christianity met this human need with a saving message: To be sure, you ought not to be the way you are but, then, no man need stay the way he is.

In every realm this same thing is true for which we are pleading in the spiritual life. It is a universal experience in physical illness to know that we ought not be as we are, and scientific medicine is trying to lift the answering cry, Men do not need to stay as they are. Lack of education is a universal experience in which people feel the need of change, and not only are all schools trying to say that man does not need to stay as he is but psychologists, like Dr. Thorndike, are assuring us that even as we grow older, fifty years old, sixty years old, we need not stop learning, that our capacity to acquire new knowledge drops no more than one per cent a year, so that, the old proverb to the contrary notwithstanding, we can teach an old dog new tricks. Everywhere one looks man's problem in life is like an unfruitful valley which long has known it ought not be as it is and now learns that through irrigation it need not stay as it is. While in other realms the sense of need may at times be dim and wavering, in the moral life it is concentrated in conscience, the inseparable companion of our pilgrimage, from whom no divorce can part us, that says, with tireless iteration, You ought not to be the way you are.

In view of this, how can men so easily consent to give up Christianity for themselves and for their generation? For what more devastating thing can we imagine than the whole race having to deal with an inner monitor demanding moral change while throwing away the voice that most has proclaimed its possibility?

In endeavoring to secure light upon this matter, consider first that this Christian gospel is the extension of the personal ministry of Jesus. He found Palestine, like the rest of the world, full of unpromising people—women of Samaria, Prodigal Sons, dishonest public servants like Zacchæus, fishermen like Peter, James, and John, getting nowhere in their lives—and he left them changed so that one would hardly recognize them. Moreover, Jesus always took it for granted that such change is an essential part of human living so that, far from being strange, it is to be expected. At no point is his attitude toward people more strikingly different from ours. We merely size people up. We look them over, take their measure, size them up. Thus and so, we say, they are, and there we leave them.

A long generation ago in London, for example, we might have seen a young man from India, smartly dressed, playing the social game with success and charm, taking dancing lessons, taking violin lessons. We would have sized him up as quite a young man about town. Why not? says some one; Why not size up a young man? To which I answer that the inadequacy of merely sizing anybody up is made evident by the fact that that young man about town turned out to be Mahatma Gandhi. Surely, not! I can imagine some one saying who knew him in the London days; that young fellow never turned out to be the toothless, half-naked ascetic living on goat's milk, holding in his frail hands the spiritual destinies of India and almost single-handed forcing the British Empire to reverse its policy? Yet that is what happened. Moreover, this which so surprises us would, I suspect, not surprise Jesus at all. He would say, That is quite the kind of thing that does occur in personality.

Have you ever been on a camping trip in the wilds with an engineer who in places where you saw nothing in particular kept saying, Think what could be done with all this power! Have you ever, in company with an educational expert, visited a backward community concerned about its schools, and felt his enthusiasm about what might be done with them? Every man who amounts to anything has at least one realm where nothing is so real to him as the possibilities. Well, Jesus was an expert in personality. When he met anyone like a Prodigal Son he sized him up. Indeed he did! No one could do that better. But he never stopped there. Nothing in that boy was so real to Jesus as what might be done with him.

If this were an argument, I should contend first that on this matter Jesus was right psychologically. It is of the essence of personal life to change. Not only can it change but it cannot stand still; it is always going up or down. And at the heart of personality is the power to direct change by throwing ahead a chosen goal and working toward it. I should also contend, in the second place, that Jesus is not only psychologically but historically right. The one thing we know that changes most is human life. The sun, moon, and stars, the planet which is our habitation, have not changed much in the race's memory, but human life has changed tremendously and in the realm of personality the possibilities contained in intellect, in creative purposefulness, and in the loves of mankind are quite incalculable. And I should contend, in the third place, that if a hypothesis must be finally tested by its fruits, this attitude of Jesus has had amazing confirmation, for he has become one of the supreme life-changers of history, in part because whenever he met anybody he started by thinking that the most significant fact in that life was what might be done with it.

Is any man here so poor in friendship that he does not know the astonishing change that can come to him when over the horizon of his discouraged soul there rises a friend who believes in his possibilities? You see, one trouble with us is not simply that we size up other people; alas, we size ourselves up! We take our own measure. Thus and so we are—so we catalogue ourselves and then go out to live with that voice which demands moral change. I know I am dealing with some one's need when I remind you of Jesus who, whenever even now he can get a man's attention, says to him, You need not stay the way you are.

Again, consider the method Jesus used when he did change people. He never gave them the impression that he was importing into them something artificial and alien, but rather that he was discovering in them something they had not known was there, and was bringing it out into the open. James Whitcomb Riley was a notorious failure in his early days at school—to quote a schoolmate, "the most celebrated failure in arithmetic in the country." Then he came under the influence of a new teacher who appreciated his literary flare and helped develop that for the world. When one contrasts the methods used by the teachers who failed to help Riley and the method used by the teacher who succeeded, there is no mistaking the nature of the difference. The teachers who failed were trying to import into that boy information which seemed to him utterly alien and uninteresting. Then the new teacher came and began at the other end. He appreciated in the boy some things whose value the others had not recognized. Before his eyes the boy saw unveiled, not James Whitcomb Riley the failure he had been told he was, but a James Whitcomb Riley he had merely dreamed of being, until, identifying himself with the newly-discovered person, he went out to be himself indeed. Well, Jesus must have had a magic touch as a teacher.

I understand the objections naturally raised to all this. Our possibilities of choice are not limitless, some one says; it is not true that anybody can become anything; rather, our lives are set within boundaries predetermined by heredity and environment and, furthermore, we are in an economic and social system which keeps many from getting out of themselves all that is there, so that to tell people that they can become anything they will is to beguile their souls with false expectations. Of course that is true. In a nursery group I know, there is now a very little boy whose major problem is to decide whether when he grows up he will be a man or a woman. Day after day he balances the relative advantages of being the father or the mother of a family and decides now for one and now for the other. Some day he will discover that his possibilities are not so extensive as he had supposed, that there is some truth in predestination and that there are limits to free will.

If some one here is trying to avoid this morning's message by stressing that range of fact, I am inclined to grant you almost anything you want, within reason. But the major truth still holds good. Of course our possibilities are not limitless but, for all that, you need not stay the way you are. No, you need not. There is more in you than ever has been brought out, and one confirmation of that fact is simply to imagine Jesus having a chance to make a voyage of discovery through your soul. What continental things he has discovered in people even like ourselves!

Again, consider the way Jesus, thus believing in man's possibilities and discovering in man the diviner self, went on, with any man he was trying to change, to give him a sense of backing so that he felt, not that he was lifting himself by his own bootstraps, but that he was being lifted. Here is where moralists fall down and only men of religious faith have an adequate gospel for human need. The moralist always has to tell a man in the end that somehow he must change himself, while the success of a high religion in life-changing has lain in the fact that it puts a man in new relationships with eternal spiritual forces so that he feels he is being changed.

Certainly, if that is true, it meets one of our most devastating needs. How many people in this congregation have been saying this morning, I have tried; Heaven knows I have tried, and still I am unchanged! Not only in this realm, however, but in every other, profound human experience bears witness to the superficiality of individual trying by itself alone. When Robert Louis Stevenson was changed from a purposeless to a purposeful young man, he did not think he had steered himself but that he had been guided by "that unknown steersman whom we call God." When Keats, reading

Spenser's "Faerie Queene," was transformed from a young lad without a vocation to a young lad who knew that his destiny lay in poetry, he did not think he had changed himself but had been changed, born from above by a vision of a world of beauty he had never sensed before. So all profound transformations of character are associated with the experience, not of lifting oneself but of being lifted, not of changing oneself but of being changed.

Indeed, consider the history of civilization as a whole and see how true it is, even in the social realm, that nothing comes merely by trying. What would we say was the first major turning point in the development of civilization on this planet? Few of us would guess that but it is plain. The first major turning point in the development of civilization on this planet came when early man planted a seed in the ground and waited. Never before had man so coöperated with the cosmic forces. He had tried to win his way by his strong right arm and the strenuousness of his will, but now a new era dawned. He planted a seed in the ground and waited. There began agriculture and with it civilization, for there man began to relate himself creatively to the eternal forces and to depend on them.

That is a parable of something everlastingly true in the spiritual life. Of course we cannot blow upon our hands and change ourselves but we can so alter our inner attitude that our whole relationship to the spiritual world will be changed. Every man instinctively knows that this is true in dealing with trouble. Many of us are not dismayed so much by our sins as by our troubles. We are outwitted and desolated by them. Yet in our best hours we know we need not stay that way. Let a man by ever so little alter his interior attitude toward trouble and the whole experience of trouble is altered. I have seen many people in these days facing tragedy in such noble fashion that what one hard-bestead person put into words I have become familiar with in life: "All the water in the world cannot sink a ship unless it gets *inside* the ship. All the sorrow in the world cannot sink a person unless it gets *inside* the mind." What is true of trouble is true of sin. Alter your inner attitude and you have changed your relationships with the whole spiritual world.

Long before this you must have felt how difficult it is to present an intimate and personal matter such as this to a great congregation.

Preachers often turn to public subjects because it is simpler to present a public subject to a public crowd, but this message is intimate and personal. Who was it said that preaching is like discharging an eye dropper out of a window into the street below in hope that the eye medicine will hit somebody in the right place? One feels the truth of that now. For all that we have been saying is quite in vain unless it reaches our intimacies. You, there, with a bad temper which is in danger of wrecking your family's happiness, you need not stay the way you are. You, there, with a sorry case of self-pity which is making all your friends miserable, you need not stay the way you are. You, there, with a habit which creeps up into dominance over you, you need not stay the way you are. You can plant the seed of faith and effort in the right soil and, lo! another era of cosmic coöperation!

Finally, think of the life-changing forces which are released by a personality who not only believes in us, discovers our diviner self and backs us up with a power greater than our own, but who cares enough to suffer for us! For if we are realistic about the life-changing forces which transform us most, we cannot leave out the people who love us into being better. Of all forces which make a man want to be better, nothing is so powerful as love. Imagine a man utterly unloved and you see a life where conscience has no leverage for its lifting power, but, just as soon as love comes in, new dimensions of desire and possibility appear. So Shakespeare made Portia say to Bassanio, when her love answered his,

> . . . Though for myself alone
> I would not be ambitious in my wish,
> To wish myself much better; yet, for you
> I would be trebled twenty times myself.

Now, when this experience of personal love is elevated and extended until we stand before great souls who have cared enough about the world to sacrifice themselves, some one perchance who died for man because he thought man was worth dying for, we are facing the most tremendous moral lifting power the race has known.

A monument, so I am told, has been erected on the coast to the officers and crew of a wrecked vessel, who at the cost of their lives kept the high tradition of the sea. The wreck came in a dreadful storm and despite their efforts the lifeboats were smashed and every one was drowned. It was noted, however, that the only bodies to reach shore were those of passengers wearing life-belts. Evidently there had not been enough for all and the officers and crew had gone without them so that their bodies sank and were lost. One day, it is said, a rollicking group of boys on a hike came to the monument, as merry youngsters as one could see, apparently without a serious idea in their heads, until one of them, out of boyish curiosity, asked what the monument was all about. So the leader told them of the officers and crew who tried to save others when they could not save themselves. The boys grew quieter and quieter until one of them took off his cap and then the others took off their caps too, and they stood there mute witnesses to one of the profoundest facts in human nature, that nothing in this world reaches so deep, takes hold so hard, and lifts so long as vicarious self-sacrifice.

If we here today could be persuaded how desperately this world needs us at our best and then could be brought face to face with those great souls who have cared enough to suffer for mankind, until we stood before the cross of Christ as those boys stood before the monument, every person here would be saying two things to himself: first, I ought not to be the way I am; and second, No man need stay the way he is.

Preventive Religion

ONE of the most important movements of our time is the gradual shift of emphasis from curative to preventive medicine. A wise family no longer regards its physician as intended primarily to cure its members when they have fallen ill, but to keep them from becoming ill. No necessary conflict exists between these two complementary aspects of medicine, yet one who sees what is afoot as the decades pass can note the changing stress. Public sanitation to prevent epidemics; quarantines, national, local, and domestic, to ward off contagion; inoculations and vaccinations to confer immunity in advance; periodic health examinations to forestall trouble—these are the signs of the times in medicine. In this realm we are taking in earnest the ancient maxim that an ounce of prevention is worth a pound of cure.

In religion, however, we are not taking it so seriously. How many controlling ideas and methods of work are still back in the age of curative religion, and how few of them have come into the age of preventive religion!

A man once went to Dwight L. Moody, it is said, with a tale of moral disaster and, after having narrated the harrowing facts, said, "Now, Mr. Moody, what would you do if you had gotten into such a situation?" to which Mr. Moody replied, "Man, I never would get into it." That is to say, true religion is not simply an ambulance at the foot of a precipice to pick up those who have fallen over; it is a fence at the top to prevent their falling in the first place. As the fine, familiar benediction of the Epistle of Jude puts it, "Now unto him that is able to keep you from falling."

Our temptation to minimize the preventive aspects of religion and maximize its curative aspects springs in part from historical causes. Christianity at first went out into a pagan world and its earliest appeal was directed to prodigals and outcasts, for whom others had no message and no help. When Celsus, the Epicurean, attacked Christianity in the second century, he poured derision on it because its devotees had so largely been, not respectable citizens, but villains and sinners. At the beginning, Christians for the most part were adults who had been converted from pagan degradation, and Paul gave a deplorable picture of their moral antecedents before they were lifted from the mire. That situation presupposes curative religion.

Alongside this historic emphasis in the New Testament one must put the medieval conceptions of heaven and hell as a reason for stress upon the religion of rescue. Hell was a desperate reality to the whole Western World, whether Christian or non-Christian, and as far down in time as 1877 Henry Ward Beecher was thundering against this belief in Plymouth pulpit, saying, "To tell me that back of Christ there is a God who for unnumbered centuries has gone on creating men and sweeping them like dead flies—nay, like living ones—into hell, is to ask me to worship a being as much worse than the conception of any mediæval devil as can be imagined; but I will not worship the devil, though he should come dressed in royal robes and sit on the throne of Jehovah." If religion be conceived chiefly as a means of escape from such a hell, it is inevitably a religion of rescue. In Adam's disobedience we all were submerged in an abysmal flood of sin and the gospel is the only Ark that can save our hell-bound humanity from eternal perdition—that was the old theology and it inevitably implied a religion of reclamation and recovery.

Even more popularly influential in causing emphasis on curative religion is the simple fact that rescue is dramatic. Few people note the processes by which fires are prevented. They are commonplace, dull and drab. But when a fire is raging and some brave fellow risks his neck in a thrilling rescue, that is dramatic and the papers are full of it. Few people are interested in the routine of inoculation, vaccination, and quarantine restriction, but let a healer come to town and loudly noise abroad that the sick are being cured, and, as in Jesus' day when all Capernaum filled up the streets, the promise of rescue from distress will thrill the populace. So, in the story of Christianity nothing is so exciting as its moral rescues.

Do not misunderstand me; they are exciting to me, too. A rescue always is thrilling. An American battalion in the Great War is lost and then after a few days is found again, and more excitement is felt over that one than over a thousand battalions never lost at all. A ship goes down at sea and a heroic tale of hazardous exploits in the life-boats comes back with the survivors, and in that single incident is more material for tears and heart-throbs than in a hundred ships that sail in safety and need no rescue. So, some men and women, sustained by an integrating faith in God and a fine companionship with Christ, live honorable and useful lives. They are dragged out of no moral hells because they get into none. They are cured of no loathsome habits because they contract none. But one must admit that they are not half so thrilling as a rescue.

From the story, therefore, of the Prodigal Son recovered from companionship with swine to sit at his father's board again, to the last narrative of a lost life found, of a smirched, dishonored soul lifted to usefulness and decency again, the most thrilling things in Christian history have been rescues. Here in this church were I to recount to you the moral reclamations that have taken place in the natural course of our work in the last few months, you would think them worth anything they might cost in time and toil. And they are. That university man who came to us morally whipped two years after getting his degree but who went out from his last interview, saying, "I am a new man in a new world," does represent one of the abiding and glorious aspects of the gospel. But without in the least belittling the power of God to cure, let me exalt the power of God to prevent. After all, one thing is far better than bringing the Prodigal Son back from the far country, and that is keeping him from going there in the first place—"Now unto him that is able to keep you from falling."

How poignantly one feels the truth of this when some life, badly mangled in a devastating crisis of practical trouble or moral disgrace, seeks spiritual recovery as an emergency measure! Why did not he feel the need of sound and healthy faith and character *before* the crisis? One cannot build his house on rock after the storm breaks; that must be done before. Granted the stirring truth in the possibilities of moral rescue through Christ, it is dangerous to expatiate upon and fairly glorify the iniquities of the saved sinner because it is exciting to see him recovered from them. Indeed, from this overdone emphasis of evangelical Christianity has come the widespread impression that only moral failures need the gospel. Plenty of people, when they see a young man collapsing morally, think that if a genuine religious experience could take hold of him it might save the day. Many parents who have lightly neglected religious training in their homes—Were theirs not dear, wholesome children? What did they need of religion?—now seeing one of these children in manhood beginning to go to pieces, wish that the minister might rescue him. Thus many regard religion as merely an agency of recovery. It is like an ambulance or a fire engine—on ordinary days no one thinks of them; only when something dreadfully amiss has happened does one turn to them.

Upon the contrary, a healthy and victorious spiritual life is something infinitely greater than an emergency measure. To be sure, for all of us life is full of emergencies. The older a man grows the more he expects unforeseen contingencies, as from ambush, to take him by surprise. There are crises of trouble, temptation, opportunity which leap unannounced into every man's experience. Such emergencies, however, cannot be adequately handled by emergency measures. When to any one an important crisis comes, the solemn fact is that either he is ready or not ready—it is too late to get ready. A man must have the resources of a strong spiritual life, grounded in faith, exercised in moral habit, in touch with adequate reserves of power, *before* the emergency. He cannot extemporize spiritual life when, in a crisis, he suddenly needs it.

Even in the external realm of economics, reliance on emergency measures is dangerous, as any one watching our national life can see. When one comes closer home and deals with the physical body, even more obviously are emergency measures a poor substitute for sound health. When, more intimately still, one enters the realm of mind, it becomes absurd to suppose that an educated intelligence can be extemporized when it is critically needed to rescue a man from failure. To this interior realm a vital religion belongs. If a man is powerfully to possess it in a crisis, he must have possessed it before the crisis. To wait until moral disaster sets one clamoring for a rescuer is a poor substitute for the radiant, healthy, triumphant spiritual life which forestalls disaster. The most important work Christ is doing on earth today is not, I think, rescuing the fallen, but producing a quality and strength of character that keeps us from falling.

In the first place, one who takes Christianity in earnest, lives in its climate and atmosphere, deals seriously with the Master's way of living and catches his spirit, does have conferred upon him as the years pass a kind of spiritual immunity. Some moral diseases he is not subject to any more. To see this exhibited one only has to think of the result of Jesus' fellowship with one of his disciples. Give John, for example, one year, two years, three years of close fellowship with the Master and an inevitable consequence ensues. Some temptations to which at the beginning John was responsive—he might even have succumbed to them—pass over into the unthinkable class. He has achieved immunity. As a man who has lived around the marshes where malaria is a real peril moves up now to higher altitudes and recognizes that somewhere along the lines of his ascent he has passed the place where malaria is a danger, so a man who genuinely lives with Christ mounts moral levels and finds at last that old temptations have no more appeal. He has passed out of the region of their power. Alas for a man who does not know what that means!

It was one of the greatest days in human history when the idea of immunity dawned in medicine. Men could be made immune so that the disease in question had no dominion over them. They could walk in its presence unafraid and uncontaminated. That was a revolutionary concept. The idea and the practise of it carry us back to the biography of Louis Pasteur, great scientist and great Christian. "Then," we read, "Pasteur jumped to one of his quick conclusions: 'Once a cow has anthrax, but gets better from it, all the anthrax microbes in the world cannot give her another attack—she is *immune*.'" That hour is comparable with the most significant moments in human history, as when man first thought the earth was round or that it moved about the sun, or that biological species are not static but mutable and evolving. It was a pregnant hour whose multiplying consequences will last as long as humanity does. People can be made immune so that devastating diseases have no dominion over them.

Well, a wholesome religion does that for character. I have before me a letter from one of the great spirits in this nation. You would recognize his name were I to mention it. He has just been going through one of those devastating tragedies which search a man's soul and he has carried it off so splendidly that those of us who know him have seen a fresh revelation of victorious living. This is the sentence with which his letter ends: "After all, religion is worth while when you need it; but you can't have it then, if you haven't had it before!" Aye, to have religion *before*, habitually to live in the fellowship of the Highest until old evils have lost their power, fine things once difficult have become easy, and the soul has grown in healthy-mindedness—that is the major use of religion. May God save us from the necessity of curative religion!

In the second place, a wholesome religion confers on its possessor the prophylactic effects of a positive purpose. Every positive purpose influencing a man's life has a prophylactic effect. Your boy becomes absorbed in some scientific interest such as building a radio set. That means that to some other things his preoccupied attention will turn a deaf ear. What Dr. Chalmers in a resounding phrase called "the expulsive power of a new affection" has come into his life. He is interested in something and when competitive interests cross his path his instinctive reaction is to call, Gangway! for his major purpose.

A psychologist tells us of a dog absorbed in chasing his master's automobile, and, says the psychologist, so intent was he on this "end motive that he 'passed up' a tempting opportunity of chasing a cat who crossed in front of him. He was observed to hesitate just a trifle but kept to his course." Well, all dogs have cats; we know well, without explanation, the meaning of that parable. And if our lives are not to be random, futile, wicked pursuits of them, it will be because in advance we have achieved the prophylaxis of a positive purpose.

When Colonel Lindbergh landed in Paris from his first trans-

Atlantic flight, his associates here sent him the offer of a contract for a million dollars. His brief, explicit, return cable is worthy of a place among the undying utterances of this generation. "You must remember," he said, "this expedition was not organized to make money but to advance aviation." A positive purpose that can make a man immune to such an offer is a spectacle which this generation should dwell upon. It kept him from falling.

Obviously such controlling spiritual purposes cannot be extemporized as emergency measures. They must have been in the man before. They run far back into his childhood and the training of his home. Consideration of them magnifies the indispensable importance of Christian families and exalts the ideal with which Dr. Bushnell startled the church of his day—that a child should be so reared that he cannot recall when he was not a Christian. Some of us came from such homes. Often, to be sure, we have been unworthy of them, but on every remembrance of them we are grateful that because of them we never needed to be rescued from some of the mires and abysses in which life can be lost. The prophylactic purposes which became ingrained in character long before we knew the perils they would protect us from kept us from falling.

In the third place, this kind of wholesome religion issues at last in the safety of established habit. Why do we commonly talk of habit as though it were a bad thing? He has a habit, we say, almost always meaning something disagreeable. As a matter of fact, habit is our best friend. The essence of character-building is the creating and confirming of such habits as that of industry, of courtesy, of punctuality, of decency, of unselfish thoughtfulness. Now, when such habits have been created and confirmed in a man, one consequence is inevitable—there are some things he simply cannot do; they are morally impossible.

Much nonsense has been talked about free will as though it meant that a man were at liberty to do anything. He could be true to his wife or false to her, he could be drunk or sober, he could be honest or rob a bank—was he not a free moral agent? Could he not do what he would? Moreover, you will find books pleading in the name of morality and religion for such free will as though it were not only a fact but a desirable fact. The truth is, there is no such free will, and it would be dreadful if there were. I am not free to forge a check—I could not forge a check; my mind would not function; my hands would not work. All the accumulated habits of my life would rise in irresistible conspiracy against the idea and the act. If by free will you mean that a man is free to do anything—commit murder, adultery, theft—thank God, the years behind us have not been altogether futile! We are not thus free. The psychologists say that good men even under hypnosis cannot be persuaded to do vile things. The experiments have established that. You cannot so hypnotize high-minded men as to make them do despicable things. The grain is set in such lives; the habits are confirmed and the result is glorious—a nobly predictable character. We can tell in advance what some of our friends will do. They will be honest, truthful, kindly, unselfish. We say they are dependable. That is to say, we know in advance that we can count on their reactions. Nothing is nobler on this earth than right-minded, predictable character.

Perhaps some one is saying, Then you do not believe in free will; you think we are all predetermined; you are a fatalist. That of course is untrue. We are not predetermined and I am not a fatalist. But it is desirable to stop our nonsense about the areas within which free will operates. We are free to have something to say in advance about which habits among all the possibilities shall be formed in our lives. And the time to begin exercising that freedom is the earliest possible moment. God save us from the necessity of curative religion! God give us preventive religion, building right-minded, predictable characters.

This holds good for the Christian experience as a life of prayer just as truly as it does for the Christian experience as moral habit. Some of the worst superstitions about prayer and perversions of it come from regarding it as an emergency measure. Prayer really is the habitual maintenance of an interior spiritual companionship. Instead of such a life of prayer sustained with radiant and powerful consequence across the years, many use prayer only when in a crisis they want some supernatural *deus ex machina* to crash through the natural order and rescue them. So Shakespeare in "The Tempest" makes the sailors cry in peril of the storm, "All lost! to prayers, to prayers! all lost!" That is the perversion of prayer. Prayer at its deepest is not an emergency measure to which one turns after disaster has fallen; it is rather an habitual spiritual companionship by which one has lived triumphantly before.

If one says that in the crisis of his last week in Jerusalem Jesus turned to prayer in the Garden of Gethsemane, the answer is that plainly he did not turn to it as an unaccustomed, emergency measure. Note the brevity of his praying! He faced an emergency indeed; there was no time for long supplication; it was too late for him to have broken an untraveled path to the presence of the Father. He could pray so briefly yet so powerfully in the garden because prayer had been his habit before. When, therefore, the ambush was sprung and the terrific crisis was on him, his feet followed a familiar path and his words were few: "Not my will, but thine, be done." What reorientation of life a moment of prayer can work in one to whom it is habitual! But if one is to have this experience when he critically needs it, he must have known it *before.*

Some of you young people, especially if you have attended revivalistic campaigns, have heard much about the power of God to save sinners. I, too, have seen some marvelous recoveries and should not count myself a disciple of Jesus if I did not expect to see them and have part in them. The number of people who have known the fine uses of preventive religion, as the number of people who have known the fine uses of preventive medicine, is so small that curative religion, like curative medicine, has a long run ahead of it. Nevertheless, be sensible! Stop talking about curative religion as though it were glorious! It is dreadful—how dreadful you never will know until you have to walk through hell with people who are trying to get out of their perdition. It would be worth while to have preached this sermon if only to drive home on some youth here this fact: you do not need to go through that experience. Many walk down Jordan most of the way on the wrong side and then cross over after the water is deep and the current strong. It is a thrilling escapade. The company gathers on the bank to celebrate so hazardous a crossing and to see the safe arrival. But this morning I celebrate another kind of experience altogether: a youth crossing Jordan near the source, where it is so narrow he hardly knows when he steps over, and coming down the right bank all the way. In spite of all our historic Christian emphasis, conversion, as it is ordinarily conceived, is not the ideal. "Now unto him that is able to keep you from falling"!

As for you older people, some of whom have been listening to this sermon somewhat aloof and personally detached, because you have been saying that you have managed your life with fair decency —let me speak to you! No moral ambulance call has ever been sent out for you. You may attribute that not to religion, but to ordinary stalwart, probably inherited character without religion. But you are wrong about that; it was religion. That same thing happens here which happens in medicine. If you have not had yellow fever, that is no credit to you. Preventive medicine built dikes against that years ago. If you have not had smallpox, that is no credit to you. Preventive medicine worked out the secret of immunity from that before you were born. You are the inheritor of the accumulating social effects of preventive medicine. So preventive religion, for all our failures, has been at work for centuries, has changed the tone of family life, has made neighborhood life better, has lifted literature to its best; national ideas have been changed because of it; great social reforms have been born out of its creative spirit. You have been protected from the beginning by the immunities created, the standards lifted, the dikes raised by the accumulating effect of preventive religion. Do you not think it would be fair to recognize that? We have a right to challenge you to the support of preventive religion.

There is an old and suggestive test for imbecility. Turn on the faucet, let the water run into the basin, and then tell somebody to empty the basin by dipping. If he starts dipping out the basin without turning off the faucet he is probably an imbecile. If he knows enough to turn off the faucet and then dip out the basin, the chances are he is normal. Alas, we Christians have not fairly met even that simple test. Too content with a few curative efforts, dipping this sinner up here and that sinner up there, while all the time the general forces of man's life, economic, educational, recreational, international, have been pouring out a flood of evil which all our curative methods could not counteract! Let us raise the standard of preventive religion, individual and social. Let us set up our banners in the name of him who is able to keep us from falling, and this morning let us begin with ourselves. For in our personal lives one ounce of wholesome, healthy-minded, religious prevention is worth a pound of religious cure.

The Service of Religious Faith to Mental Health

THESE are days when we need all the resources we can find which will assist in creating and maintaining mental health. The mental, moral, emotional consequences of living in a disturbed, threatening generation like this are terrific. Is there anybody here this morning who one way or another, for himself or for somebody else, does not feel the strain? Listen, then, to this message from the second letter to Timothy: "For God hath not given us the spirit of fear; but of power, and of love, and of a sound mind." Aye! that would be something to get out of one's religion.

This word from the New Testament, so close to our present need, at once suggests that it probably never has been easy to attain a sound mind. We moderns often pity ourselves in this regard. Our new civilization, we say, has so complicated life that the strain is breaking down the mental balance of many: insanity is increasing and nervous breakdowns multiply. To be sure, it is easy to recount those factors in modern civilization which so overstrain many and unbalance some. But let us remember that even though it be true that our modern civilization has in some regards increased the difficulties of healthy-mindedness, in other ways it has decreased them. Think of ancient fears and superstitions that once haunted our fathers which are not in our world at all—mysterious plagues that in a single year took off a large part of England's population, cause unknown, cure impossible; or belief in demons that scared sanity out of generations of common folk; or the paralyzing fear of hell; or the dread of torture for heresy; or in the economic life masses in penury so hopeless that even today it is difficult for us to imagine it. No, my friends, it probably never has been much easier than it is today to win that inner victory without which no good life is possible—a sound mind.

When, therefore, an ancient character like Paul talks to us about the contribution which his Christian faith has made to healthy-mindedness, he comes close to our need. For through Paul's burdened lifetime he was a healthy-minded man. He faced the contentious ingratitude of his followers. He faced the limitations of physical ill health, most bitter to an active man. He was brutally maltreated by his public enemies. He endured poverty, always skirting the ragged edge of destitution and ever and again falling over. And at last, after a long-drawn-out imprisonment, he met martyrdom. But through it all he kept a high morale and his last cry came from an unspoiled and unembittered soul: "I have fought the good fight, I have finished the course, I have kept the faith."

I do not see how we can avoid the challenge of a healthy-minded man like that. We had better listen to him when out of so rich an experience he writes, as despite some scholars I hope he did write, in this particular portion of the second letter to Timothy, "God hath not given us the spirit of fear; but of power, and of love, and of a sound mind."

Let us clarify our thought on one matter. "Healthy-mindedness" and "sick-mindedness" are not the common vocabulary of the pulpit. "Righteousness" and "sin" are the preacher's ordinary words. But while "righteousness" and "sin" are good words and have a long future ahead of them, they sometimes confuse the issue. What would you call pride, for example? A sin? Let us rather say that a conceited man has a sick mind. To see the truth of that, turn the matter around and consider the impression made on us by a fine specimen of humility. Mr. Einstein, for example, in his own lifetime by consensus of scientific opinion was ranked along with Newton and Galileo. Already he is among the immortals, and he was told so, so that I suspect a similar thing has seldom, if ever, happened in the history of science. Listen, then, to Mr. Einstein himself: "Many times a day I realize how much my own outer and inner life is built upon the labors of my fellow-men, both living and dead, and how earnestly I must exert myself in order to give in return as much as I have received."

What is your first comment on that? Mine is that that man had a healthy mind.

If some one, now, is fearing that it is dangerous so to translate righteousness into healthy-mindedness and sin into sick-mindedness, I simply ask, What did Jesus call himself? A physician. How did he describe the people he tried to help? "They that are whole have no need of a physician, but they that are sick." Aye, they that are sick!

Indeed, thinking of you young people in particular, I ask you which ideal is the more attractive to you, to be righteous or to be healthy-minded? You know well that some of you here, if I called you sinners, would be moved not at all except, it might be, to hidden mirth, but if I could make you even dimly suspect that you are not healthy-minded, you would be disturbed. Behind all our callous consciences every one of us does want to be healthy—physically, emotionally, mentally healthy.

What tragedies have come from the changed meanings of a word! If in this pulpit today I should cry, "O young men and women, be holy!" what a mistake! Who wants to be holy? Nevertheless, go back to the original meaning of that word "holy"—whole, wholesome, healthy. That is what it means. Well, God hath given us not the spirit of fear; but of power, and of love, and of a sound mind.

In the first place, note that those most competent to interpret the meanings of vital Christian faith unmistakably testify that it does release interior resources of spiritual *power*, and if that is true nobody can afford to neglect it. For, as all the psychiatrists say and as every man must plainly see, one of the commonest sources of mental ill health is the consciousness of deficient resources and of consequent inadequacy for life. Why should we not feel inadequate for life? Look what it does to us! I have just been reading a new biography of George Eliot. When she was a young woman she loved Herbert Spencer. And, what is more, he was very attentive to her, so that their friends supposed of course they were going to marry. But he was coldly philosophical. One day he took a shilling and flipped it: heads he would marry, tails he would not. And it came down tails. Months afterwards, out of her convalescence from heartbreak, the young woman who was afterwards to be George Eliot wrote to a friend: "I am very well and 'plucky'—a word which I propose to substitute for happy, as more truthful." How many of us have had one way or another to learn to substitute "plucky" for "happy" as more truthful!

Multitudes of people today, faced by the cruel things that life sometimes does to them, are pounded quite to pieces, and the consequence is what the New Testament describes as "the spirit of fear"—that is, an appalling sense of inadequacy for life. If there were time, I could unroll a long list of unhealthy tricks which the human mind is guilty of in such a case. For some people, running away from their appalling sense of insufficiency, take to boasting; they talk and act as if they were as conceited as Lucifer, pathetically covering up with a crust of seeming pride their real humiliation and inferiority. Others fall into a persecution complex, blame somebody else for their inadequacy, brood over being hurt and wronged, and end, many of them, in the asylum with paranoia. Others take to day-dreaming, run away from these unhappy situations where they always feel inferior, into a fantastic world of make-believe, where they are always superior and come out on top, and so comfort themselves. Some become downright sick, fall into physical illness, frequently of an hysterical variety, their subconscious minds devising for them this escape, as often happens in shell shock, whereby they may be pitied instead of blamed for their inadequacy.

What consequences a man who works with individuals sees arising from this familiar feeling of inadequacy for life! And all the time, my friends, there is only one healthy way out: power, personal power in life, spiritual resources that can be tapped, in the possession of which a man goes out into life saying like Paul, even though he was in prison when he said it, "I can do all things in him that strengtheneth me."

A religion that does not do something like that for a man is not functioning. Many people suppose that a man has so much power and no more. A man's energies, they think, are in a closed reservoir and when the demands are too much, they are exhausted. So they picture themselves, and the damage done by that familiar but false way of thinking is incalculable. For the seers of the spiritual life agee that the truth is something else altogether. We are channels of power,—not closed reservoirs,—open channels of power, and at the fountainheads of our being it is possible to release power, set it flowing, so that one may not easily put limits around the quantity of power that might conceivably be let loose even through a simple life.

Consider. You are exhausted, limp, done for, and you come into the presence of a radiant personality who touches hidden springs in you and, lo! the channels of your soul fill up and the riverbed of your power overflows. You are not a closed reservoir; you are an open channel through which power can flow. Here is a woman, apparently at the end of her resources, whose child falls ill, and mother-love in her sets free energies and staying power that will see her through long months of tireless watching. This thing we are talking of is not miles up in the air and mystical; it is solidly founded. Now, Christ had a similar effect on men. Simon Peter was not a closed reservoir; he was a channel, limited in size, to be sure, but still a channel, and when Christ released the fountainhead of his passionate loyalty and purposefulness, a power flowed through him that those who knew him in his early days never would have dreamed.

How can we put this, so that some one here who needs it can practically get hold of it? To believe in God, not far off but here; to understand prayer, not as a form of words but as an inner opening of the life to the Divine resources, and so to experience what the prophet said, "They that wait upon the Lord shall renew their strength"; to go out into life, in consequence, not afraid of being overborne, because you know you are not a closed reservoir that can be exhausted but a channel in touch with inexhaustible resources, and that therefore as your day is so shall your strength be— that is vital, personal religion. If you have a little of it, deepen your experience. If you have none of it, for your own soul's health fulfil the conditions of getting it. For some day the sense of inadequacy stands on every threshold.

In the second place, the New Testament tells us that God has given us not a spirit of fear, but of power, and of *love*. Now, the word "love" in the New Testament has nothing whatever to do with soft sentimentalism. "Love" in the New Testament is one of the strongest words in the vocabulary, representing the kind of undiscourageable goodwill that could carry Christ to the cross or float a soul like Paul's unembittered through many an angry sea. If there is any force on earth, religious or not, that can help a man to keep that undiscourageable goodwill about living, it is worth investigating for, as every one of us can plainly see, one of the most familiar causes of mental ill health is bitterness, plain bitterness about life. It may be some one says:

> Why not? Why should one not be bitter? See what life does to us. The idea of pious sentimentalists that this world is just to the individual simply will not hold water; it is not just. Who hung on those three crosses? Christ and two thieves. That is life—the best and the worst nailed up together and no justice anywhere. The poets indeed may sing:
>
> Truth forever on the scaffold, Wrong forever on the throne,—
> Yet that scaffold sways the future, and, behind the dim unknown,
> Standeth God within the shadow, keeping watch above his own.
>
> Does he? Does he indeed? Well, he waits a long while sometimes before he acts. And in the meantime the merciless heel of the world crushes innocence and guilt alike.

How easy it is to grow bitter about life! And in personal, human relationships, as on an autumn day one walks through a rough country field and comes back covered with nettles, how easy it is to walk through life and accumulate stings! One knows well that some people here this morning are sorely tempted to bitterness and therefore to mental ill health.

For as soon as you see the other thing, an unembittered soul, generous, magnanimous, full of radiant and undiscourageable goodwill, you know that *that* is healthy-mindedness.

Consider a homely illustration of this. A century ago a French citizen left to the French Academy a fund which, increased by others, year after year furnishes prizes for conspicuous exhibitions of virtue discovered in the French population. Here is a typical case: Jeanne Chaix, the eldest of six children—mother insane; father chronically ill; she with no more money than the wages she earns in the pasteboard factory where she works, brings up the family, maintains the entire household, which, says the record, "subsists, morally as well as materially, by the sole force of her valiant will."

With these few facts, what do you know about Jeanne Chaix, standing there to receive her prize from the French Academy? You know this: she had not grown bitter; life had done hard things to her but she had not been embittered; she must have been sustained by an undiscourageable goodwill. She was a healthy-minded girl. Moreover, I suspect that, being French, she was a good Catholic too and that more than once, when the burden did seem unjust and she was tempted to be bitter, she went up to the church and prayed to the Blessed Virgin and came down again sweetened and reinforced. Have we any religion that does anything like that to us?

Bitterness imprisons life; love releases it. Bitterness paralyzes life; love empowers it. Bitterness sours life; love sweetens it. Bitterness sickens life; love heals it. Bitterness blinds life; love anoints its eyes.

In the third place, the New Testament tells us that God has given us not a spirit of fear, but of power, and of love, and of a *sound mind.* The Greek word for "sound mind" is not easy to translate. The Revised Version calls it "discipline." I suspect that the new psychological word "integration" comes close to it. That is to say, Paul's Christian faith pulled his life together, integrated it and so made it sound, saved him from a split, scattered, aimless life, gave it direction and guidance and so unity and discipline, made life seem abundantly worth living, put purpose in it worth living for, and so incalculably contributed to healthy-mindedness.

If Christian faith can do anything like that for anybody, we might well look into it. For we know mentally sick people. What is the matter with many of them? Cynicism, futilism, disillusionment, nothing in life for them, they say, no meaning in the universe to live by, no purpose in the universe to live for—and that is essential irreligion. There are multitudes of people who never will get a healthy mind until they get a vigorous religious faith.

Here in this church, as you know, we are not interested in the minutiæ and peccadilloes of religion. So, I beg of you, do not erect against this truth we are driving at small matters of obsolete church custom, or of belated theology, or of perverted forms of religion that burlesque reality. What we are driving at now is basic.

Listen to this from a contemporary writer: "Is this, then, all that life amounts to? To stumble, almost by mistake, into a universe which was clearly not designed for life, and which, to all appearances, is either totally indifferent or definitely hostile to it, to stay clinging on to a fragment of a grain of sand until we are frozen off, to strut our tiny hour on our tiny stage with the knowledge that our aspirations are all doomed to final frustration, and that our achievements must perish with our race, leaving the universe as though we had never been?" Is this, then, all that life amounts to? Well, is it? If a man consents to the idea that it is, he has accepted a philosophy which, as a matter of fact, theorize about it as you will, is leading many into cynical contempt for life, an abysmal sense of futility in living life, a disillusioned unwillingness to sacrifice for life. And cynicism, futility, and disillusionment are diseases of the mind.

Look out in imagination on that world we left today and must go back to tomorrow. If ever out of its chaos order comes and a more decent world for our children after us, who will be the builders of that better day? We may be sure of this: it will be the healthy-minded. The cynics and futilists? Never. The disillusioned and discouraged who can find no profound meaning or purpose in life? Never! The healthy-minded must build the better day, and we never will get a robust, vigorous, radiant, hopeful, healthy-mindedness out of the kind of irreligion that reduces man to a hapless victim stumbling by accident into a universe that does not want him, and clinging to the fragment of a grain of sand until he is frozen off.

For myself, I have lived long enough now and have seen enough of the appalling tragedies that fall on man and the broken social hopes that make his progress halting and unsure, to understand how deeply indebted to religion—even though a man may have got only a little of it by indirect contagion—we all are for any healthy-mindedness we may possess.

How strong faith does pull life together, put meaning into it, run purpose through it, put horizons around it! How, when we lose a battle, it reassures us that we may lose a battle and still win the war! In parched years how deep and cool a well it is into which to drop the buckets of our need! And in days like these, when evil seems triumphant and cynicism is easy and courage is hard, how it does unveil upon the surrounding hill tops the horses and chariots of fire!

Inadequacy for life, bitterness of soul, cynicism and futility—these are prevalent diseases today, and because so many are afflicted with them one may be sure that some are here in whom is the last consequence of all these evils, the innermost and final enemy of healthy-mindedness, the sense of guilt. As the psychologists are telling us, behind many nervous breakdowns, emotional maladjustments, insanities, lies the sense of guilt. And we cannot push it out of our souls; it will not go. We cannot argue it out of our souls; it is not amenable to argument. We cannot thrust it down into the pit of our minds and deliberately forget it because always what we try to forget we must remember. There is only one healthy way out from the sense of guilt: penitence, confession, restitution, forgiveness, a new start, and new reserves of strength. How many thus have found, not the spirit of fear, but of a healthy mind!

Christian Faith—Fantasy or Truth?

FOR many reasons these are difficult days in which to hold the Christian faith. The major events of our time are so essentially anti-Christian that against their terrific background Christian faith seems to many to be mere wishful thinking, a pleasant fairyland. Indeed, its very desirableness is used as an argument against it. Granted, men say, that the Christian faith is comforting, sustaining, bringing solace and encouragement to men in trouble. But, they add, that is precisely the reason why the Christian faith has developed —not because it is objectively true but because it is subjectively comfortable. So in one book after another we are told that Christian faith is a lovely fantasy, creating a world of make-believe where men and women, up against cruel facts, find encouragement by fooling themselves. As one of Galsworthy's characters put it: "There *is* something about a Church . . . there's beauty in it, it's a pleasant drug."

No preacher today can plead for Christian faith because it is desirable without knowing that some in his congregation are thinking, To be sure it is; it is comforting and encouraging; that is why people are religious; the stark facts of this cruel universe and the dreadful ills of human life are insupportable for most of us unless we conceal them, dress them up, decorate them in some comforting faith. Did not one poor woman in Robert Lynd's *Middletown* exclaim, "Land sakes! I don't see how people live at all who don't cheer themselves up by thinkin' of God and Heaven"? That is the origin of religion, men say; it is an illusion that cries, Cheerio! In our disappointed hours; it is spoofing on a grand scale. As one youth put it: "Religion is nothing but a chloroform mask into which the weak and unhappy stick their faces!"

Augustus Caesar was barely five feet seven inches tall, pale and delicate, with a weak throat and poor circulation, who all his life had to live on a strict diet and constantly struggle against bodily frailty. Yet see what Augustus Caesar did! One element in his amazing career is undoubtedly the fact that in his youth he visited Theogenes, a famous astrologer, to have his horoscope cast, and when Theogenes saw the young man's horoscope, so runs the story, he was so impressed with the marvel of it that he fell on his face and worshiped him. You and I do not believe in astrology, but you see Augustus did. It was a superstition, but, being believed, it worked. All his later life through difficulty, peril, burden-bearing, and inner struggle for self-conquest, he kept an undiscourageable faith in his destiny, which the stars had foretold. Such, men say, is Christian faith; it is a psychological shot in the arm, not objectively true but subjectively stimulating.

Over against this prevalent view we put today the testimony of the New Testament. The Fourth Gospel was written about 100 A.D., when the Christian church had had time to take the measure of Christ's meaning and to see his gospel against the background of one of the most difficult periods in human history. And at the heart of the Fourth Gospel, again and again repeated, is the conviction expressed in the words attributed to Jesus. Jesus said, "I am . . . the truth." Not a stimulating ideal merely, not a consoling faith, not a happy stroke of wishful thinking, but the realistic truth! Pretty much everything in our Christianity today depends on the issue we thus are faced with: What is our Christian faith—comforting fantasy, or reality?

All we can hope to do in dealing with so vast a subject here is to block out a few areas where the evidence lies that the Christianity of Christ is not a pleasant spiritual drug but is true.

In the first place, we may well ask, Since when has great religion been primarily pleasant and comfortable anyway? This whole picture of religion as mainly a search for comfort contradicts obvious facts. Look even at orthodox Christianity! Is it comfortable? Was Calvinism comfortable? Predestination, the damnation of non-elect infants, the eternal torture chamber of hell—there was small comfort in that, and some of us in our boyhood were driven by it nearly to hysteria. That is why Henry Ward Beecher had to challenge the orthodox religion of his day with its terrific doctrine of God, insisting, as he put it, that God is not a thunderstorm that has to be approached under an umbrella.

Of course, Christian faith can be caricatured. It is often perverted into a religion for comfort only, but the main tradition of Christian thought and life never has been primarily comfortable. The religion of Christ was not chiefly comfort. Without the cross we cannot understand him at all; in the cross his life and teaching centered. He had no light-hearted view of life that let him stay, pleasantly drugged, in Nazareth, but a heavy-handed, serious view of life that caused him to walk at last the dark road to Golgotha, saying to his disciples: "If any man would come after me, let him deny himself, and take up his cross, and follow me."

What does one mean by talking, then, of religion's being a pleasant drug? Listen to Gandhi, one of the most serious religious spirits of our time, as he says of God: "He is the most exacting personage in the world and the world to come." Gandhi could have lived countless times over an easier, more peaceful life had he not believed so deeply in God and his purpose for India and the world. God did not so much save Gandhi from trouble; God got Gandhi into trouble. Everybody here who has ever had any serious dealings with faith in God knows what Gandhi means by calling him an "exacting personage."

To be sure, there is another side to Christian faith, represented in Whittier's lines:

> Drop thy still dews of quietness,
> Till all our strivings cease;
> Take from our souls the strain and stress,
> And let our ordered lives confess
> The beauty of thy peace.

Nevertheless, even Whittier's religion is not half expressed there. Whittier was first of all a social reformer. In his elder years, when he was a famous poet, he wrote this: "I set a higher value on my name as appended to the Anti-Slavery Declaration of 1833 than on the title-page of any book." Many think of Whittier in mystical seclusion writing pious and consoling verse. We should think of him also in Concord, New Hampshire, going to speak at an anti-slavery meeting, facing a crowd on the way that pelted him with rotten eggs until his black Quaker coat ran yellow with the stains. We should remember him bitterly hated, and lampooned for years in the press of the United States as a traitor. No, when we find a man who has deeply entered into the Christian faith, we find a man who has discovered not fallacious comfort but a deep, demanding seriousness in life. Great religion has always been not first of all a search for comfort, but a search for righteousness and truth.

In the second place, let us now go further and see that Christian faith at its best, far from being fantasy, meets one of the basic tests of reality. If in any realm we fulfill conditions and get results, if when we meet the law-abiding requirements the universe responds, we know that we are handling reality.

Behind this whole idea that Christian faith in God, and in the creative power of the Spirit, is nothing but elaborate spoofing and wishful thinking, lies the presupposition that only the materialistic aspects of the universe are real. Men take for granted the physical cosmos and then say, Well, the spiritual is a mysterious something that we make up to comfort ourselves with. But, my friends, the physical aspects of the universe are just as mysterious as the spiritual. This whole physical structure is incredibly made up of negative and positive poles of invisible electricity, arranged in patterns of mathematical equations. How can any man take it for granted? As Balfour says, "We now know too much about matter to be materialists."

Nevertheless, we are sure that in dealing with the physical aspects of the universe we are dealing with reality, and for this reason: When in that realm we fulfill the law-abiding conditions, the universe responds. Something real is there, When Archimedes leaped from his bath and ran about the streets crying "Eureka," why the excitement? He was having one of the most thrilling experiences in human life. He had tried an experiment; the universe had responded to him, and he knew that he was dealing with reality. When Newton discerned that the movements of the heavenly bodies could be subsumed under one law and that his figures were working out correctly, he fell into an agitation so intense, we read, that he could not go on with the computations and "was obliged to desire a friend to finish them." His emotion was justified. He was trying an experiment; the universe was responding to him, and he knew that he was dealing with reality.

Well, throughout the ages, in all great religion, men have fulfilled conditions in the spiritual world and the spiritual world has given response—creative, transforming, powerful response. To be sure, religious ideas have changed, just as scientific ideas have changed, but in both realms great spirits have fulfilled conditions and the universe has responded to them. In both realms the cosmos has answered, saying, Something real is here. Indeed, out of that experience in the spiritual life have come the most towering characters in history, so that Benjamin Kidd, in his classic work on society, says that that kind of religion has been the most powerful element in the social progress of mankind. To laugh all that experience out of court as fantasy and spoofing is incredible.

Are not ideas real? Nobody ever saw them. They are not physical. An idea is as invisible as God and yet we can discern what happens when the conditions are fulfilled in that unseen realm. As John Eglinton put it: "Without an idea man is frivolous, anarchic, dissatisfied, despicable. With an idea, the long-hoarded initiatives of his nature are liberated, he strains forward to new consummations." To explain away the world of ideas as our delusion, imagined to make this materialistic cosmos more meaningful, will not do. Whenever in any realm we fulfill conditions and the cosmos responds, we are dealing with reality.

Listen to Paul, praying that "ye may be strengthened with power through his Spirit in the inward man; that Christ may dwell in your hearts through faith; to the end that ye, being rooted and grounded in love, may be strong to apprehend with all the saints what is the breadth and length and height and depth, and to know the love of Christ which passeth knowledge, that ye may be filled unto all the fulness of God." That does not sound like spoofing. That does not sound like a weak and unhappy man sticking his face in a chloroform mask. That sounds like a great character fulfilling conditions in the spiritual world, to whom the spiritual world has made response. Innumerable souls across the ages, experiencing such response, have heard Christ saying clearly, "I am . . . the truth."

Let us go further now into a third area of evidence. Whenever in any realm one runs across powerful personality—not now ideas in the abstract any longer, but personality itself, potent, creative, smiting the world with rememberable impact—one can have a fairly impressive confidence that he is handling the real.

I would not say that every idea my father had corresponded with the real. My father would not have said that himself. But my father was real, and were anyone to argue that the essential factors producing that potent character were fantasy, self-deceit, and make-believe, that kind of argument would run into this insuperable difficulty: It must take more than fantasy, self-deceit, and make-believe to produce anything as real as that. To believe that so much reality can come from unreality calls for a credulity I cannot attain.

This attack on Christianity, therefore, as a chloroform mask, confronts its insuperable difficulty in Christ himself, and in people who have shared his spirit, his quality of character, his kind of life. It must take more than a chloroform mask to produce anything as real as that. The trouble with this new attack on the Christian faith is that it proves too much. It explains away as the result of self-deceit, not simply the great religious characters, but the great spiritual characters in every realm. For if this universe were basically materialistic, and all our spiritual life were but our endeavor to conceal, dress up, and decorate for our consolation the cruel facts, then that would be true not simply about religion but about art. That is what Joseph Krutch, one of the most honest atheists of our time, frankly says in his book on *Experience and Art*. So *that* is another chloroform mask into which the weak and unhappy stick their faces; and music is another, and poetry another, and love another. If once you let this argument get started, it does not stop with religion. It takes in art, music, poetry, love, the deepest faiths undergirding human personality, and the ultimate hopes of society. They are all engulfed in the same absymal explanation, as nothing but our comfortable way of making an intolerable world more livable. It would make even the supreme creative characters of history, the Platos, Beethovens, Michelangelos, great saints, great prophets, great lovers, great seers, and Christ over all, the greatest fools of all, most beguiled by fantasy, most misled by deceptive and consoling imaginations.

Well, any theory that makes the greatest characters the most deluded of the fools has something the matter with it. *Ex nihilo nihil fit*—"Out of nothing, nothing comes." That the noblest aspects of human life are mere creations of fantasy is an incredible creed. I have seen too many people who, coming under the influence of Christ and discovering through him not only ideals of character but resources of power, have been transformed, as Paul said, from character to character, ever to believe that creed. One who lives beside the ocean and sees the tide come in to fill bays and inlets as they never could fill themselves, cannot be persuaded that nothing real and deep is needed to explain that. What is happening in this little bay cannot be explained without the whole ocean and the gravitational pull of the skies upon it. Something real and eternal is evidenced in that rising tide. No more can we explain great character as due to mere delusion. There, at least, I hear Christ clearly say, "I am . . . the truth."

To one more area of evidence I ask your thought. Strangely enough, it is this present world itself—this terrible, upset, catastrophic world, trying to manage its affairs on anti-Christian principles. Many people, who would not have been concerned with philosophic arguments that the Christian faith and way of life are delusive, are thinking today that Christianity is delusive because this present hideous and diabolical world scene shows Christianity up as utterly impractical. To which I answer: The Christian way of life impractical? Do you think, then, that what is going on in the world today is practical? This demonic regime of anti-Christianity—would you call it practical —economically practical? in terms of human happiness—practical? in terms of hope for the kind of world our children will have to live in—practical? Do you call this essence of all evil, war, practical? Rather, this world disaster with all the voices of its need cries out that unless we can achieve the hard-headed realism of the Christian ethic and put it into practice, we are personally and socially sunk.

Granted that religion can be the opiate of the people! As one of

Warwick Deeping's characters says: "Anything to escape, to colour the spectacles." So some turn to drink and color the spectacles that way; some turn to drugs and sleep it off; some in daydreaming build an unreal world and live in it; some do turn to a religion of fantasy where wishful thinking takes possession of their lives. Their religion is a chloroform mask where, weak and unhappy, they stick their faces.

But it is a cheap and superficial habit to estimate great matters by their burlesques. We do not judge architecture by filling stations and wayside huts; we judge it by its great exhibitions. We do not judge music by its cheap and tawdry expressions; we judge it by its classic and abiding forms. What business have we to throw religion out of the window because of its caricatures? Great religion has been the source of the most creative ideas in human history. And today the Christian faith and ethic with its central principles—the sacredness of personality, the inescapable membership of all mankind in one body, the absolute necessity, therefore, of goodwill not as an ideal but as a working principle, the need of individual regeneration if we are to have a regenerate society, the call to seek first the Kingdom of God on earth, that is, the welfare of all, if there is to be any welfare for each, and the reality of God himself, above all nations, races, and classes, calling for one human family—this religion is no fantasy, no opiate. Rather, look at the mad world today, trying to live on the opposite principles, and see if the closing words of Jesus in the Sermon on the Mount, as Dr. Moffatt translates them, do not ring true: "Everyone who listens to these words of mine and acts upon them will be like a sensible man, who built his house on rock."

In the New Testament the very words "ideal" and "idealism" are not to be found. They are not there. But the word "truth" is there again and again. The Christian gospel was not idealism but realism, not a message, first of all, about what ought to be, but about what is. God *is*, Christ *is* his revealer, man *is* the child of the Eternal Spirit, there *is* an eternal purpose which he purposed in Christ, all men *are* inextricably members of one body, love *is* the law of life—such are the basic realities.

Surely some of us need to take this to ourselves. We are growing older. Forty years old, fifty years old, sixty years old—the decades pass, and with the years, by an inevitable drift, we are thinking about life one way or another. Happy the man who with the passing years is more and more persuaded that what Christ stands for is the truth!

On Learning How to Pray

AS FAR as the records go, only one thing did the disciples explicitly ask Jesus to teach them—how to pray. At first sight it seems strange that they should have asked him this for those disciples had prayed all their lives. When, however, they came under the influence of Jesus and saw what prayer meant to him, it dawned on them that although they had prayed from their youth up they did not know how. "It came to pass," says the Gospel of Luke, "as he was praying in a certain place, that when he ceased, one of his disciples said unto him, Lord, teach us to pray, even as John also taught his disciples." Evidently they had been observing what prayer meant in his life. He went into it in one mood and came out in another; power was released; praying to him was not a form but a force. And when beside his prayer they put what they called praying, it was plain that, while the same word covered both, the meanings of the two were far apart. So these religiously trained disciples, who always had prayed, wanted Jesus to teach them how.

Note that this awakened interest in prayer came not at all from new arguments about it but from a new exhibition of its power. Here before their very eyes they saw a personality in whom prayer was vital and influential. The more they lived with him the more they saw that they never could explain him unless they understood his praying, and so, not at all because of new arguments but because of amazing spiritual powers released in him by prayer, they wanted him to tell them how to pray.

It is an impressive experience to face a personality whom we cannot explain until we understand his prayer. A superficial brook can be explained without going far but the river Nile is inexplicable until one knows the high mountains in the center of the continent and the rains that fall there. Personalities like that we do discover, not simply among great figures of history, but in homely places. Here, for example, was a woman who, comparatively young, was left a widow with five children and who resolutely shouldered the practical and spiritual responsibilities which that entailed. By careful management she saw the children through college. On the day of her burial, in her ninety-sixth year, one of the children said they never had seen her impatient or distraught to the point of giving up, even in the most troubled times. One son became president of a great railway system; another became president of a state university; another became a leading pioneer in his department of medical research. That kind of consequence in a family is no accident. That mother was an extraordinary personality. It was the university president who said to me that no one could understand her who did not understand her prayer. It was a force, he said; it released radiance and power.

I think I know all the arguments for and against prayer and I would not minimize them. No one wishes to pray unintelligently. But prayer as a force in personalities so powerful that we cannot explain them until we know their praying, goes deeper than argument. Some young man fresh from a college class in philosophy assures me that prayer is nonsense, quite irrational in this modern world. All the while he is talking I keep thinking of some hard-hitting, hard-living man like Henry M. Stanley, coming out of hell in Africa and saying that prayer made him stronger morally and mentally than all his non-praying companions and lifted him hopefully over the wilderness of forest tracks, eager for each day's labors and fatigues. What I want to ask is, What is that force? Never mind about the name! What is that power and how does one get into contact with it and handle it? As the disciple said to Jesus, "Lord, teach us to pray."

Let us condense into a brief statement some of the things the great pray-ers of history and the Master, above all, would tell us about how to pray.

For one thing, they surely would say, Pray *receptively*. That is one of the primary meanings of prayer: "Spirit of God, descend upon my heart." Yesterday, let us suppose, you had a busy schedule. You put your back tensely and aggressively into the morning's work, and then in the afternoon you went to Carnegie Hall and heard a glorious symphony. You had to change your technique. You had been active; you became receptive. You had been aggressive; you became appreciative. You had been doing something to your world; now you let another world do something to you. What a new kind of experience that is, and how indispensable!

The failure of much popular praying arises from the fact that when we pass from our ordinary, aggressive, workaday world into what we call prayer, we do not thus change our technique. Despite our supposition that we are praying, we still are secular. That is, we are aggressively trying to force our selfish will upon the world. To many people prayer is only an additional way of getting what they want, a kind of spare tire to be used when the others fail. They are as much go-getters when they pray as at any other time, and the whole tone of their praying is, "God, get me what I want!"

Indeed, so prevalent is this idea in popular religion that, alas! many ministers still preach it. The angriest letter I have received this year came from a minister who, having correctly understood something I said over the air about prayer, came back with wrathful protest, insisting that, to use his phrase, "prayer moves the arm of God." So! A mortal man dares desire to move the arm of God! My friends, nothing much more essentially irreverent than that is conceivable. Upon the contrary, true prayer begins only when a human soul desires above all else that the arm of God should move him.

"I would fain be to the Eternal Goodness what his own hand is to a man." Who said that? A contemporary liberal? No. An old German mystic. "Not my will, but thine, be done." Who said *that?*

All great souls have prayed receptively. "I will hear," said the psalmist, "what God the Lord will speak." Prayer is the hospitality of the soul entertaining the Most High.

A young man who had recently graduated from a Western university once sought membership in this church, and when I asked him the effect of his college course on his religious faith he said that on the whole his faith was stronger at the end than at the beginning. When I inquired how he explained that, he said, "Mountains." "Mountains!" I exclaimed. "Yes," he answered, "mountains." And when I inquired what mountains had to do with it, he replied: "A part of every year I spend among the high mountains. I have seen sunrise on too many mountain peaks ever to doubt the reality of God." Have we anything remotely approaching that in our lives even though we have to experience it amid the cañons of these city streets? Sunrise on mountains!

In the second place, pray *affirmatively*. The trouble with much popular praying is that it is mainly begging. It conceives the Eternal as a universal organized charity and of ourselves as impecunious applicants, saying, Give me! Clearly, that involves a pagan theory of God, but, worse than that, in actual practise it so damages men's souls that any minister, dealing intimately with individuals, should welcome the chance to sound a warning. One repeatedly hears the familiar complaint: I prayed long and earnestly about this temptation, this habit, this need, and it did no good. Of course it did no good. Habitually behind that complaint one finds a kind of praying which, far from doing good, does harm. Prayer holds the object of its wish in the center of attention; the more earnest a man's prayer, the more stoutly his need occupies his thought. Picture, then, a man praying about sickness, for example, holding some illness in the center of his solicitude and saying in effect, I am sick, very sick, see how sick I am; give me health! Any one intelligent about psychological processes knows that the more earnestly a man prays like that the more sick he is likely to be. Run your imagination out, therefore, into other realms of need—sexual passion, discouragement, anxiety. You see, the more we hold such things in the center of attention, even in prayer, the more they will obsess and control our living. In consequence, many people come to the minister saying, Long and earnestly I prayed about this need and it did no good. And a wise minister says, My friend, when one considers the way you have prayed, you are lucky that it did not ruin you.

One finds no praying like that in the New Testament or in the lofty areas of the Old Testament, or in the great souls of the church at their best. True prayer is affirmative. It turns its back on our wretched, miserable needs and stretches out a taking hand to appropriate the inexhaustible resources of the divine grace. It says,

The Lord *is* my shepherd; I *shall not* want.
He *maketh* me to lie down in green pastures;
He *leadeth* me beside still waters.
He *restoreth* my soul.

Every one knows that at Worms Luther defied the emperor at the risk of his life, but most people do not know what Luther was praying when he did it. But he has told us. "O Thou my God, stand by me, against all the world . . . do Thou do it, Thou must do it, Thou alone. It is indeed not my cause, but Thine." That is affirmative prayer. It is like drums and bugles to a man's soul. In sickness it gives tonic thoughts; in anxiety it orients life around sustaining faiths; in discouragement it centers attention on inexhaustible resources. In such praying a man retires for a little while from troubled foregrounds to the great resources in the background and actually appropriates what he needs. Such is affirmative prayer. It does not so much ask as take; it does not so much beg for living water as sink shafts into it and draw from it. It starts as Jesus did: "Our Father who *art*."

In the third place, pray *dangerously*. To many people the idea that prayer can be dangerous never has occurred. Of all safe things in this world, they think, a comfortable retreat from trouble, an anesthetic even for life's pains, prayer is the safest. That shows how little some people understand prayer. As a matter of historic fact, prayer has been one of the most perilous things great spirits have indulged in.

I have personal friends who prayed and now they are in the heart of Africa, living sacrificial, missionary lives. If they wanted easy lives, they prayed a few times too often. Once there was a man who could have escaped crucifixion if he had trimmed a little, but instead he went into a garden to pray and, issuing from that experience, he could not trim at all but walked straight to the cross. Behind that man there is another whom one scholar has called "the father of true prayer," Jeremiah, who often desperately wished that he could escape the severe compulsions of his duty, but who was always prevented from running away by the habit of prayer, where the Will that was greater than his will laid hold on him again and sent him back. As Jeremiah himself put it, God said to him, "Call unto me, and I will answer thee, and will show thee great things, and difficult."

That is a consequence of praying which the superficial pray-ers never expect but which great spirits know. What a sight it is to watch them retiring into their high backgrounds and then emerging again carrying on their consciences great things and difficult! Every forward step in the moral advancement of the race goes back to some experience like that.

The other evening I sat at home comfortably stretched out in an overstuffed chair, thinking among other things about this sermon, when of a sudden my eyes rested on a book upon the table. It is a beautiful, old, leather-bound book which once belonged to Hugh Latimer, who was burned at the stake for his faith in the sixteenth century. It still carries his name upon the flyleaf, written with his own hand. As I watched the book, I began in imagination to see Oxford Square that day they led him out to burn him, and across the centuries I heard again the words he spoke to his companion in martyrdom: "Be of good comfort, Master Ridley, and play the man; we shall this day light such a candle by God's grace in England as, I trust, shall never be put out." Then I thought Hugh Latimer turned his eyes on me. Said he:

> So you are going to preach on prayer. What do you know about praying? I am going now from my knees to the stake. Have you any idea what tremendous moral issues prayer, when it is earnest, can present to a man's conscience? You modern preachers have made prayer safe, easy, comfortable, fitted for narcotic purposes. Tell them something about dangerous praying, in which a man's duty becomes to him the compelling will of God, which he cannot escape. And you there, in your overstuffed chair, if you are going to preach about such praying, experience it a little!

So with wide and fascinated eyes I watched the old man as he walked on, going from his knees to his sacrifice.

Of course, I cannot be sure just where this may apply to each of us, but it applies. Lord, teach us to pray dangerously about some moral issue in our lives today!

Once more, pray *undiscouragebly*. As Jesus said, men "ought always to pray, and not to faint." Now, most of our prayer is scaled to a short term. We ask for things immediate. We want what we want when we want it. Even in our praying the spirit of 'get rich quick' irreverently enters. That is not great praying. Great praying is always scaled to a long-term enterprise. "Thy kingdom come. Thy will be done, as in heaven, so on earth"—prayer like that is handed on from one generation to another.

To be sure, at this point some one is certain to be saying, What good does that do? We want international peace and economic justice and we had better work for them, but praying does not bring them and what use is there pretending that it does? To which I answer, If by prayer you mean saying prayers or expecting God to hand out peace and justice because we request them, you are right. We, however, are taking for granted here sufficient intelligence to have thrown over long since childish praying which casts on God problems that God never will solve except through us. There are some kinds of prayer that are distinctly wrong and should never be indulged in. Some of the most excoriating things Jesus ever said were about ways of praying he disbelieved in. No more sarcastic picture did he ever draw than the portrait of a man who went up to the temple to pray and "stood and prayed thus *with himself*" a narrow, mean, and selfish prayer. There was plenty of praying in which Jesus cordially disbelieved, but he did teach his disciples out of the depths of their desire to lift up the great prayer for the kingdom of God on earth. Now, when he did that and when he filled that prayer with the ethical and humanitarian content which he put into it, he *did* something.

Put it this way. Beethoven wrote music far beyond the capacity both of the instruments and of the technique available in his day. We read, for example, that the solo of the C minor Concerto was played on "a miserable little box of wires, hardly more sonorous than a spinet." So Beethoven wrote music that could not adequately be rendered on the instruments of his time, music which, therefore, was in itself a prayer: Give me instruments, create for me instruments so that I can be really played. As you know, Beethoven's music, by being itself, compelled the creation of new instruments and new technique. As his biographer puts it, "Born into a day of small things he helped the day to expand by giving it creations beyond the scope of its available means of expression. So it was literally forced to improve these means and thus to grow with them—a method much used by emancipators of humanity." Indeed, yes! almost always used by emancipators of humanity. For what they do is to give men music—great ideas and ideals of justice and equality, peace and brotherhood—far beyond the implementation of their time, music which is itself a prayer: Give me instruments, create for me in practical social life instruments so that I may be played. *That* the emancipators of humanity have always done.

Suppose that you, devoutly believing in Beethoven, had heard the C minor Concerto at its first rendition. You would have known, would you not? that that could not possibly be the end of the story; that though it might be a long time from Beethoven to Toscanini and the Philharmonic, yet the music would bring to pass at last an orchestra which could play it properly. So we, who deeply believe in Christ and hear his music being ruined by our economic disorder and our international policies, know that that is not the end of the story. Underline this in your faith: *The future belongs to the music and not to these wretched, obsolete instruments.*

When, therefore, I say to my own conscience and to yours, Believe this and pray and work undiscourageably for this, I am saying something real. If, as Mrs. Browning says,

> . . . every *wish*
> Is like a prayer, with God,

then millions of Americans are not praying for peace and justice. Listen to the prayers that rise from the people. Many of our people are praying,

> Bless me and my wife,
> My son John and his wife,
> Us four, no more. Amen.

Many are praying to get back to the lush days before 1929, despite the poverty that blasted the lives of millions even then. Munitions manufacturers are praying for profits from military and naval armaments, and every heart has its egoistic prayers. What a world of crazy praying!

When we think of it so, praying is no light matter, is it? Columbus' search for a sea route to the Indies was prayer; Edison's search for the secret of incandescence was prayer; the long accumulating desire for democracy was prayer. Yes, Napoleon's ambition to rule Europe was his prayer, and Pasteur's ambition to glorify France by making a discovery to bless mankind was his prayer. On its deepest levels, human life is a battlefield of conflicting prayers. The strongest forces in this world are these importunate desires, and when a multitude of people share a common desire, when a great prayer rises within millions like the tide called by the sky and filling all the bays and crannies of the human shore, it is irresistible. Prayer, when it is a caricature, is a futile retreat from reality. Prayer, when it is real, can turn the stream of centuries into new courses. Look to your prayers, then, your deep, real, genuine demands on life. Only when a great multitude that no man can number stands before the throne and with a voice like many waters cries, We are through with war and poverty; we demand peace and justice and brotherhood—only then will men invent the instruments on which such music can be played.

If some one says, This deep, interior attitude which you have been describing as prayer is certainly very different from merely saying prayers; it is rather the habitual and constant highlands and backgrounds of great living, I answer, Of course it is. What do we suppose Paul meant when he said, "Pray without ceasing"? We cannot imagine a busy man like Paul saying prayers without ceasing. To be sure, all the year ought to be more unselfish because of Christmas Day, every month more grateful because Thanksgiving comes, every day more triumphant because of Easter, all our married life the sweeter because we remember the anniversaries. There is value in special times and places. Prayers can help prayer, but prayer itself is spiritual life at its creative origin.

If some one says, Much that you have been talking of I know in my own experience but I never have called it prayer, I answer, Of course you know it. There is no possibility of high, strong life without it, and it is prayer. I beg of you, do not be so misled by the pettiness and ignorance of popular religion as to miss the fact that not only now but in all the centuries, in the great seers and saints, this has been prayer. Do not let it remain unconscious and unrecognized in you. Lift it up; make it radiant and powerful. Make your life one that people cannot fully understand unless they understand your prayer.

When Prayer Means Power

THERE are three ways in which men get what they want—thinking, working, praying. Concerning the first two no one has any doubt; if we are to fulfill our desires, of course we must think and work. But concerning the third, doubts are plentiful. In many minds such baffling questions rise concerning prayer that that whole area of experience is nullified.

In part, this difference is due to the fact that thought and work have not been ritualized. We are supposed to think wherever we happen to be, to work wherever our tasks carry us. These two ways of getting what we want run through the common hours of every day. They are not centered in a special building with a steeple on it, and we do not cast ourselves into a special posture, like kneeling, when we engage in them. But prayer has been ritualized; it is associated with sacred places, sacred practices, special moods, and special postures. So for many people prayer seems a formal, conventional, technically religious performance that they do not understand, and so they are left with only two ways of fulfilling their life's desires—they think and work.

Yet even casual consideration suggests that from such lives something has been left out whose omission is a personal tragedy. Powerful personality is never created simply by thought and work. Powerful personality has deep interior resources of inspiration and intake. Call it what we will, we find in every great soul something that goes beyond thinking and working—inner receptivity, sensitiveness, and hospitality to a world of truth and power higher than the self. Great living is not all output in creative thought and work; it is also intake, the openness of the soul to the Over-Soul, the quietness that can hear a still small voice, an inflow, as though, in William James' figure, we were bays open to a great deep where the tides rise. Everybody here knows that this third area of experience is real, not simply religiously, but psychologically, factually real.

One of the major tasks of the church today is to help people to recover and to make effective in their lives this third realm of experience, which is the realm of prayer. After all, that area of experience is no more intellectually mysterious than thinking and working are. There are philosophical problems involved in the process of thinking that never have been solved; there are theoretical questions about the operation of free initiative in working to which no one knows the answer; and there are profound mysteries in this inner enrichment and empowerment of life when the tides of the Over-Soul flow in. But all these three are factually real, and it takes all three to make a strong life.

Especially in these days we need them all. In this tremendous generation, of course we must think and work, but who of us does not feel that the more strenuous our thought and work become, the more we need that third realm of experience? Paul, in his letter to the Ephesians, called it being "strengthened with power through his Spirit in the inward man," or, as Dr. Moffatt translates that verse, "a mighty increase of strength by his Spirit in the inner man."

At the start, it may help some of us if we clear away certain common misunderstandings of prayer. Almost all of us as children start praying by asking for things. Prayer then is begging, and just as we use our fathers and mothers as means for obtaining what we want, so we try to use God, saying, Give me this or that. But when we grow up—if, indeed, we do grow up—that early, egocentric universe of childhood dissolves and we find ourselves in this vast cosmos whose God is no errand boy of ours. So one boy who grew up in the last generation described his experience:

> As wider skies broke on his view,
> God greatened in his growing mind;
> Each year he dreamed his God anew,
> And left his older God behind.

That greater God can no longer be an errand boy, prayer to whom means saying, Bring me this or that.

In consequence, many modern people swing over to the opposite extreme. Prayer, they think, is merely autosuggestion. It is purely subjective, a kind of psychological dumbbell exercise by which one raises one's own spiritual muscle. God thus is left altogether out of prayer, and a man alone with himself gives to himself, as it were, a spiritual massage. But, my friends, that does not account for the facts. Ages ago Isaiah described a fact when he said: "They that wait upon the Lord shall renew their strength." And centuries later Dr. Alexis Carrel, one of our foremost scientists, described it again: "Prayer is . . . the most powerful form of energy that one can generate." All the way from Isaiah to Alexis Carrel, ask anyone who ever entered into this experience what its nature is, and he will say that it is not simply a man alone tinkering with himself; it is more like a man gone spiritually dry within, who far down in his soul clears away the clutter of impeding obstacles until the cool water of a rising spring, whose sources are far beyond himself, wells up to refresh and reinvigorate his life. To use a modern figure, prayer is plugging in on a current whose sources are cosmic and not simply individual, a current that brings light and power. That is the way Professor Wieman of the University of Chicago put it: Prayer is completing the circuit.

This then, in general, is what we mean by the third realm of experience necessary to great living. It is not begging God, as though he were our errand boy; it is not self-isolated autosuggestion. It is an inner openness to the Spirit from whom comes, in Paul's words, "a mighty increase of strength." What, then, are some of the elements that enter into this experience?

For one thing, if we are to get it we must deeply feel the need of it. In all great matters the sense of need must precede the discovery of the experience. Of what possible use to some of us is the higher mathematics? Most of us can go on month after month and never think of the higher mathematics. But were we bridge builders, trying to throw a great span across some river like the Hudson, then we would have to have the higher mathematics.

So some kinds of persons feel no need of prayer. They can think a little and work a little, and get by. That is all they want of life. But they are not the persons who most have elevated and dignified the human race. Out of that group who feel no need of this third realm of experience, we never get our great musicians, saying with Handel about the "Hallelujah Chorus": "I did think I did see all Heaven before me, and the great GOD Himself"; we never get great prophets, saying with Ralph Waldo Emerson: "When I watch that flowing river, which, out of regions I see not, pours for a season its streams into me, I see that I am a pensioner"; we never get anybody remotely like Christ, saying: "I am not alone, but I and the Father." Such creative souls did think and work, but the deeper secret of their greatness was that far within themselves they knew how to complete the circuit and become the media of liberated power.

In ordinary life two experiences call out the conscious need of this deep kind of prayer—being up against something too much for us, and undertaking something too hard for us. If someone here is not up against something too much for him, or is not undertaking something too hard for him, the chances are that he will not know what we are talking about and will not care. What, to him, is all this higher mathematics? But can it be that in these days that is true of anybody here?

The question is often asked whether there is now afoot in this country a return to religion. No general answer seems possible, but here is a typical individual whom I meet more and more frequently. He has been conventionally a Christian, believing in God, thinking the church a good thing to belong to, valuing his Christian heritage and, it may be, hard at work on many Christian tasks after the fashion of those women whom Jonathan Swift once described, who, "out of zeal for religion, have hardly time to say their prayers." But today such merely outward and expressive Christianity is to this individual not enough. He is up against something in this terrific world and in himself, and to meet it he must be something that he now is not. He faces, as never before, the need of inward resources of strength for daily life. He is thinking and working as hard as he can, but such thought and work are life's branches, the expression and output of one's self, while rootage is his need—not more branches but rootage—by which life strikes deep into the solid earth and draws vitality and strength from unfailing sources. I have seen some remarkable transformations of life in this congregation recently, in people who for the first time have discovered what that kind of experience can mean: "A mighty increase of strength by his Spirit in the inner man." They needed it.

For another thing, if we are to gain this kind of experience, we must not only need it, but clearly see that it cannot be achieved merely by trying hard. The comon property of thinking and working is to try hard. We put our wills into our thought and work. But now try your will out in this deeper realm, where the profound issues of your soul's life are concerned. Will to have resources of inner spiritual power that makes you adequate for life! Will to have what Wordsworth called

> . . . central peace, subsisting at the heart
> Of endless agitation!

Concentrate on the matter, and, focusing your volition, will to have a mighty increase of spiritual strength! Where will such futile straining of volition get you? For here is a basic psychological fact about every one of us—we cannot will such experiences of inner enrichment and power. They do not come by trying, but by another method altogether: "Spirit of God, descend upon my heart."

To be sure, we may have to put our wills into it in order to get to Carnegie Hall on time. We may have to think hard and work fast to make the schedule click. But when now we are in Carnegie Hall, and a glorious symphony is being played, if all we can do then is to try hard, we might just as well not have come. That occasion, like all supreme occasions, calls for another realm of experience—receptivity, spiritual hospitality, the sensitive and understanding openness of the soul to the Over-Soul, the capacity to let the tides flow in when the sky calls to the deep. And if someone says, That is easy; being receptive and responsive is a simple matter, I say, No! It is a thousand times easier to be the kind of person who can hustle, put his back into it, and get the things that trying hard can get, than to be the kind of person who also can complete the circuit until he becomes a medium for liberated power.

What mature person can escape facing this problem sometime or other as the most practical issue in his life? Soon or late, life confronts every one of us with situations that cannot be handled well merely by trying hard. In a crushing grief, an irretrievable bereavement, is there nothing one can do except try hard? In an overwhelming temptation, when the emotional floods are too strong for our volitional resistance, is there nothing to do except try hard? In a day of world-wide catastrophe on a shaken earth, where no one can see a week ahead, is there no source of steadiness, no fountain of fortitude and courage, except trying hard? The phrase "practical Christianity" has generally been associated with activity, doing something useful and serviceable. I agree. That is practical Christianity. But there is another aspect of Christianity that for ages our fathers and mothers have called prayer, from which at their best they have gained interior resources of spiritual power that enabled them to carry on when carrying on was hard, and that in days like these is practical, if anything is. It is not begging God for things; it is not a man's tinkering with his own soul; it is inwardly establishing contact with a resource of power whose endless supply comes from a great deep. "The water that I shall give him," said Jesus, "shall become in him a well of water springing up." My soul! That is practical.

Consider still another element in this experience. If it is to be real, we must apprehend the fact that when we are alone we are not alone. This is one of the most profound and mysterious facts in human life—the consciousness that, being alone, we are not alone. We may well see in the Garden of Gethsemane a picture of a universal human experience. Jesus left the world outside the Garden gate; he left the major group of his disciples at the Garden gate; he left his three closest friends within the Garden gate, and then in solitude he went out under the olive trees—

> Into the woods my Master went,
> Clean forspent, forspent.

But there, alone, he was not alone.

Explain that experience as we will, it cannot be explained away. Elijah amid the loneliness of the desert all the more clearly hearing the still small voice; Socrates ascribing all that was worth-while in his life to the guidance of his inner angel; Epictetus, the Stoic, saying: "When you have shut your doors, and darkened your room, remember never to say that you are alone; for you are not alone, but God is within"; Jesus saying: "Enter into thine inner chamber, and having shut thy door, pray to thy Father . . . who seeth in secret"—there is a fact of human experience, antedating and outside the Christian tradition as well as within it, not to be explained away. And if someone says that this is an ancient matter, that will not do.

> Thou Life within my life, than self more near,
> Thou veiled Presence infinitely clear,
> From all illusive shows of sense I flee,
> To find my center and my rest in thee.

That is modern.

Here, indeed, is the truth that Professor Whitehead of Harvard was dealing with when he said: "Religion is what the individual does with his own solitariness." Well, what do we do with our solitariness? What do we make of this mysterious inner companionship, this sense of presence, this strange effect of solitude that makes a still small voice more audible? Some of us are not making much of it, but possibilities are there to which no man knows the limit. The major gift of science to the world is a mighty increase of power. Did science then create that power? Not a bit of it! Science discovered that power in the universe and set it free. Science found out the conditions, fulfilling which, the endless dynamic forces of the cosmos are liberated. Electricity is none of man's making, but man has learned how to fulfill the conditions that release it. Atomic energy is a force that man did not create, but that some day man may liberate. Man by himself is still a puny animal; a gorilla is much the stronger. Man's significance lies in another realm—he knows how to fulfill conditions so that universal power not his own is set free. The whole universe as man now sees it is essentially a vast system of power waiting to be released.

In the spiritual realm this is what prayer means. Prayer is inwardly fulfilling conditions so that power is released. I do not believe in miracles in the old terms of broken or suspended law, but I have to believe in these scientific miracles, incredible things done by science through the releasing of cosmic power; and I have to believe in personal miracles, incredible things happening in people and to people and for people who have liberated the divine resources. Listen to Dr. Hadfield, one of the leading psychiatrists of England, describing his failure in trying to cure certain nervous patients until he brought to bear on them, he says, "faith in the power of God which is the substance of the Christian's confidence and hope. Then," writes Dr. Hadfield, "the patient has become strong." So he wrote a book entitled *The Psychology of Power*, that might be called a psychiatric sermon on our morning's text. For the old experience at the heart of great religion is going on still in those who discover that when they are alone they are not alone.

To play fairly with our subject, however, we must note one more element in this experience. It is not simply comforting, reassuring, enriching, empowering; it is also searching and demanding. Someone here, up to this point, may have resisted the impact of this sermon on himself, saying, After all, what mankind needs today is people who will put their minds to the task and go out and do something for the world. Surely, mankind needs that. But who of us does not know what it means to face a situation where we cannot do much for the world until, first of all, we have done something with ourselves? The longer an orchestra plays, the more it needs to be tuned up. The farther an airplane flies, the more it requires ground service to put it into shape again. There is no evading that law in any realm. When an orchestra or a personality is out of tune, it cannot do anything well for others until it has first done something with itself.

At that point, the profoundest experience of the race has been that there are regenerative forces, not within our power to create, but within our power to appropriate and assimilate. That is true about our bodies. The days come when we cannot physically do anything more for the world until we have done something with ourselves. We are played out and done in. Would any physician say to us then, Think it through and work it out; hard thought and labor are what you need. But it is hard thought and labor that have depleted us. Now we must have intake. Now we must re-establish relationships with sunshine, fresh air, and the open country, and drink in what we never could create, but can appropriate. Why do we try to live as though that universal law, obvious in our bodies, were not true also in our souls?

Nevertheless, when that experience is translated to the spiritual realm, it is not simply comforting and reassuring, but searching and demanding, too. In that deep and inner companionship where we face the still small voice and seek to be made right within, costly and sacrificial things often must be done. Before Niemoeller faced Hitler, we may be sure that Niemoeller faced God. Before he did what he did do for the world, he had to do something with himself—and it was not easy. I am not promising anyone ease and comfort only in this profound experience of prayer. Jesus did something for the world on Calvary, but behind that lies his experience in the Garden, where he sweat blood, praying, "Not my will, but thine, be done!" Whatever form this inner communion takes, this is true: No powerful personality ever brought saving help to the world without this third realm of experience within him. All through this congregation, made up of people who spend their days thinking and working, this problem runs today. We are not going to do what we could do for the world until, far within, we have done something with ourselves.

If that regenerating, re-empowering experience is to be ours, then we must give God a chance. We said at the start that one reason why thought and work seem real and prayer seems unreal is that prayer is ritualized, and thought and work are not. But that is not the whole truth. Any serious thinker does have special times of seclusion and quiet which he gives to thinking. Any serious worker does have special places and methods by means of which his work gains competence. Many of us, however, vaguely and in general agreeing with what we have been saying this morning, never give the inner companionship of the divine Spirit any special time. Less and less frequently we nourish it with worship, deepen it with reading, enrich it with meditation. John Owen lived in the seventeenth century, but one could almost think he had airplanes in mind when he wrote: "When Christ comes . . . upon the soul, he hath no quiet landing-place."

Personally, I should hate to live through days like these without the deep experience of divine companionship, and of available resources greater than my own. I know that the old Hebrew story about the three Israelites cast into a burning fiery furnace and walking through it without so much as the smell of fire upon their garments, is a tale and not actual history, but it is a symbolic tale and a true parable for our times. For this is written of them, that there walked with them through the burning fiery furnace one like unto "the Son of God." Who here does not need that experience? No furnace so fiery hot that there does not walk through it with us a divine companion, from everlasting to everlasting God.

Finding Unfailing Resources

THESE days we are living through make a heavy demand on our strength. Action, output, work—to this energetic side of our lives, our time appeals. And because the church must and should feel the generation's characteristic needs, it is Christianity's active aspects that Sunday after Sunday we naturally think about. Our Christian responsibilities and obligations, what we should do and stand for and sacrificially bring to pass—this is the staple of our preaching. Yes, but the more the output, the greater the need of replenishment—that is universal law nowhere more manifestly operative than in personal experience.

Our situation today, therefore, little as it may outwardly seem to do so, leads our thought straight into the realm of prayer, and that, too, by a route that should make the matter cogent. In quiet, easy days we may approach prayer speculatively, arguing our differing theories concerning it; but having myself done that aplenty, it is not my interest now. Today one needs intake to match output. If prayer means that, as the great exemplars of prayer have said it does, then let us have it somehow or other! A disbeliever argues with me that prayer is theoretically irrational, but all the time he is talking I keep thinking of some one who is finding in prayer a sustaining source of power that sees him through troubled and laborious days. What I want to know is, what is that power and how does one get it?

Jesus came to the crisis of his life, when he knew once for all that the cross confronted him, and taking his disciples to the lovely retreat of Caesarea Philippi, under the shadow of Mount Hermon, he told them so. It was a tense and nervous time in the Master's life. He was going to Jerusalem to face the cross. Then we read that Jesus prayed. For a moment, at least, put aside theoretical skepticism about prayer and face the realistic facts. "As he was praying," we read, "the fashion of his countenance was altered." Had he too looked tense and drawn, harassed and afraid? Had his face, too, revealed his inner struggle, as he felt today's strain and foresaw tomorrow's peril? While he was praying, so Dr. Moffatt translates it, "the appearance of his face altered." Faith for fear, strength for anxiety, confidence for hesitation, inward power adequate for outward tension—that showed in his face. Theory or no theory, call it by what name we will, if that kind of experience is possible today, we need it.

In these difficult times this need is critical. Nine times out of ten, what breaks us down is an external strain plus a sense of internal inadequacy to meet it. Suppose we ask ourselves now what we are worrying about. We are worrying about the threat of war, about economic conditions, about our work, about our personal relationships, and endless other strains and problems. But press the matter more intimately home, and what each of us is really worrying about is himself and his own stamina. Many of us feel like trees in a high wind, and asked what occasions our anxiety, we naturally say, These tempests. But what we are really anxious about is our own rootage. If we knew that we had roots deep-set enough to stand tempests, our morale would not be shaken.

At this point the deepest need in us meets the deepest fact in Christianity, and if today these two could be brought together, the result might change the course of many a life. Some of us are like cisterns—we are good as far as we go; we have our uses, but we cannot count on ourselves; the sources of our supply are superficial; our reserves are limited; we cannot stand a prolonged drought. But some are like artesian wells, with resources that run deep, not at the mercy of transient circumstance. As Jesus said, "The water that I shall give him shall become in him a well of water springing up."

If such an experience of unfailing interior supply, that the great exemplars of prayer have borne witness to, is really possible, we need it, and this deep need in us corresponds with the deep resource the Christian Gospel offers: "Strengthened with might by his Spirit in the inner man." Many religious people never experience this. Christianity involves a great theology, and all of us reared in the churches have absorbed at least a smattering of that. Christianity involves a great ethic, and we have, by contagion at least, caught some of its ideals and accepted some of its obligations. Christianity involves a great fellowship, and we have in some degree assumed responsibilities for the church. Theology, ethics, church—these three make up the Christianity of multitudes. They have everything, that is, except the pith of the matter—the vital inward transforming climax of it all—God in us, a dependable resource of daily power, an unfailing well.

Asked whether we believe in God, most of us would say, Yes. But how little that affirmation sometimes means! What God do we believe in? To which some would answer, We are not materialists; we believe that the basic creative reality in the universe is Mind, not matter; and with that I, for one, would cordially agree. But is that all? To which others would say, We believe in Christ as God's revealer, and see the light of the knowledge of the Divine Glory in his face; and with that, also, I would agree. But again, Is that all? God, the creative Mind, behind and in the universe, God revealed in the supreme historic Character—is that all? Too few of us, with any accent of genuine experience, would be able to go on to the affirmation that makes the New Testament a book of triumphant living in a desperate time—God a spiritual presence in us: "Know ye not that ye are a temple of God, and that the Spirit of God dwelleth in you?" Resource, backing, power available for daily need, making us wells and not cisterns, until in sober fact, in him who strengthens us we are able for anything—that is the deepest fact in Christianity. The New Testament glories in a three-fold experience of God—God the creative Mind, God revealed in the transcendent Character, God the indwelling Spirit whose presence, as at Pentecost, is always accompanied by the promise, "Ye shall receive power."

It is commonly not weaklings but men of competent, aggressive will-power who need this experience most. Here is one who always has been adequate for life; naturally dynamic, strongly volitional, able to tackle life hard, he has been unaware of any vital lack of power. If you want anything, like a leopard, leap for it—such admirable directness of aim and effort has distinguished him. He belongs to the aggressive activists, whose very Christianity sings,

> Awake, my soul, stretch every nerve,
> And press with vigor on!

I never see people like that without knowing what will come some day; soon or late it will inevitably come, their confrontation of an experience where that whole method will be as inapplicable as hammering on water.

Real sorrow, for example. My friend had a lovely five-year-old daughter killed, by accident, in front of his own house, and in his own arms he carried her shattered body into the home. What does one do for one's friend in a time like that? Certainly not talk about "stretch every nerve, and press with vigor on." A great word in the English vocabulary our preaching too commonly neglects: endurance. Active vigor needed, yes, but not that alone—vigor by itself will not cover the case. We need the inner resources that make endurance possible. And that means that a man must be a well, not a cistern.

So one watches people starting out in life quite adequately, handling life with active vigor, as they run, one after another, into experiences where something deeper than vigor is needed. Serious failure, for example. Some night in his lifetime everyone comes home to find a new guest there—disappointment. What he had set his heart on has gone. In such a time, when a man cries, like Beethoven with his hearing lost, "O God, give me strength to conquer myself," how futile is mere appeal to vim and vigor, like a football coach's pep-talk to his team between halves! That is an impertinence at such a time. If one is to come through difficult experiences unembittered, unspoiled, still a real person, one needs deep resources. One must be more than a cistern.

Not alone in such experiences as sorrow and failure does this need arise but in man's search for the indispensable spiritual requirements of a satisfying life—inner peace, for example, some serenity in the soul to come home to at night and go out from in the morning. Who does not need that? But no one can get inner peace by pouncing on it, by vigorously willing to have it. Peace is a margin of power around our daily need. Peace is a consciousness of springs too deep for earthly droughts to dry up. Peace is an awareness of reserves from beyond ourselves, so that our power is not so much in us as through us. Peace is the gift, not of volitional struggle, but of spiritual hospitality. Peace is a power-question. Cisterns are anxious; wells have peace. There too, man's deepest need meets Christianity's deepest fact.

There are two aspects to every strong life—rootage and fruitage, receptivity and activity, relaxation and tension, resting back and working hard. A man who cannot do the former, can never do the latter well. He who cannot rest, cannot work; he who cannot let go, cannot hold on; he who cannot find footing, cannot go forward—never! The offices of psychiatrists are littered up with folk who have mastered the techniques of activity and aggressiveness, and who are going all to pieces now because that other technique they have failed to master: they have nothing to rest back upon.

"Let my soul take refuge from the crowding turmoil of worldly thoughts beneath the shadow of Thy wings; let my heart, this sea of restless waves, find peace in Thee, O God." That was Saint Augustine's prayer. A weak man? One of history's most momentous characters, from his early struggles with himself until at last, after an immeasurably important contribution to the world, Bishop of Hippo in North Africa, he fell on sleep, while the invading barbarians were at the city's gates and the Roman Empire was tumbling down about his ears. There is no understanding such a life without such prayer. He had something to rest back upon, and many a perilous and troubled day he prayed, and the fashion of his countenance was changed.

There are two ways to learn to pray. One is to try to argue it all out first, solve all the theoretical difficulties, and then, having our questions answered and our doubts resolved, say, Now I will try to pray. I have seldom seen that method issue in profound experience. But I have often seen another kind of thing happen—folks, that is, who started with the need of backing greater than their own, the desperate need of it, and who, theory or no theory, reached out for God and found him there, some power indubitably there that they could rest back upon, so that now they face all gainsayers with firsthand experience no speculative argument can confute. Prayer is real. "Strengthened with might by his Spirit in the inner man"—that is real!

On the Maine Coast a boy asked an old sailor, "What is the wind?" and after a long pause the old man answered, "I don't know. I can't tell you. But I know how to hoist a sail." To someone here today I am saying, Try it, will you? Endless unanswered questions yet about the wind, but still the wind is real. Hoist your sail, and see!

The kind of prayer that thus brings power always involves affirmation, positive affirmation of faith and confidence in God, putting divine strength in the center of the picture and crowding apprehensions, anxieties and fears off the edge. Who does not face hours when doubts and dismays, anxieties and apprehensions crowd up into the center of his mind? How obsessing such hours can be! And when they come something must be done about it. The Master too had such hours. Did he not cry, "Now is my soul troubled; and what shall I say?" Did he not in Gethsemane exclaim, "My soul is exceeding sorrowful, even unto death"? So, too, at Caesarea Philippi his anxieties and forebodings crowded up into the center of his thought, and then he prayed, and lo! the perspective changed. Confidence and courage marched in; the great convictions that sustained him and the great resources that supported him moved up into the center of his soul.

Real prayer like that is always more than begging; it is affirmation.

> Though I walk through the valley of the shadow of death,
> I will fear no evil; for thou art with me—

that is prayer.

> Therefore will not we fear, though the earth be removed, and though the mountains be carried into the midst of the sea;
> Though the waters thereof roar and be troubled, though the mountains shake with the swelling thereof . . .
> The Lord of hosts is with us; the God of Jacob is our refuge—

that is prayer.

> They that wait for the Lord shall renew their strength; they shall mount up with wings as eagles; they shall run, and not be weary; they shall walk, and not faint—

that is prayer.

> I. . . am persuaded that he is able to keep that which I have committed unto him against that day—

that is prayer. It carries up into the center of the soul convictions and reassurances that crowd out apprehensions and fears. How do folk live without that?

John Bunyan wrote *Pilgrim's Progress* in Bedford Jail. Anxieties crowded up on him—for himself, yes, but more for his family, and especially for that blind child of his whom he most dearly loved. It was his own personal experience he was describing when he wrote about Apollyon, the foul fiend, who "stradled quite over the whole breadth of the way, and said . . . prepare thy self to die, for I swear by my Infernal Den, that thou shalt go no further, here will I spill thy soul."

Yet Bunyan's soul was not spilled; no, nor countless others' souls who have known his inner secret. Prayer can be drums and bugles in one's spirit; faiths and reassurances come marching in with it to hold one's central square and drive out the saboteurs, and great convictions blow trumpets in us. All through this congregation are lives deeply in need of that.

The way the expressions of our faces change depends a great deal on the company we are in. In one group we may look dour, but let certain persons come within our view and see how our countenances light up! The Master's prayer did that for him; it introduced him to a spiritual companionship that transfigured even the way he looked. "I am not alone," he said, "the Father is with me." We can choose our interior, spiritual company—in that brief statement lies a truth that could remake our lives. Many things in the outer world we cannot choose; there we are the victims of necessity, and during these days in particular we have to live often in depressing company. But within ourselves we can choose our spiritual companionship. There we are masters of our hospitality. There we can live in a great and stimulating fellowship.

Prayer is establishing ourselves "in a sense of God's presence by continually conversing with Him." Brother Lawrence, a medieval Catholic saint, said that. Prayer is making "frequent colloquies, or short discoursings, between God and thy own soul." Jeremy Taylor, a Protestant leader of the seventeenth century, said that. This thing we are saying now is no modern thinning out of prayer, but the essence of prayer's meaning as the great souls of the church have experienced it: the maintenance of an habitual, spiritual fellowship.

We talk much today about practical Christianity. I am all for it—Christianity that gets down to hard brass tacks, that feeds the hungry, clothes the naked and works for social reformation; the Christianity of the Good Samaritan serving those of whom Jesus said, "Inasmuch as ye have done it unto one of the least of these my brethren, ye have done it unto me." Such Christianity calls for fruit on the tree; it wants practical results. But the tree's roots are practical too, critically practical, and watching modern Christians I am concerned about that aspect of the matter. Says the Psalmist,

> He shall be like a tree, planted by the streams of water,
> That bringeth forth its fruit in its season.

Many of us need that double emphasis—rootage and fruitage. Even the Master's life reached the place where all his stress on practical service would not fill the bill. Despite that he would have been long since forgotten; what saw him through was something underground, not visible to the eye, his rootage, "a tree planted by the streams of water."

This aspect of the Master's life and of our own becomes most clear to some of us as a real experience when we think of it in terms of the companionship we live in. Thank God for our friends! When the Master's face was transfigured he too was in the company of his friends. But there was more to it than that. Even when his friends failed him, and the world turned on him a forbidding face, he still had stimulating companionship within. When he was alone, he was not alone.

Such prayer as we have been talking of releases power and that phrase ought to have vivid meaning now. Turn to an old dictionary and this is what we read about "uranium"—"A rare, heavy, white metallic element . . . has no important uses." So! Uranium—no important uses! But it has now shaken the world to its foundations, because science has released its power. Such is the task of science in the physical realm—to fulfill conditions that release power; and in the realm of the spirit that is prayer's effect too.

Christian prayer is not the endeavor to get God to do what we want. Christian prayer is the endeavor to put ourselves into such relationships with God that he can do in and for and through us, what he wants. All the worst misunderstandings and perversions of prayer start with egotism—ourselves at the center, and we endeavoring to get God to do our will. But Jesus' prayer started at the other end—God first, what he wants predominant, and prayer opening up the way for the release of his purpose, giving gangway to his action and free course to his power: "Not my will, but thine, be done." Without such prayer God can never do in, and for, and through us, what he wants to do.

For such praying these present days urgently call. For action, yes—determined, courageous, tireless action—but all the more because of that, for those interior resources that only great praying can supply. Ah Christ, two things happened to your face in those trying days. First you prayed, until your face shone; and then, we read, you set your face steadfastly to go to Jerusalem.

The High Uses of Serenity

A FEW miles from Wiscasset, in the State of Maine, is a beautiful, old New England meeting house which was dedicated to the worship of God about the time the Constitution of the United States was adopted. Separated now from any large center of population, it is generally closed, but once a year at least the countryside makes pilgrimage to worship in it. A few weeks ago, sitting in one of the old box pews, I listened to a well-known writer and student of English literature speaking on the influence of the New England meeting houses on the character of the Maine people. What most I recall, however, and expect never to forget, is a condensed statement evidently born out of long brooding over the classics of our English speech: "There is no great art without serenity." Even an amateur can understand that. In music, literature, and painting, there is a difference between the fussiness and sensationalism of cheap and superficial work and the impression made on us by things supremely beautiful, and, when one stops to consider it, the speaker in that old New England meeting house was right. An essential element in all great art is serenity.

If some one says that great art has come out of troubled souls, as Chopin wrote his music often in an agony of creative turmoil, that is true, but the nocturnes themselves have poise, symmetry, proportion, peace, as truly as the Parthenon has, which even in its ruins fills the eye with rest.

If some one says that in their works, as well as in themselves, Wagner and Beethoven, Goethe and Shakespeare could be tumultuous and stormy, of course they could, but it was never like a tempest in a little pool roiling everything up, but always like a storm at sea, with wide distances around and undisturbed depths beneath. Think of the great music which we love the best, the great books which have meant most to us, the great paintings before which, if we could go back to Florence or Dresden, we would sit down quietly. The speaker was right. There is no great art without serenity.

Now, the highest of all arts is not music or literature or painting but life, and there, too, without serenity there can be nothing great.

This may be a dangerous thing to say, for nothing much more degenerating to character can be imagined than to make serenity an end in itself. One might almost as well make sleep an end in itself. No healthy person would do that. Sleep is not an end in itself, but it is a grand place to start from in the morning. A physical organism which has no background of tranquillity can have no foreground of activity. That truth, translated from the physical to the spiritual plane, is, I should suppose, in days like these one of the most important that a man can get his eyes upon.

The high uses of serenity are plainly indicated in the family life. The members of a family ought to be engaged in many diversified and exciting enterprises; a home should be a beehive and in and out of it parents and children go on eager errands; all of which is gloriously possible if at the heart of the home there is serenity. Tennyson said about his wife: "The peace of God came into my life before the altar when I wedded her." When home means that, what great things may come out of it! When home lacks that, what great thing can come out of it? For here also the basic law holds good: nothing great without serenity.

Let us get our eye clearly, then, on what we are talking of—not serenity as an escape from life, but as an indispensable part of life, what rest is to the body, what peace is to the home, what roots are to the tree, what depth is to an ocean. Nothing in heaven above or the earth beneath great without it!

Consider, for one thing, that our personal happiness is profoundly involved in this. How much of happiness consists in interior serenity and how impossible is any happiness without it! Give us the loveliest of autumn days that the artistry of nature can create, with peaceful and resplendent trees around us and every circumstantial factor fortunate, yet even there a man cannot be happy if within him his spirit has lost its serenity. On the other hand, consider how strangely circumstanced some of our happy days have been, not set in autumnal trees or in any fortunate environment, but in difficulty. Yet we were happy and the reason is plain—our spirits within us were serene.

If some one says that serenity is not the whole of happiness, that excitement, sensation, thrill are part of it, of course they are. Alas for a man who has nothing exciting to do or to enjoy, and who does not sometimes cast his harness off and have free pasturage to kick his heels in! Nevertheless, of all pathetic things few are worse than the familiar sight which one sees on every side in a town like this—people, I mean, who are trying to substitute thrills for serenity. Having no serenity at home within themselves, they run away into sensations, spend as much time as possible away from themselves amid their thrills, and then at last have to come back again to no serenity. That is the very essence of unhappiness.

On an average, twenty-two thousand people commit suicide in this country every year and the month when the largest number of them do it is May. It is a lovely month; all nature stirs with prophecies of coming summer—and they kill themselves. Moreover, for the most part it is not the poor and hard-put-to-it who do that. Listen to one of them who killed himself in the month of May: "I have had few real difficulties. I have had, on the contrary, an exceptionally glamorous life—as life goes—and I have had more than my share of affections and appreciations. . . . No one thing is responsible for this and no one person—except myself." Hearing that, what do we know about that man? Surely this much that, for all his excursions into life's successes and thrills, he kept coming back to a spirit where there was no serenity.

This human need for tranquillity has always inhered in life but in days like these it is accentuated. An Englishman is reported to have said that on three trips to the United States he came to three different conclusions as to what was the major passion of Americans. After one visit he concluded that this passion was power, after another he decided it was wealth, after the third he was sure it was acceleration. Well, acceleration is a towering fact among us. Speed becomes a mania and the pace is sometimes frantic, and in the midst of it one who cares about man's happiness and quality looks on the wreckage of that inner grace without which there can be nothing great in life or art, serenity.

In view of the prevalent unhappiness because of this, some of our modern sophisticates might well cease their attacks on our forefathers because they were dour, grim, and unhappy. Sometimes they doubtless were. Their theology at times was dreadful. But, while they may have been dour, grim, and unhappy, they were not cynical, flippant, futile, and unhappy. The more one deals with first-hand evidence, the more one is inclined to stake the Puritans themselves against many of our modern sophisticates in point of happiness.

In a biography of Louisa Alcott, author of *Little Women*, one gets the impression that in her generation life was not so steady and calm or so dour and grim as we have pictured it. At any rate, in the first twenty-eight years of Louisa's life her family moved twenty-nine times, which is a record even for New York. Life then was not calm and easy. In the Alcott household it was very difficult. But one gets the impression also that it was happy, fundamentally happy; serenity in the soul, serenity in the home, something profound and peaceful in themselves and in their relationships with one another and with God—a haven to come back to from the storms of life. We moderns desperately need that and a vital Christianity gives it. For whatever else a real religion has done or left undone, it has ministered to those who understood it best a profound resource of inner power, a margin of reserve around their need, so that even in a prison Paul could sing about the "peace of God, which passeth all understanding." He had within himself a serene spirit to come home to. Without that, nothing in the world can give abiding happiness.

Consider also that not only personal happiness but personal character is involved in this. A great deal of our so-called modern badness is not malicious; it is simply life, lacking deep wells of quietness, trying to make up for the loss of serene meaning by plunging into sensations with a kick in them. When Dante turned his back, an exile, on his loved city of Florence, he described its wickedness as like the restlessness of a sick woman in a fever who keeps changing her posture to escape the pain. So, in a town like this, men plunge into debauchery and women fly from one sensation to another and live like whirling dervishes, for the same reason that small boys pull false fire alarms to feel the thrill of the converging fire engines. People behave so because they have missed something in their lives. The boys have missed the old and simpler happiness that some of us who lived in the countryside knew. They have no normal resources to fall back upon. And men and women who act like that have missed an inner quiet, a serene meaning in life that makes cheap sensation seem intolerably tawdry.

Some things we cannot imagine being cared for by a man with any serenity of life. Why should he be attracted by drunkenness or by the hectic chances of a gambler's existence? Why should he find life's satisfaction in artificial excitements, with the hours between them but a dull interlude? This mad living, this constant change of posture to escape our pain, is a psychological compensation on the part of people who have missed serenity.

One of the finest things ever said by one man about another John Morley said about William Ewart Gladstone: "He was one of that high and favoured household who, in Emerson's noble phrase, 'live from a great depth of being.' " If that had been said about Gladstone by one of his coreligionists, it would not have been so impressive, but Morley was an agnostic; he was no coreligionist. Only, closely watching his lifelong friend, he saw where the secret of his moral power lay—he lived from a great depth of being. In a world like this and in a generation such as ours, there is no separating the problem of character from that. That pretty much *is* character.

Indeed, let a man ask himself what spoils serenity and he cannot answer without plunging deep into his moral life. Remorse ruins serenity; our infidelities, which we so eagerly anticipate and which pass from expectation through enjoyment into memory, haunt us evermore. Illwill spoils serenity, as does the cherished grudge, the mean vindictiveness. Jealousy wrecks serenity, as in the old story where, from the day he began enviously eyeing David, Saul never had a peaceful moment more. Engrossing ambition, where a man's ego becomes the clamorous center of the universe—that exiles serenity. Here we come to grips with our theme. Some at first may have supposed we were speaking of an easy virtue. No, one of the most costly. If serenity were easy there would be more of it. At its wicket gate there stand conditions to be satisfied—no unforgiven sins, no cherished grudges, no jealousy, no egoistic ambitions—the profound moral conditions of serenity.

To be sure, in this realm as in every other, there are caricatures and fakes. Man so instinctively knows that inward calm is to be desired that every conceivable device for getting it without fulfilling its serious conditions has been tried. One of the commonest, I suspect, is to seek a serene mind by shrugging one's shoulders at life, saying that nothing much matters anyway so that one need not bother much about anything. That provides a bogus serenity.

In Maine, one summer, so Bishop Fiske writes, he and three friends spent a vacation with their guide, an old Maine fisherman. It was the summer when William Jennings Bryan was making his last attempt at the presidency and rock-ribbed Republican Maine was worried. One of the men in the party was a research physician; one was a geologist; another was an astronomer. They talked about the ages of the rocks and the evolution of life from the creatures of the sea and the immeasurable distances of the stars, and the Maine fisherman listened. At last even his taciturnity broke down and he poured out a flood of questions. Were the rocks really so old? Did life evolve from the sea creatures? Were the stars so far away? Was everything so inconceivably vast and ancient? And when at last he got it in his mind, he heaved a sigh of relief. "I guess," he said, "it won't make a powerful lot of difference even if William Jennings Bryan *is* elected!"

Such detachment born of a long look can have wholesomeness in it but it is not of that we are thinking now. Rather, serenity is the basis of powerful activity. There is no art, no creativeness, no release of moral power even to rebuild society, without it. If a man is going to help lift the world he must have some solidity within him to lean his lever on. Some here doubtless said at first, In days of social and economic tension such as these, how can a man waste his time talking on serenity? I am thinking of these social questions. What else can an intelligent man think of in days like these? One who cares about them walks the streets and sees how few people are constructively and unselfishly thinking about public matters. How can they? They have no leisure from themselves. They have no serenity. They are harassed and agitated about themselves. They are afflicted with an appalling self-preoccupation. They have no inner steadiness to lean their levers on. And considering the case, one begins to understand some things not so clearly seen before.

Consider the Quakers, for example. Of all the Christian groups, which, would you say, has been right about more social questions than any other? The Quakers. Well, then, what have they stressed? It is very strange! They have stressed serenity—

Dear Lord and Father of mankind,
Forgive our feverish ways.

Yet when we stop to think of it, is it so strange? Can we think of any supreme soul in history without this quality within him? We cannot understand Christ without it. When he talks about inward peace one well may listen. A young man he was, dangerously plunging into revolutionary matters that would shake the world; yet he talked about inward peace. He never could have done anything without it. In the Garden of Gethsemane he might have lost it. That was the struggle under the olive trees, to maintain his serenity. Everything depended on it. There was a victory when he was sure of it, the interior leverage of the divine Archimedes by which he moved the world. It is of that we are talking. Lacking it, there is no powerful character, and it belongs only to those who live from a great depth of being.

So, inevitably, we come to our third fact: not only are personal happiness and personal character involved in this but personal religion. Some time since, an invitation came to attend a conference of humanists, non-theistic humanists, who are trying to build churches on a moral program only, and I was asked to tell them frankly what I thought was the trouble with the humanists. It was impossible to go but, could I have done so, I know what I would have said in candid criticism of my humanistic friends. All profound religion ministers to three basic human needs: the need of a great metaphysic, a philosophy of life to put meaning into living; the need of a great morality, principles of conduct, personal and social, to ennoble living; the need of a great mysticism, profound resources of interior power by which to live. All profound religion has made to life these three major contributions: a great philosophy, a great ethic, a great resource of power. The trouble with the humanists is that they are trying to limp along with one of them, the ethic. All complete religion has three dimensions. It has height, an elevated philosophy of life; it has depth, a profound resource for life; it has extension, a noble way of living life. The trouble with the humanists is that they try to keep it one-dimensional, to preserve the moral extension without the height of faith or the depth of power, and I, for one, am certain that that essentially is incomplete and that, for psychological reasons, if for nothing else, it will not work.

Humanism, however, is more than an organized movement. It is a modern mood, an attitude, a drift that affects us all, so that every Sunday these pews have people in them powerfully tempted to a one-dimensional Christianity of moral demand only. Then, when trouble comes, people have no high philosophy of life or deep resources of power to give serenity. And sometimes, alas, they discover that, in facing heavy hours, bearing heavy griefs, handling heavy tasks, when a man loses serenity he loses everything.

I plead today for a kind of religion which helps a man to live from a great depth of being. You young people in particular, eager, enthusiastic, devoted, as many of you are, to the noblest causes of today, beware of a Christianity that merely adds one more demand on life without being a resource for life. The demands of life are terrific enough already. As the years pass they often mount appallingly. What if, then, a man has a Christianity which merely piles on him a further demand for more sacrifice and more toil but which does not at the same time help him to meet the demand from a great depth of being? There is much eager, youthful, one-dimensional Christianity like that today.

My friends, if we are to have a profound religion we may indeed throw away our old, childish, anthropomorphic ideas of God, but we may not throw away God and leave ourselves caught like rats in the trap of an aimless, meaningless, purposeless universe. There is nothing in that philosophy of life to help a man live from a profound depth of being. And while we may throw away our early, ignorant ideas of prayer, we may not throw away prayer, the flowing of internal fountains that keep their freshness when all the superficial cisterns peter out. These are the other dimensions of religion which, helping us to meet demand with resource amid the strain of life, bestow serenity.

Young man or woman, some day you are going to be forty years old, fifty years old, sixty years old, and the years between now and then will not be easy, either. We will take it for granted that morally you will try to live a good life and socially a useful one. All *that* I pray for you, and something more beside, that as age comes on you may deserve the salutation which in the old days of titled nobility stood high on the list—'Your Serene Highness.' After a long life, that is a crown of praise—Your Serene Highness.

What Keeps Religion Going?

THE Book of Job is one of the great dramas of the ancient world. It is not easy to translate, and the best endeavors are not the standard versions but the freer renderings of independent scholars. So Dr. McFadyen, in the fifteenth chapter, translates the accusation that Job's false friends, speaking through Eliphaz, hurl at Job because he doubts the current theology: "See!" they cry, "thou art destroying religion." More than 2000 years ago men were saying that. On a man like Job, who doubted the contemporary creed, they brought down the stunning charge: "Thou art destroying religion." Nevertheless, while the old creed that Job doubted has long since perished, religion still is here. Men like the friends of Job have thought they saw religion being destroyed innumerable times, but it persists. What keeps religion going?

This fact is clear, that religion is one of the little group of fundamental interests in human life that everlastingly change, and yet everlastingly persist. Are not these two characteristics, persistence and change, the marks of the most important elements in human experience? Some things we cannot get rid of—they persist; but at the same time, we cannot keep them static—they change. Whenever we find those two qualities, persistence and change, in the same field, we may be sure that we are dealing with something important.

Some things mankind can finish and be done with, but not music, that persists, and changes from tom-toms to Beethoven and beyond; not architecture, that persists, and changes from mud huts to Chartres Cathedral and beyond; not agriculture, that persists, and changes from Ruth's sickle to McCormick Harvesters, soil chemistry and beyond; not science, that persists, and changes from ancient Chaldeans studying the stars to a new telescope with a 200-inch reflector and beyond; not religion, that persists, and changes from old credulities and world views to new thoughts of God and larger apprehensions of his meaning. Religion is like language. Languages have perished, but language goes on.

Now this is not only a historical matter of great import, it is a personal matter too. Who of us has not had some cherished theological idea smashed to pieces, seen some old religious world view disintegrate, until we too cried, Thou are destroying religion? Everyone here has used these words of the friends of Job. Today we consider the fact that men have said that from the beginning, and still religion goes on. What keeps it going?

In handling so large a subject, all one can hope to do here is to suggest certain deep sources from which religion perennially rises in man's experience, so that not only can mankind as a whole not escape it, but you and I personally are inevitably bound to deal with it one way or another.

One such profound source is obviously the need of spiritual meaning in our life in this mysterious universe. Ages ago a wandering star passed too near the sun, and drew out from it by its gravitational pull this planet that ever since has swung around its solar center, has gradually cooled off, given birth to life, and become the habitat of our strange human race. What does it all mean? Macbeth calls life

> . . . a tale
> Told by an idiot, full of sound and fury,
> Signifying nothing.

Is that the answer? That would be strange, for we here live in two worlds, one material, physical, tangible, visible, the other spiritual, intangible, invisible, the one made up of things we can weigh and measure, the other made up of ideas, ideals, of intellect, conscience, creative genius, of faith, hope, love. In that latter world, invisible, we really live, and not by bread alone. In Santayana's phrase, man's oddity is "that interest of his in things not edible." What does it mean?

If only increase of scientific knowledge cleared up the mystery the case would be simpler, but it does not. The more we know about this universe, the more mysterious it is. The old world that Job knew was marvelous enough, and his description of its wonders is among the noblest poetry of the race, but today the new science has opened to our eyes vistas of mystery that transcend in their inexplicable marvel anything the ancients ever dreamed. What does life in such a world mean?

Now meaning is spiritual. If this cosmos is an accident of electrons and protons going it blind, then there is no ultimate meaning. But if God is real, if his purpose runs through all creation, if we are spirit, the children of Eternal Spirit, and so can be fellow workers with God for an end unseen and unimaginable, but worth everything that its achievement costs, then this universe and our lives within it are packed with meaning. That is the profound issue involved in religion, an issue persistent, tenacious, inescapable, outlasting the rise and fall of all special theologies. Demolish religion's theories a thousand times, and it will still lift its head in men, crying, Life does have eternal meaning!

Here is the explanation of an experience familiar in our time. Many people have given up Christianity, supposing that they were merely surrendering faith in religion, only to discover that what they really had surrendered was faith in life itself. They thought religion was a mere parenthesis in the sentence of life. They supposed they could drop the parenthesis and not miss it. But now, having dropped the parenthesis, they find they still have the main sentence on their hands, with the insistent question rising, What does it mean? And it begins to dawn on them that Christian faith is all about that. Christian faith is no parenthesis. It concerns the meaning of the whole sentence of life.

As a Christian minister, I should not particularly mind people losing faith in religion if that were all there were to it. Plenty of things go under the name of religion that a man had better lose faith in. One does care, however, about the shattering experience coming to countless people who have lost faith in life itself. When a fine-natured, socially useful atheist of our time comes to his life's end, saying, "The outstanding fact that cannot be dodged by thoughtful men is the futility of it all," one does care about that.

When one of our fine dramatists, whose plays we all have enjoyed, says in his autobiography, "There is no reason for life and life has no meaning," one does care about that. Such men have not simply dropped a religious parenthesis; they have lost meaning out of the whole sentence.

Many a time in my life I have heard the cry, Thou art destroying religion! This or that creedal or customary appurtenance of religion became incredible, and men thought the Christian faith was done for. No, my friends, the deep fountains of Christian faith are not so easily dried up. Forever it rises in man's soul, crying, There is a basic, ultimate, eternal, spiritual meaning in this universe, and in our lives! That keeps religion going, because that keeps life going. One man has just written a brief biography of his friend. His friend was a success in business, and died worth over $40,000,000. But at seventy years of age his verdict on life was "Vanity of vanities; all is vanity." "He died," writes his friend, "in the midst of luxurious surroundings with a handful of ashes in his grasp." So a man can stand almost any adversity if he keeps a strong faith that there is ultimate meaning in life; but if he loses that faith, then though he gain the whole world he has lost his soul.

Another perennial source of religion that will never be exhausted is the presence in our lives of profound personal experiences that no materialism ever can adequately account for. Every one of us has them. Life is shallow enough, but not so shallow that any one of us escapes the deep hours when we stand face to face with some spiritual reality that no materialism can adequately explain.

The evidence for this lies in the very fact that when we sing, for example, "Dear Lord and Father of Mankind," we know what Whittier means. That experience of inner spiritual companionship is not alien to us. When Helen Keller was a little girl they brought Phillips Brooks to her to teach her something about God, and with the sign language he did his best to describe the inner presence of the unseen Spirit, until suddenly her face lighted up and she signaled back that she had always known there was a God, but had not before known his name. There is revealed one of the profoundest truths about the human soul.

It is a strange thing that when the supreme seers of the race describe their profoundest insights, something deep within us understands. When Elijah, after the earthquake, wind, and fire, heard the "still small voice," we know what that means. When Jesus says: "Go into your room and shut the door, pray to your Father who is in secret," we may not do it, but we understand it. When Wordsworth says,

> . . . I have felt
> A presence that disturbs me with the joy
> Of elevated thoughts,

we have felt that presence too. And deep in man is an unconquerable conviction that in such experiences there is something that materialism cannot account for.

In how many different ways men have tried to explain the persistence of religion! Some have said it was the work of priestcraft. That now is recognized as nonsense. Some have said it was man's desire for a comfortable opiate, but that explains only the perversions of religion. The basic reasons for religion's perpetuity lie deep in man himself, in those experiences of the spiritual life of which materialism can give no adequate account.

We all have hours when beauty plays upon our souls like winds on an aeolian harp. We all know hours of love—deep, true, and tender, asking nothing, willing to give everything, like parents with a little child. We have hours of intellectual illumination, when our minds are quickened and a new idea reorients our lives. We have hours when the sense of honor is regnant, and to our consciences, commanding a hard duty, we give a strong affirmative reply. We have hours when a power greater than our own is mysteriously at our disposal, and Paul's words, "Christ in you, the hope of glory," are real. And then materialism tries to explain these, and other experiences like these, saying, as one modern atheist has just written: "The realm of spirit" is "a sort of invisible vegetation flourishing in some of the stars." My word! Raphael's sense of beauty, Einstein's intellect, Christ's spirit, a sort of invisible vegetation that flourishes on some of the stars? No! Demolish religion endless times and it still will come back, crying, That explanation explains nothing! These experiences of men's souls are too real, too deep, too universal, too significant, too transforming to be so cheaply disposed of.

See what was troubling those false friends of Job! They had a theological theory that God must immediately bless all good men with prosperity and curse all bad men with misfortune, and that, therefore, all prosperous people were thereby proved to be good, and all unfortunate people were thereby proved to be bad. That was the current theology. And Job did not believe it; he saw through it into its shallowness and falsity, and he vehemently denied it. It was because of that Eliphaz said: "Thou art destroying religion!" And now history, looking back, calls those friends fools, and blind. That theology of theirs and countless others like it have gone, but deep beneath them all, persistent, fundamental, inescapable, are the great experiences of the human soul in its supreme hours, which no materialism can adequately account for. In the old days when Phillips Brooks held consultation hours at Harvard University, one student came to his office and said with an anxious air: "Dr. Brooks, I would like to talk over some of my doubts; but I don't want to disturb your faith." And Brooks broke out into uncontrollable laughter. Disturb his faith, he who knew the deep experiences of the soul that only God can adequately explain!

A third source from which religious faith forever rises in the life of man is found in human history. Though religion were destroyed countless times, it would still come back, sure that hands stronger than ours are on the reins of mankind's life. Man did not make himself; he was made. It was not man who brought the organic out of the inorganic, and created life. It was not man, the animal, who deliberately set out to climb the ascending road toward Christ; he was set upon that road by a power greater than his own. Man is not the original creator of goodness, truth, and beauty; he discovers them. Something greater than man has been making man and dealing with man.

Now this general truth out of which religion perennially springs is made vivid in one special experience repeated again and again in human history, namely, where right defeated turns out to be stronger than wrong triumphant. That is a strange, recurrent fact.

The defeats of righteousness are stronger than the victories of evil. How far can evil go? It can go a long way, even far enough to crucify Christ. But it has its limits. For lo! even though it goes so far, yet that defeat on Calvary turns out to be a victory, as though evil contained within itself the seeds of its own destruction, so that Caiaphas and Pilate, who thought themselves the winners, are the losers, and Christ's day, far from being over, is yet to come. What is it, in a merely materialistic world, that could make that kind of event possible?

Professor Charles A. Beard, one of the leading historians of our time, was asked sometime since what major lessons he had learned from history, and he answered that he had learned four. Here they are: "First, whom the gods would destroy they first make mad with power. Second, the mills of God grind slowly, yet they grind exceeding small. Third, the bee fertilizes the flower it robs. Fourth, when it is dark enough you can see the stars." So! That is what secular history teaches.

This self-defeating quality of evil that Professor Beard sees everywhere in history has been plainly exhibited in our generation. In *Mein Kampf*, for example, Hitler wrote this: "By means of shrewd lies, unremittingly repeated, it is possible to make people believe that heaven is hell—and hell, heaven. . . . The greater the lie, the more readily will it be believed." Skillful and audacious mendacity can be a powerful element in public policy. That is true. But Hitler should have remembered the old German saying: "Lies have short legs." So the old Germans said. Lies can go a little way, but then they reach their limit and their nemesis. First, your enemies will not believe you; then the onlookers will not believe you; then your allies will not believe you; then even your friends will not trust you. There is in mendacity itself, whether it be Hitler's or our own, a self-defeating quality. Lies have short legs.

If this world and ourselves within it were but the chance by-product of mindless dust going it blind, why should lies have short legs? Why should crucifixions turn out to be supreme triumphs? Why should Nero from his golden house put Paul to death upon the Appian Way, and centuries after, Nero be a by-word and derision while Paul's insights sway the minds of multitudes? Why should not only a poet sing

> Though the cause of Evil prosper, yet 't is
> Truth alone is strong,

but a hard-headed historian say that history teaches that "whom the gods would destroy they first make mad with power"; that though "the mills of God grind slowly, yet they grind exceeding small"; that "the bee fertilizes the flower it robs"; and that "when it is dark enough you can see the stars"? Some power greater than man has hold upon man. All our pictures of him are but children's drawings. All our imaginations of him are but fable and parable. But though our theologies about him change and our theories perish, still religion will rise forever in the mind and spirit of man, saying, The Lord God omnipotent reigneth!

From at least one more deep source religion perennially rises in the soul of man—from the fact of great personality. For personality at its best is a momentous fact. Amid the horror of the world and the shame of man's degraded life, one thing cannot be taken from us—we have seen in great souls what personality can mean. The modern mind balks at miracles, but after all, how miraculous a supreme person is, a comprehensive intellect, a luminous character, a creative genius, a sacrificial spirit! How ever did anything like that come to pass on this wandering island in the sky? Einstein may explain the cosmos, but if he does, who, then, can explain Einstein? Bach may account for the deep secrets of great music, but if he does, who, then, can account for Bach? Christ may elucidate the mystery of spiritual life, but who, then, will elucidate the mystery of Christ himself?

There are only two things that ultimately can be believed about great personality in this world. Either it is an accident, or else it is a revelation, one or the other. Either it is mere chance, like a spark luckily struck off by falling stones, or else it is the unveiling of an eternal quality at the heart of all things.

Now materialists have to see great personality as an accident. Stones and stars are to them revelations; atoms and electrons tell us something everlastingly true about the universe, says materialism, but intellect, character, spirit, are accidents; there is nothing like intellect, character, and spirit, eternally at the heart of the cosmos. Over against that, religion stands, and will not have it so. Great personality is not an accident, it cries, but a revelation! Whenever goodness, truth, or beauty shine in human life, they are rays of an eternal sun. As Professor Montague, of Barnard College, put it: "What is highest in spirit is also deepest in nature." On that conviction religion takes its stand. Destroy its theologies endless times, it will come back, crying, Great personality cannot be an accident! It is a revelation, the light of the knowledge of the glory of God in the face of Jesus Christ. So to many of us in dark days when theories break down and abstract arguments fail, some strong, inspiring person comes, a soul that matter cannot explain, nor yet explain away, and lo! our faith comes back again, as in the New Testament, crying, "I know him whom I have believed."

Our little systems have their day;
They have their day and cease to be;
They are but broken lights of thee,
And thou, O Lord, art more than they.

All through this congregation now are folk who have been tempted and are being tempted to surrender Christian faith. I beg of you, take the measure of what you would be surrendering. That human life has in it basic spiritual meaning; that the deepest experiences of our souls represent reality and can be explained only as the impact of an Eternal Spirit; that human history is under a sovereignty greater than man's; that supreme personality, Christ above all, is not an accident but a revelation—against that religion even the gates of hell shall not prevail.

The Towering Question: Is Christianity Possible?

MANY people find it difficult to believe in Christianity. They picture Christianity as a creed, concerning which they have to decide whether or not it is credible. When, then, they do not find it credible, they think that ends the matter and say, often wistfully, that they cannot believe in Christianity.

Surely, there is a radical mistake somewhere in this picture of what Christianity is all about. Let us at the start put the case bluntly. Christianity is primarily something to be *done*. It is not first of all a finished set of propositions to be accepted; it is first of all an unfinished task to be completed. It is a way of thinking about life and living life to be wrought out personally and socially on earth. The question to be asked about it is not simply, Is it true? but, Can we ever in this world make it come true? not simply, Is it credible? but, Is it possible?

So blunt a statement of the case may well call out the protest that, after all, Christianity does involve ideas, doctrines, truths, which must be believed if the Christian task is to be Christian. To be sure it does. A full-face photograph and a profile are not contradictory, and because today we are talking about the full-face view of this matter we are not denying the profile. Of course, the Christian task to be done is associated with Christian ideas to be believed. Many people, however, are living spiritually arid and pointless lives because they never have put the Christian task first and then seen the Christian ideas as instruments in its accomplishment.

One who is fearful that thus we may belittle Christian truth should consider science. Nobody would suspect science of minimizing ideas. Nevertheless, science also is a deed to be done and every idea is an instrument for a task. Could steamships cross the seas? Men theoretically said, No: no ship could carry coal enough to stoke its engines across the Atlantic. That disputed matter never could have been settled in debate alone. The crossing of the ocean by steam was an enterprise not simply to be thought out but to be worked out.

Could men fly? Leonardo da Vinci dreamed it long ago and throughout the succeeding centuries of debate the same thing could have been said about flying which we just have said about Christianity. The question was not simply, Are the ideas of aviation true? but, Can we ever make them come true?

Of course, yellow fever was stopped by a process involving ideas. Nevertheless, there is a man still living in this country, permanently invalided because long ago he deliberately and courageously let himself be bitten by an infected mosquito to find out what really did cause yellow fever and hence how to stop it. Science is not simply ideas to be accepted but deeds to be done.

If that is true in the realm where pure intelligence is most exalted, how much more in other realms much nearer Christianity, such as art? Many of us recall the long process of this church's building, the ideas which went into it, the theories and formulas which were involved, and we recall, too, how all this came to point and meaning, was lifted up and made significant, because every theory was embodied in a task, every idea an instrument for getting something done.

In no realm can anybody understand the full significance of an idea until he sees it as a means of achievement. Many minds are in confusion because they never have thought of Christianity in such terms. Is Christianity true?—they have debated that without end, but not, Is it something that we can make come true?

In facing this issue we well may look at the world about us with its tremendous problems—like war. The oldest historic monument on earth concerns war. Take camels and go out into the Sinaitic Peninsula, down the valleys where the Pharaohs' turquoise mines used long ago to be. You will see it carved there yet on the great rock face, the oldest known monument on earth. It is a Pharaoh with uplifted weapon about to crush the skull of an Asiatc captive forced to his knees before him. That represents war thirty-four centuries before Christ; and now, nineteen centuries after Christ, with weapons more terrific than any Pharaoh could have dreamed, we are at it still.

Or consider the tragic human consequences of our economic life, organized around self-interest. Edwin Markham put it in a quatrain:

> "Two things," said Kant, "fill me with breathless awe:
> The starry heaven and the moral law."
> But I know a thing more awful and obscure—
> The long, long patience of the plundered poor.

See, then, this present world on one side, with its tragic human problems, and, on the other, Christ and what he stands for—noble character, the ideal of brotherhood, the method of love, belief in the victory of righteousness. What is the towering question rising out of that contrast? Surely, not first of all, Are Christ's ideas theoretically credible? but, Are they, in a world like this, possible? not simply, Are they true? but, Can we make them come true?

In saying this we are getting back to the first impression which Jesus made upon his hearers. Of all personalities who have swayed the thought of humankind, none could have been less speculative and theoretical than Jesus. Nobody ever met him and went away thinking that he had been faced with a theoretical problem. Moreover, the reason for that is plain: every element in Jesus' teaching is livable. Run through the Sermon on the Mount and note that each element in his teaching can be tried out in life: brotherliness, cherishing no inward hate—that is livable; purity which even in thought respects womanhood—that is livable; sincerity, so that a man's "Yea" needs no oath, his word as good as his bond—that is livable; and generosity which unostentatiously helps its fellows, the right hand not knowing what the left hand does—that is livable; inner fellowship with God in the shrine of the spirit, and faith in the victory of righteousness—that is livable. Every emphasis of Jesus' teaching in the Sermon on the Mount can be tried out in life. No wonder, then, that after finishing it he said, "Every one therefore that heareth these words of mine, and *doeth* them. . . ."

If, then, all Christ's teaching can be lived, every presentation of it was a call, not for debate but for decision. Will you? he said. Here is a task to be done, a life to be lived, an idea to be worked out. Will you? That is far from the manner of facing Christianity to which many of us have grown accustomed. We older ones, especially, have lived through a generation when one factor after another pushed into the foreground of attention the speculative, argumentative aspects of Christianity. First, the theory of evolution made many accustomed doctrines obsolete. Then fresh light on the Bible outlawed old beliefs about that. Then the new cosmos broke up the ancient molds in which ideas of God had long been fabricated. Then a fresh vision of the historic Jesus so humanized him as to make ancient dogmatic statements about him seem both untrue and unlovely. The total consequence was to push the argumentative, controversial elements in Christianity into the foreground. We even split into fundamentalists and liberals and, vehemently arguing, hurled back and forth the question, Is it credible? Some of us here were in the thick of that. We are not denying that it was necessary and had its use but, with all the difficulties of this present time, it is healthier to be here.

Look out on this generation. History repeats itself. After an era when the Christian churches contended in vexed theological argument, so absorbed in intellectual adjustment that often they forgot what the intellectual adjustment was about, we are plunged into an era which faces us with a towering task. Can we ever in this world make Christianity come true? Can the principles of Christ and his ways of living life be victorious? Is Christianity possible? On that question hangs everything which matters most in the religious life of our time.

Note again that this way of getting at the matter is not a cheap evasion of intellectual difficulties in order to make Christian faith easier. Some may have said, This preacher is trying to escape the intellectual problems of Christian belief by reducing Christianity to a practical task only. To which I answer, Tell me which is easier, to believe in the credibility of a formal creed or to believe in the possibility of a Christian world? No, when one chooses that latter as the center of the matter, he is not dodging difficulties or making faith easier.

Some of us can well remember the halcyon days of mid-Victorian optimism, when calling any one a Cassandra or a Jeremiah was to insult him. Cassandra prophesied the fall of Troy; Jeremiah prophesied the fall of Jerusalem. Who wanted to be called names like that when it was the fashion everywhere to be optimistic? But now we are soberer and remember that both Cassandra and Jeremiah were right. Troy did fall; Jerusalem was destroyed. So in a civilization shaken to its center, with some of the dearest things we ever believed in and worked for, like liberty and democracy, a hissing and byword in nations where they were once established, no one can say we are dodging difficulties when we raise the question, Can we make Christ's way of life come true?

This shift of emphasis is particularly wholesome for us who are modernists. For on one point our critics were right: we were Brahmins, what the world calls 'high-brows.' We faced Christianity mainly on theoretical levels and made it an affair of the philosophic academy. In consequence, many of our modernist churches, as any one can see, are spiritually dead and morally futile. For the heart of the common man understands better where the real problem lies. Here is this actual world, blood-drenched, pagan, filled with tragedies so cruel that even in this church they are the hardest things your ministers have to face. Alongside this actual world stands another thing, this strange, unearthly, enchanting thing, this way of living that was Christ's, his dream of a world where peace and brotherhood, integrity and humaneness reign, of which Walt Whitman sang:

> Is it a dream?
> Nay but the lack of it the dream,
> And failing it life's lore and wealth a dream,
> And all the world a dream.

The heart of the plain man understands that the central question of Christianity is, Can we ever in such a world make Christ's vision come true?

When we modernists discover *that,* we discover something else in Christianity which commonly we have lost. I mean the cross. That is where the cross came into Christianity in the first place, and always will come into it again, not in the acceptance of a theory but in the assumption of a task. If Christianity is a finished set of propositions to be believed, it is not costly. But if Christianity is an unfinished task to be completed in this terrific world, and if Christian faith is faith that this is the kind of world where that can be done, we are back again at Calvary. "If any man would come after me, let him deny himself, and take up his cross, and follow me"—that is Jesus, calling not for the acceptance of a theory but for the assumption of a task.

Consider, for another thing, that some of us need this truth more than we need anything else if we are to keep our spiritual life from drying up. We pay our speculative intellect a higher compliment than it deserves when we suppose that the main reason for the loss of Christian faith is argument. Upon the contrary, in any realm if one abstracts an idea from its appropriate task and tries to keep it in isolation as a mere belief, it always dries up. The only way we can keep any idea, Christian or not, real and vital is to do something with it. A generation ago, one of the most prominent professors in Yale University described the process by which he lost many of his religious beliefs, in a way both accurate and revealing. Said he: "I never consciously gave up a religious belief. It was as if I had put my beliefs into a drawer, and when I opened it there was nothing there at all." Inevitably so! Take one look at the life of the Man of Nazareth and see that the last place where it would be possible to keep any real faith concerning him would be in a drawer. When you opened it, there would be nothing there.

If some one insists that something still is there, let me describe it to you. It is possible for man to abstract from the Christian faith a selected list of comforting ideas—the fatherliness of God, the inward retreat to his peace, and such like—a carefully selected list of consoling ideas. These a man puts into a drawer. Once in a while, when he wants comfort, he takes them out and puts them back again. Ask him if he is a Christian and he will say, Yes! Undoubtedly he does possess Christian ideas and beliefs. How many millions like that do you think are in our churches? It is the commonest caricature of Christianity, the reduction of the amazing faith of Jesus in the possibility of a Christian world to a few solacing ideas in a drawer.

I know atheists who are much better Christians than that. As was written of Moses, "When Moses was grown up . . . he went out unto his brethren, and looked on their burdens," so these, my unbelieving friends, have put their lives alongside humankind, hurt by the hurt of others so deeply that they have cried out in agony of soul that no good God would ever suffer this to be. For very pity's sake they have surrendered faith in God and then have gone out to try themselves to be God to men and help the race. They have rejected the Christian theory; they have accepted the task. If I know anything about Jesus, he would look on them as long ago he looked upon another, saying, "Thou art not far from the kingdom of God."

Is some one saying, This means that the preacher thinks it makes small difference what a man believes? No, that is not true. But I am sure that what does make a difference was put by Walter Rauschenbusch into a true and ringing phrase: "Wanted: a faith for a task."

Of course it makes a profound difference what a man believes. As Thomas Huxley said, "the most sacred act of a man's life is to say and to feel, 'I believe. . . .' " But do not mix up that high and sacred matter with belief in the accumulated odds and ends of ecclesiastical opinion which never yet made any difference to Christian character or the prosecution of great social causes. Listen to Jesus: "Seek ye first his kingdom, and his righteousness." Aye, first the task; then, Wanted: a faith for the task. That makes Christian belief in God, in man, in the Master, real.

It does one thing more. It challenges each of us, if we will have it so, to be in our daily, homely life defenders of the faith. From Henry VIII on, some queer people have been handed that title. I suspect that even now most of us would think that the real defenders of the faith are the men who argue for it, construct speculative reasons in support of it, help others to adjust their minds to the new knowledge of the world so that faith can claim the consent of all their faculties. How important I think that is you know well. But, my friends, the most convincing thing in the world is never an argument. It is always a deed. Men kept on arguing that transatlantic steamships were incredible until a steamship crossed the Atlantic. That proved it possible and, since possible, credible. Men kept on arguing that habitual flying was unbelievable until men like Lindbergh flew. That proved it possible and, since possible, believable.

Nine times out of ten the real conviction of mankind that anything is credible has come not from an abstract argument, but from deeds which showed it to be possible. If this is so in such realms, of course it is more obviously so in the kingdom of the spirit. James Russell Lowell was right:

When a deed is done for Freedom, though the broad earth's aching breast
Runs a thrill of joy prophetic, trembling on from east to west.

If, then, the most convincing persuasiveness in life lies in right deeds, you and I, plain people, are involved. Mark Twain once had a Negro servant, named Lewis, who worked around his farm. One day Lewis in an extraordinary exhibition of skill and daring stopped a runaway and saved the lives of three of Mark Twain's family circle. This is what Mark Twain wrote about him: "When Lewis arrived the other evening, after having saved those lives by a feat which I think is the most marvelous I can call to mind, when he arrived hunched up on his manure-wagon and as grotesquely picturesque as usual, everybody wanted to go and see how he looked. They came back and said he was beautiful. It was *so*, too, and yet he would have *photographed* exactly as he would have done any day these past seven years." Always, a right deed is beautiful and convincing.

I believe in the possibility of a Christian world, not because I have been argued into it but because I have seen Christian living *done*. I have seen it in persons, firm as steel and beautiful as music, who poured out into this pagan world a Christlike integrity and humaneness which made spiritual life real. I have seen it in homes where what Jesus said ought to be the law of life was the actual principle of fellowship. It was not Christianity argued: it was Christianity achieved. I have seen it in social movements that leaped high barricades, belied the scoffing of cynics and the fears of friends, and opened the doors of new eras. It was not Christianity debated; it was Christianity done.

Could there ever have been a generation in history with more need of such defenders of the faith? If to defend Christianity were mainly to argue its credibility, how little most of us could help, but if to defend Christianity is to exhibit its possibility then every one of us is called for. Victory for decent government in this city would make multitudes believe more in the reality of the spiritual world. The triumph of peace over war, when it comes—as come it will, however long delayed—will lift up innumerable souls into a fresh faith in the reality of the spiritual world. Even when one man stands out, to use George Eliot's phrase, with "the impressiveness of a fine quotation from the Bible . . . in a paragraph of to-day's newspaper," he makes it easier for every one who knows him to believe in God. Is Christianity true? Millions ask that question and the answer will never be in words. It must be in deeds. We must make Christianity come true!

The Essential Elements in a Vital Christian Experience

THE worse the world is without, the deeper we all need to go within. The profound meanings of inward, personal, Christian experience become not less but more important in a turbulent and dismaying era. What, then, are the essential elements in a vital religious life, so basic that from Quaker to Roman Catholic all Christians at their best have shared them? Are they not a great need, a great salvation, a great gratitude, and a great compulsion?

Often the doom of Christianity has been announced. Many a time it has sinned against light and fallen on evil days. It has been used as a mere counter in a political game, as Napoleon used it and as more than one dictator would like to use it now. Often it has faced new world views and refused new knowledge. Time and again it has identified itself with some contemporary social *status quo* and has seemed to collapse with the downfall of the system it was tied to. How often the cry has risen which Voltaire voiced in the eighteenth century: "Ere the beginning of the nineteenth century Christianity will have disappeared from the earth"! But it has not disappeared. Its expressions change but at the heart of it are creative factors that everlastingly keep their hold: a great need, a great salvation, a great gratitude, and a great compulsion.

First, then, a great need. No one achieves a vital, personal, Christian experience without a profound sense of need. While many think of need as a sign of weakness, the fact is that there is no truer test of the status of any creature in the scale of existence than the size, amplitude, and quality of his needs. See this strange creature, man, that the materialists tell us is but an accidental bundle of atoms drifting toward oblivion. That estimate of man seems to some of us incredible if only because of what it takes to meet this creature's needs. If he wanted only food for his body, like some animals, then an animal he would be. But he has curiosity that must explore the farthest stars and build great telescopes to get at the stars he cannot see. That is an incredible thing for a mere bundle of atoms to need to do. The badge of man's dignity, the sign of his greatness, is this outreach of want without whose satisfaction he cannot be content. He needs music and books and art—not telephones and airplanes only, though that is mysterious enough, but ideals for himself and his society, a clear conscience, great purposes to live for, and high faiths to live by, if at his best he is to be content. Such need is incredible in a mere bundle of atoms. Need, first of all, is not a sign of weakness but the mark of a creature's status in the scale of existence. Consider, then, the fact that age after age millions of folk have sought a personal experience of Christ because they needed him.

To different people this need comes in different ways. With many it appears as a sense of inadequacy in meeting the demands of life. For the demands of life can be terrific. A father lately had to say farewell for the last time to his sixteen-year-old son. There on the hospital bed lay the boy, ill of an insidious disease but with no idea that he was going to die. And one evening the father, as though it were a matter of course, not at all revealing what he knew, had to say "Good night, son," and hear the boy say "Good night, Dad," knowing all the time that that was the final good-by and that before morning the boy would die. What demands life makes on us! Who can meet them? Not simply when they come suddenly but when they come slowly in the long drag of the years, putting burdens on us difficult to sustain, who can face life's demands, whether in youth or age, without a need of spiritual reinforcement to meet the strain?

To others this experience comes mainly through moral failure. For sin is a Trojan horse. We welcome it through a breach in our walls as the ancient city did, expectant of happiness, but it has inside it many hostile forces we never suspected, that in the night come creeping out! Habit, for example, so that we start free to sin and then wake up to discover that we are not free to stop. Guilt, for example, so that we begin with high anticipation of pleasure only to find that our sin passes from anticipation through committal into memory, and, changing its visage, becomes guilt and settles down to haunt us like a ghost. Explicit punishment, for example, for there is something terrific in this universe that finds out a man's mistakes and even at long last lays a heavy hand upon them. Perhaps, worst of all, we sin thinking only of ourselves and our pleasures and then discover that we have involved others and that the consequences of our evil blast the hopes and happiness of those for whom we really care. So, age after age, people facing moral failure and its tragic aftermath have sought a personal experience of Christ, his forgiveness and re-establishment, because they needed him.

To others this experience comes not so much from life's demands or even from moral failure, as from a positive vision of life's possibilities. When I was a boy I do not recall that I needed great music. I had little chance to hear any. Once, as a lad, I was taken to a symphony but I did not like it. Then one day some really great music broke through. That was a strange experience; to use Wordsworth's words, it disturbed "me with the joy of elevated thoughts." I awoke to a new need, something that ever afterward I must have to be content—a solace, comfort, incentive, and inspiration. That is a strange experience, to break into a new realm of need, where something you have not known before becomes necessary to you, and that experience is most often reduplicated through the awakening influence of great personalities. Remember Alcibiades saying of Socrates: "There is one experience I have in the presence of this man alone, such as nobody would expect in me; and that is, to be made to feel ashamed; he alone can make me feel it. For he brings home to me that I cannot disown the duty of doing what he bids me, but that as soon as I turn from his company I fall a victim to the favours of the crowd." Above all others, Christ has so disturbed people. They could not live beside him and still be what they were. They awoke to a new sense of need from a new vision of possibility.

Whatever way it comes to us, this is the first element in a vital Christian experience. If someone says he feels no such need, that is a pity. Some feel no need of music, or of books, or of the beauty of God's out-of-doors, and that fact is a revelation of their status in the scale of existence. What kind of person do you think he is who does not need interior resources of spiritual power to face life's strains, conquer its temptations, and fulfill its possibilities?

The second element in a vital Christian experience is a great salvation. To be sure, that word troubles me. Words can fall into bad company and be dragged down by their associates. When St. Paul's Cathedral in London was finished, the architect displayed it to the king on a state occasion and the king called it amusing, awful, and artificial. The architect was overjoyed at the royal compliment for in those days "amusing" meant "amazing," "awful" meant "awe-inspiring," and "artificial" meant "artistic." So words change their meaning, and "salvation" has often walked in undesirable intellectual company and gotten incredible connotations. I beg of you today to use the word, since there is no other to be used, in its finest and best sense.

If a man has ever been lost in the woods at night or on the sea in a fog in a small boat without a compass, and then help has come, he ought to know what it feels like to be saved. If a man has ever been unemployed and the long succession of days that were hard and nights that were terrible have worn him down, and then employment has come again, he ought to know what it means to be saved. If our family life was ever in peril and we had almost given up hope, and then a better spirit came and the rift in the lute was mended and what we cared more for than anything else in the world became lovely again, we ought to know what it means to be saved. And in the same realistic sense, if we have ever known a desperate need for help to stand life's strains, overcome its temptations, and fulfill its possibilities, and then victory has come through the revelation of power that Christ has brought, the word "salvation" ought to have a vivid place in our vocabulary. At any rate, across the ages millions of people have found a great need thus met by a great salvation.

This experience comes to most of us in two general ways. To many it is opportunity for a second chance. They have failed, messed up their lives, and have only the remnants left of their first opportunity. Then they face that amazing, unbelievable offer of a second chance. A friend of mine attended cooking school sometime since and the title of one of the announced lectures has fascinated my imagination ever since—"Putting the Lure into the Leftovers." That lesson is needed far outside a cooking school. Who has not needed *that?* The Prodigal in the far country with only the remnants of his first opportunity left needed something that would put the lure into those leftovers, and, all the ages since, men like Augustine—afterwards St. Augustine—who ran away from home and lived with his mistress, and even after he had felt Christ's attraction cried: "The worse that I knew so well had more power over me than the better that I knew not," have needed something or someone who could put the lure into the leftovers. Who of us here has not thus failed, made a mess of some first chance, stood with only the remnants left, and then faced that incredible miracle of forgiveness that reestablishes the old relationships as though we had not broken them, and offers a second chance?

Along with this first factor in a saving experience goes strength to make something of the second chance. For any kind of failure, moral failure in particular, is a Svengali to the soul. It hypnotizes us, and, casting upon us its horrid spell, towers over us, saying, You cannot; you have failed; you are whipped. Who has not experienced that? And who has not cried out for someone who could defeat that incantation, break that enchantment, and lift him up to answer back, as Paul answered even in a Roman prison, I can—"In Him who strengthens me, I am able for anything."

Sometimes I think we preachers, overawed by the formal dignity of the pulpit, talk too anonymously and impersonally. Here I am today, an older man talking to you about the secret of spiritual power in general, when all the time what I am really seeing in my imagination's eye is that young man I was years ago, shot all to pieces, done in and shattered in a nervous breakdown, foolishly undertaking too much work and doing it unwisely, all my hopes in ashes and life towering over me, saying, You are finished; you cannot; you are done for. People ask me why in young manhood I wrote *The Meaning of Prayer*. That came out of young manhood's struggle. I desperately needed a second chance and reinforcement to carry on with it. I was sunk unless I could find at least a little of what Paul had in mind when he said, I can—"In Him who strengthens me, I am able for anything."

That is salvation—forgiveness, a second chance, reinforcement, power, the voice of a friend out of the fog where all direction has been lost, saying, I am here, and, You can! Across the ages Christ has meant that to men—a great need met by a great salvation.

The third element in a personal experience of Christ is a great gratitude. One cannot understand the New Testament or the driving power of the Christian church at its best without taking the measure of the fact that a profound need met by a profound salvation has issued in a profound gratitude.

Mark this strange fact that the church is the only organization in the world that advertises itself as a company of sinners. That fact is worth walking around. In the second century Celsus the pagan jeered at the Christians because of this. To the heathen world it seemed a ridiculous, incredible thing that a great company of people should advertise themselves as sinners and to their fellowship welcome sinners. And still it is a unique phenomenon. Where else will you find people standing up to say that they have done those things they ought not to have done and have left undone those things they ought to have done and there is no health in them? And even when we do not use those words, how difficult it is to find a scripture or a hymn without the accent of penitence!

> When the worldling, sick at heart,
> Lifts his soul above;
> When the prodigal looks back
> To his Father's love;
> When the proud man, from his pride,
> Stoops to seek thy face;
> When the burdened brings his guilt
> To thy throne of grace.

Here is a unique phenomenon, the founding of a world-wide fellowship explicitly made up of sinners. One cannot understand what that means until one sees that a great need, met by a great salvation, has issued in a great gratitude.

That, of course, is the reason why the Lord's Supper, to a Christian who understands it, is the climax of Christian worship. The early Christians called it the Eucharist. What does Eucharist mean? It is the Greek word for "thank you." Just as in France we say *Merci*, or in Italy, *Gratia*, so in modern Greece we say *Eucharisto*, that is, Eucharist, thank you. The Lord's Supper is the church of Christ, knowing that it is made up of sinners, having faced a profound need, met with a profound salvation, going up before the cross of Christ, the symbol of the price paid for our help, to express a great gratitude.

The ethical implications of such gratitude are immense. Gratitude, someone has said, is the mother of all virtues. That is a defensible proposition. Here is a man who has no spark of gratitude anywhere concealed about his person. He thinks life has been egregiously unjust to him. He is resentful and rebellious about life. You will get no great living out of him. Or here is another man who thinks life consists in getting what you have earned. It is *quid pro quo*, so much for so much, and he suspects he is breaking about even; he is getting what he earns and is earning what he gets. You will find no superior living in such a man. But here is a man who feels that no matter what he does he never can pay back the debt he owes. To be sure, there is injustice in his experience and *quid pro quo* too, but when life is taken as a whole, he feels that he has received what he never could deserve or earn. In all ages the finest living has come out of folk like that.

This is not simply a matter of religion. Consider, for example, the millions of us born in democratic nations, who have strolled into the privileges of democracy and nonchalantly have settled down there without a grateful thought. We have even been dominated by resentfulness over the failures of democracy or by nonchalance toward its liberties. But who can take the measure of these present days and not rise to another attitude? Freedom is precious in the world today. It was won for us, before we were born, by our fathers, who with thought, labor, and sacrifice built a democratic nation where the rights of individual souls and of minorities would be respected. We should be grateful. Our lives, our fortunes, our sacred honor are owed to democracy. There is something to be said for the idea that gratitude is the mother of all virtues. Certainly, there is no such thing as a vital Christian experience without it. Need of Christ, salvation in Christ, gratitude toward Christ—those three phrases are, as it were, the stethoscope where we can hear the very heartbeat of the gospel.

The fourth element in a creative experience of Christ is a great compulsion. For it stands to reason that if a man has known a deep want, met by a great redemption issuing in a profound thankfulness, then something has gotten hold of him. He is not his own. He has been taken possession of. He is under a powerful inner compulsion.

Now compulsion is a part of every man's life. One way or another, life coerces all of us and no one of us can escape the word "must." But how vast the difference between those mere creatures of circumstance, pushed and pulled by outward chance and fortune, on one side, and, on the other side, the elect spirits of the race whose compulsion is from within! The great musicians, the Beethovens, Tschaikowskys, Brahms, must write music. Why must they? No one makes them. But they know the need that only music can supply; they have had an experience of music bringing to them its saving satisfaction; they have a gratitude toward music that no words can express; and so they are under a compulsion strong as steel and ineluctable as destiny. They must give their lives to music. The elect spirits of the race know this compulsion from within.

So Paul said: "I must also see Rome." Why must he? No one made him undertake that risky adventure that ended with his beheading on the Appian Way. I must see Africa, said Livingstone. Why must he? No one coerced him from his Scottish home to die in his tent in Africa with his face fallen into the open pages of the Bible, a sacrifice to his high endeavor to paint the dark continent white. Here is the secret of man's greatness and his liberty, to have compulsion not from without but from within. And in quieter lives among our friends or in our families, who of us has not known such characters, who could have said: "O Love that wilt not let me go"?

No need of the modern world is so deep as the need for this kind of character. We could muddle along without much more scientific invention. We could get by with no more skyscrapers and gadgets. But we cannot get by without more Christian character if by that we mean what we have been talking about. Theologies change; creeds alter; the world views of one generation are incredible to the next; the mental patterns that Paul, Augustine, Calvin used we cannot exactly copy. But when we range up into this experience of profound need met in Christ by a great salvation, that issues in a deep gratitude so that we are inwardly taken possession of by a high compulsion, we not only overpass the differences between our contemporary sects but the differences between the centuries. Paul would understand *that,* and St. Augustine and Luther and Phillips Brooks. In that experience is the real communion of the saints. When one pleads for that one is pleading for the basic structural material without which no decent society can be built. When one pleads for that one is pleading for a quality of character without which man at his best cannot be satisfied. If you lack it, seek it. If you have a little of it, deepen it—a great need, a great salvation, a great gratitude, a great compulsion.

Christians in Spite of Everything

MANY find it difficult, if not impossible, to be Christians because, as they see it, they are living in so powerfully unchristian a world. They might make a success of the Christian life if the social environment would only give them a decent chance, but how can one be Christian, they think, in a world like this? Even Jesus got himself crucified for trying it.

The mail from the radio audience often expresses this mood. In a world of war and economic injustice, amid the down-drag of pagan customs, why torment our individual consciences with urgent appeals to be Christian, when we can never get good Christians until we have a good world? So they write, and much of what they say has so much truth in it, and yet is so inadequate to cover the case, that I invite your consideration of the matter.

First, let us put it biographically. Paul in his Roman prison writing to his Philippian friends, ended his letter saying, "All the saints salute you, especially they that are of Cæsar's household." Saints in Cæsar's household! That was a strange place in which to try to be a Christian—in the imperial retinue of Nero among the lesser nobility, it may be, but especially among the freemen and the slaves. We continually complain at having our fine ideals of brotherhood knocked about and battered by militant nationalism, but think of trying to be a Christian in Cæsar's household! We lament the grossness of our commercialized amusements which vulgarize and sometimes brutalize the public taste but, recollecting only the frescoes of Pompeii, think of trying to be a saint at Nero's court! We complain against the greed and cruelty of our social order and the nonchalance and carelessness with which our life proceeds in the face of it, but think of Nero's palace and the Colosseum as a background against which to try to be a Christian! When we have allowed all the justifiable excuses we can muster from our social environment, there still remains something more to say about people who have been Christians in spite of everything.

In other realms than Christian faith and character—the arts, for example—this same truth holds. Creative genius has risen into splendor in many places outside the areas we would have thought fortunate for its emergence. There are times, to be sure, like Elizabethan England, when a confluence of factors creates a culture out of which artists rise with prolific prodigality. But that does not cover the case or remotely suggest the infinite diversity of circumstance, often fiercely antagonistic, where great art has risen in spite of everything.

Mozart was so poor that all his life was a heartbreaking struggle and he was buried in a pauper's grave, while Mendelssohn was so well-to-do he never had to think of self-support. John Keats was so crippled by proverty that it is an agony to read his life, while Browning from his youth up was amply cared for by his patrimony. Infinite has been the diversity of circumstance within which creative genius has burned like fire. We commonly think of art as beautiful. Of course it is, but behind the beauty and indispensable to it is this tougher, hardier matter—a man who has the stuff of creative genius in him will be an artist in spite of everything.

Abstract that spirit from Christian faith and character and we have emasculated it. Surely, some one here today needs to hear that said.

For one thing, if we are to stop blaming spiritual failure on outward circumstance and are to achieve a spiritual victory in the midst of hostile environment, it will be in part because we take antagonistic circumstance for granted as a natural, inevitable part of the problem. Christianity essentially means winning a spiritual victory in the face of hostile circumstance; that is what being a Christian is about. From a rocky farm in Connecticut, across which one could almost walk on the stones without touching the ground, comes a story which, though seemingly irreverent, voices a healthy philosophy. A minister visited one of his parishioners on a farm which, hitherto a failure, was now, by dint of tireless labor, being made a success. "So," said the minister, "God and you are getting on very well here." "Yes," said the farmer, "but you should have seen this place before, when God was trying to handle it alone." Exactly! To start thus with a difficult situation as a place to begin being what Paul called a fellow-worker with God, is the very stuff of robust Christianity.

Many in our time, however, are powerfully tempted to another and a softer attitude, in part because attributing inward failure to outward circumstance is always popular and in part because social pessimism is now in the ascendency and we think we have a dreadfully bad external situation on which to blame spiritual collapse. When my generation was young we were optimistic. We came at the climax of an amazing accumulation of social encouragements crowned by the doctrine of evolution, which to our young and kindled eyes made the whole cosmos seem a going and growing concern. Social optimism was then in the ascendency but it is not so now. The catastrophe of war has broken through the thin veneer of our civilization and revealed the savagery beneath. Some of our contemporary pessimism is healthy. The optimism was pleasanter but much of it was unjustified and cheap. We have a chance now to be more soundly realistic than we used to be. But some of our current pessimism works a disastrous consequence in that it gives multitudes of people, who are glad enough to take it, a chance to say that in so crazy and disheveled a world they see no use in trying to be Christians at all. I want another slogan to sound in the consciences of some here today tempted to take that attitude—Saints in Cæsar's household. A spiritual victory won in the face of hostile environment—that is what being a Christian is all about.

Of course, I understand the protest which is already rising in some minds. Some may be saying:

> This is a high-sounding exhortation, telling us to be Christians in spite of everything, but, so far as millions of our population are concerned, it is nonsense. To be a Christian in spite of being born and reared in the depth of some city slum, to be a Christian in spite of being a child in a share-cropper's family with never a decent thing to civilize and elevate the soul, to be a Christian despite the fact that, like

multitudes of young people, one finds it economically impossible to marry and found a home, or despite the insanity of nations periodically plunging their youth into the hell of war—what absurdity is this! Far from saying that we should be Christians in spite of everything, it would be fairer to say that we must change pretty nearly everything in order to get Christians at all.

To all of this I should answer, That is handsomely said, but you have forgotten one thing. Make that kind of excuse for everybody else but not for yourself. Never! For yourself no default! Go out, indeed, to help change circumstance, which so crucially needs to be changed. Strength and courage to you as you try to lift the handicaps that so cruelly rest on human souls! But for yourself, no excuses, no defense mechanisms, no passing of the buck! A clean conscience whatever happens, a saint even in Cæsar's household, a spiritual victory despite circumstance—that is every man's business *with himself*.

Cannot we imagine John Keats lamenting the lost poetry of young and kindled souls in whom beauty might have sung its way to immortal fame but who, crushed by poverty, found their songs quenched before they started? So Keats might have lamented and one can imagine his laboring sympathetically and indignantly to change circumstance so as to make poets possible. But for himself, though he was so poor that often his days were misery, he took no leave from that to stop his singing. For himself, no default. "I think," he said once, in one of the most wretched periods of his life, "I shall be among the English poets after my death."

So, wherever one looks—in science, the arts, music, Christian character, practical success even—one finds this basic duty: endless sympathy for any one else crushed by external circumstance, but for oneself no blame of inward failure on outward environment!

Consider, again, that if a man is to make a high success of his spiritual life in the midst of hostile environment, it will be in part because he centers his attention not so much upon his outward pressures as upon his interior resources. Whenever in any realm you find a saint in Cæsar's household, you may be sure that deep within him this thing has happened: he has cultivated a keen awareness of his spiritual resources so that in the orientation of his thinking they have become most real to him and his consciousness of the outward environment has been secondary. *That* constitutes one of the profoundest differences between people.

How many great books, for example, have been written in prison! Paul wrote his letter to the Philippians in prison, Cervantes started *Don Quixote* there, and John Bunyan worked on *The Pilgrim's Progress* in Bedford Jail. When one considers how they could do that, it is evident that they must have concentered their attention on their interior resources rather than on their outward circumstances. Like all the rest of us, they lived in two worlds: first, the external system of circumstances alien to their wishes, antagonistic to their finest aspirations, a veritable prison house; but, on the other side, the inner world where a man's mind may be his kingdom, where there are doors of the spirit which a man can open and which then no man or circumstance can shut—realms, principalities, and dominions of the soul where one walks at liberty. As between these two, they so minimized the outer and maximized the inner that they proved to themselves and to mankind that

> Stone walls do not a prison make,
> Nor iron bars a cage.

Granting that this illustration is drawn from extraordinary experience, it is still true to our ordinary life. For it is our externalism that commonly ruins us, our absorption with things, our obsessed attention habitually given to the setting of our lives, so that were we to be in Bedford Jail it would be a long time before we thought of anything except the jail; not readily would it occur to us that even there the soul might walk the Delectable Mountains. So, because we take our cue for everything from circumstances, when we face circumstance hostile to high character we blame moral failure on that. We take our moral cue also from environment. One hates to think what some of us would have been in Nero's court. We would have gone native with a vengeance and the excuse would have been ready, What else do you expect in Cæsar's household?

As a matter of fact, as I understand my own soul, that is an illegitimate excuse. The worst foes of my spiritual life have never been hostile circumstance. Upon the contrary, sometimes hostile circumstance has been like a strong wind on a flying field, a grand force to take off against for a flight, if one knows how to do it. The deepest foes of my spiritual life have had their origin far down within the soul. There is no situation into which life ever put me that I could not have handled better than I did if I could have gotten my eyes more on, and made more out of, the interior resources of the soul, until *that* was the realest world to me.

Does some one say that it is hard work being a Christian if one is very poor? Of course it is. But imagine yourself very rich. Do you think it would be easier then? You know who said it was easier for a camel to go through a needle's eye than for a rich man to enter into the kingdom of heaven. It is hard to be a Christian if one is very poor and, if anything, it is harder if one is very rich. That is to say, it is hard to be a Christian anywhere in a world like this and, whether rich or poor, in whatever environment life may be set, there is no such thing as triumphant living save as one learns the secret which Mrs. Browning once put into four simple but profound words: "Life develops from within." So! Show us any great soul that has risen triumphant out of trouble. That is the secret—life develops from within. If a man lets his life develop from without, if he takes the moral dent of circumstance, drinks intemperately because everybody drinks, is sensual because this is a sensual generation, copies Nero in Nero's court, then he belongs truly to the congregation of the damned, who have literally lost their souls. But to have life develop from within, to have the origin and fountainhead of one's living come from deep resources in the soul, that *is* living. And obviously it is only out of such living that one ever becomes a saint in Cæsar's household.

Consider once more these saints in Cæsar's household. Not only did they take difficult situations for granted and have lives that developed from within, but they allied themselves with whatever saving elements they could find in their environment. Hitherto we have talked about their experience as though it were merely individualistic. No! Saints in Cæsar's household—they were plural. They were a group; they stood together. They had a strong fellowship harnessed to the help of their souls, else how could they have stood their ground in Nero's court?

A great teacher of ethics, T. H. Green, said once, "No individual can make a conscience for himself. He always needs a society to make it for him." Surely, that proves its truth in our experience. A man's conscience never is merely or mainly individual. It is always socially created and sustained. In Cæsar's household both the Christians on one side and Nero's cronies in debauchery upon the other had consciences socially produced—the debauchees' conscience created by the general society they lived in, the Christians' conscience created by a special society they had deliberately picked out to live in.

How many people do you think are here this morning, accustomed vaguely to talk about being Christian, who need powerfully to be laid hold on by this truth? An individual cannot make a conscience for himself but always needs a society to make it for him. Behind our artificial and highly organized churches one wishes we could get back to the original idea of a church. *Ecclesia* is the Greek word used in the New Testament for 'church,' and it means 'called out,' 'selected.' It suggests that a man can have a world of his own to live in within the larger world. Out of the hodgepodge and potpourri of the social mass, with its down-drag upon life, a man can choose those saving elements that elevate, purify, and empower the soul. In the fellowship of such selected elements he finds his ecclesia, his church, where his conscience is rekindled and from which he goes out again to face the wrath of devils and the scorn of men. No man ever yet lived a great life without having in that sense of the word a 'church.'

My soul, think what your ecclesia has done for you! For out of the general mass of the world you have selected some special things for your intimate companionship—the beauty of the green earth by day and the stars by night, great books, great music, great friends, the noblest traditions of the race, its finest faiths, its most illustrious souls, Christ over all. See how out of the mass of life you have chosen your ecclesia. No one can ever live a great life without such a church.

If some one asks what all this has to do with the actual churches, the answer is that the meaning of the actual churches lies in the endeavor to make this experience easy of access, available to all who want it, real, and effective. All organizations fall short of their ideal significance, as courts fall short of ideal justice, but the meaning of a church is this: it tries to help people to have a society within society, a world within the world, an ecclesia of ideas and ideals, of faiths and purposes, of great souls, the noble living and the noble dead, and Christ over all, in whose fellowship they will have some chance of being saints in Cæsar's household.

I beg of you, do not let your idea of the church grow stiff and formal. Keep it plastic and vital. Paul did. In prison, where he needed, if ever a man needed it, a world within the world which so dragged him down, he had an ecclesia. He wrote to one friend who was coming from the East, "Bring when thou comest . . . the books, especially the parchments." So the great books of his race were part of his ecclesia. And his friends were part of it, not simply those whom he could see and touch, like "Luke, the beloved physician," but that larger body of Christians across the Empire who kept reminding him that he was not alone but a member of a beloved community to whose ideas the future belonged. And his interior world of thought was part of his ecclesia also. Listen to him there in prison: "Whatsoever things are true, whatsoever things are honorable, whatsoever things are just, whatsoever things are pure, whatsoever things are lovely, whatsoever things are of good report; if there be any virtue, and if there be any praise, think on these things." What an ecclesia!

This is too tough a world to try to be Christian in without that. The whole consequence of what we are trying to say this morning will in many lives depend on just this point. If you go out vaguely expecting as an individual to be a Christian, Cæsar's household will get you. You need an ecclesia.

Finally, let us try to satisfy some here who have been discontented. For probably some have been troubled by the fact that what we have been saying seems to leave this wicked world unchanged with merely a few people trying to be Christian within it. That, however, is not the end of the story. Cæsar's household was not unchanged. Cæsar's household was abolished. As one of the leading scholars of our times has analyzed it, the early Christian movement gradually undermined and destroyed the old order of the ancient world by withdrawing the spiritual allegiance of millions of souls from it and giving that allegiance to another set of values altogether. What consequence came out of those saints in Cæsar's household almost passes belief.

Two young sisters were disputing about which was the last book of the Bible and one was heard to exclaim to the other, "Barbara, I tell you the Bible does *not* end in Timothy; it ends in Revolutions." History validates the truth thus unwittingly stated, so that none should leave this sanctuary saying that the conclusion of the matter is a few individuals lifted out of the wicked world. Rather, this is the conclusion of the matter, that if this desperately needy world is ever to be saved, with not souls only but the societies of men redeemed to a kingdom of peace and righteousness, there is one indispensable prerequisite for which no substitute will ever be discovered: men and women, namely, who do not wait for Cæsar's household to be redeemed before they begin living redeemed lives within it—Christians in spite of everything!

What Are You Standing For?

OUR morning's thought concerns one of the most significant aspects of human life: our representative capacity. We all have in us the power to stand for something, and the way we use it determines, as hardly anything else does, our personal quality.

In the first chapter of the book of The Acts, for example, Jesus is reported to have said to his disciples, "Ye shall be my witnesses." He is making, that is, a direct and definite appeal to their representative capacity, as though to say, You can be more than yourselves; you have the power to stand for high principles and worthy enterprises in your generation; hardly any element in you is more influential than this power so to identify yourself with something greater than yourself that when people think of you they think of that; I want that representative capacity on my side; you shall be my witnesses.

As we turn to consider the application of this matter to our personal lives, note two or three facts which underlie our truth.

In the first place, we all do possess this representative capacity. A new-born babe is a baby only, but even in the early years of developing personality the child begins to accumulate suggestiveness. A young child soon achieves interests and ambitions so distinctive that whenever you think of the child you think of them. And when the man is grown and such interests are confirmed, he has identified himself with what he stands for, so that Galileo and astronomy, St. Francis of Assisi and saintliness, Napoleon and militarism, Captain Kidd and piracy, Florence Nightingale and nursing, are done up in one bundle of thought. A man does have this mysterious power to accumulate personal suggestiveness, so that when we think of him we think of that.

Charles Dickens has been often laughed at for the exaggerated way in which he used this fact in the depicting of his characters. How many of Dickens' people are simply lay figures for some mannerism or personal quality! Micawber stands for waiting for something to turn up, Scrooge for churlishness, Squeers for cruelty, Uriah Heap for mock humility. In all this, to be sure, Dickens did exaggerate but there is truth in it. Think of the people whom you personally know and see how inevitably they have achieved personal suggestiveness so that when you think of them you think of what they stand for. What, then, do we remind people of when they think of us?

Under our morning's truth a second fact lies, that the right use of this representative capacity is man's glory. This is the only thing about war that by the wildest stretch of imagination I can conceive as good. War is irremediably evil and yet one experience associated with it we never should forget. Multitudes of men, living monotonous lives, absorbed in answering physical needs for food and shelter, never having known the thrill of a consuming loyalty, heard the national cause saying, Be my witness; stand for me; it may cost you the ultimate self-sacrifice, but the need is great. Multitudes of men, answering that appeal, felt like ciphers that had had numerals put in front of them. They achieved value; they were lifted into self-respect; at last, after many years, they were really standing for something. Remembering the gruesome slaughter of war and the disillusionment of its futile aftermath, let us never forget this revelation we had of the amazing power of men's representative capacity when it is once aroused. We never can tell when the most unlikely man may find his cause, identify himself with it, and by it be lifted to a greatness that will make us ashamed.

One of our American schoolmasters has told us about two young college men whom he personally knew, who went to a moving-picture theater one afternoon. The film was a salacious one, as its advertising made clear. They could have planned their time to better purpose. That afternoon a fire broke out in the theater and the young men, sitting near a fire escape, could have stepped to safety on it. Looking back, however, they saw what was going on inside the theater. A riot had broken out, women and children were being trampled, and a tragedy was inevitable on that fire escape unless something was done immediately. So the youths deliberately stood on each side of the door, held back the struggling crowd, handed women and children to safety, until one of them was pushed off the landing by the mob and the other caught fire from the encompassing flames. "Don't cry," he said to his mother before his death three days later; "I have no regrets. . . . I think I was the last to leave the theater alive." Strange duality in human nature! Think what they went for. Think, then, what they did.

So it is with the lowest of us—much, to be sure, that is deplorable in us and yet, on the other side, the capacity, when the right call comes, to identify ourselves even with so high and difficult a cause as vicarious sacrifice and find in that our glory! For the real worth of a man is not in himself alone; it is in what he comes to stand for.

Under our morning's truth there lies a third fact, that the least of us can stand for the greatest things. It is not difficult to see the operation of our principle in those capacious personalities that have bestridden the world. One sees it plainly, for example, in a character like Lincoln. Abstract from Lincoln the things he came to stand for and we have a queer remainder. For Lincoln, taken by himself, was unprepossessing and ungainly, came from lowly origins and small opportunities, had no superficial graces that cover inward lack. Rather, like a very plain wire grown incandescent, Lincoln shone with what he came to stand for. He achieved a personal suggestiveness that is one of the marvels of our history. Think of him and see how inevitably you are reminded of magnanimity, patience, steadfastness under strain, devotion to the nation's unity, love of liberty, deepening faith, and spiritual life! He came to stand for those things which man must love or else perish. And so, plain man though he was, he achieved an undying name.

In such capacious personalities it is not difficult to see the operation of this principle, but the more important thing for most of us to see is that the least of us can stand for the greatest things.

Water is indispensable; the whole earth's fertility depends upon it, but its representatives differ widely in magnitude. Not the ocean only, fruitful mother of all moisture, nor the Great Lakes, nor continental rivers, but every rill, every mountain stream, every wayside spring, every drop of rain must represent that indispensable necessity. So the smallest of us can stand for the greatest things.

Honesty is indispensable. It is needed in high places, as one must see who looks upon the crying shame of our municipal governments. In any schoolroom, however, any child, refusing to cheat in an examination, can stand for that indispensable quality. Unselfishness is indispensable, and in personalities like Father Damien, immolating himself among the lepers, the man, as Stevenson said, who "shut to with his own hand the doors of his own sepulchre," it is famously exhibited. But in any home, in everyday, commonplace relationships we can see that indispensable quality, as a wayside spring might stand for the same cause the ocean represents.

This challenge no one of us can evade. The smallest of us can stand for the greatest things. A lantern can represent the same cause of light that the sun stands for, and in its corner of the world a lantern can often do what the sun could never do. So no one of us can escape the question: What are we standing for?

If our truth is so deeply imbedded in the soil of human nature, let us turn to two special applications of it in our human relationships.

In the first place, in this confused and turbulent generation, what are we standing for in our moral loyalties? There are two kinds of great men. Some by the sheer brilliance of their intellectual genius are lifted to the heights, but others, much less highly endowed, find greatness in another way. They perceive in their generation the real movements of thought and life to which the future belongs, identify themselves with them and stand for them. The first kind of greatness, individual brilliance, is the gift of destiny to a very few. The second kind of greatness, identifying oneself with the real movements of one's time, is open to us all.

To be sure, it is not easy to achieve the insight to know what the significant movements of one's time really are. About 1400, Tamerlane, the Tartar emperor, swept across Asia in campaigns of conquest which for ruthless slaughter and practical success have few parallels in history. Naturally, he filled the public eye; he caught the public ear. The multitudes thought that he was the great event of the time. About 1400, however, a boy was born in Mainz, Germany, who soon would be experimenting with and then using movable type on a rude printing press, and that lad, Gutenberg, had in his hands more power over the future of humanity than many Tamerlanes. So it is difficult to achieve the insight to see what the real movements of our day are, but blessed are the men and women who achieve it and who come to be what Emerson called "representative men."

In saying this I am not sure whether I am thinking more about the progress of good causes in the world or about the welfare of individuals, who never will achieve health and happiness until they find something outside themselves to stand for. For while on the one side it is true that if a cause is to have success it must have witnesses who will speak up for it and be devoted to it, on the other side it is true that no individual soul can ever find life worth living until he has discovered a cause for which to stand.

One feels that especially now when so many thousands of our people, well-educated, well-to-do, are flocking to the psychiatrists to have their dislocated and emotionally upset personalities put together again. What with complexes, inhibitions, repressions, suppressions, and neuroses, not to say psychoses, with men and women, especially women, flocking to the psychoanalysts to tell all that ever they have done and much that they never did at all, one can readily understand the saying, "Whoso among you is without insanity, let him think the first think."

Now, I am sure that this new psychiatry is making and is going to make an incalculable contribution to human happiness. But there are multitudes of people who never would need to go to a psychiatrist if, in the first place, they would achieve a little healthy-minded objectivity about living, discover in this amazing generation a few things to be interested in, identify themselves with something greater than themselves and stand for it. To be carried out of yourself by something that you serve, so that you forget yourself in something other than yourself and so enlarge yourself—that is the secret of a healthy and a happy life.

There must be some here who ought to be ashamed of themselves. So often these dislocated and emotionally upset people are not the poor, the really hard-bestead, but the softly situated, the comfortably circumstanced, the selfish, the ingrowing, parasitic minds who never have found anything outside themselves that took their thoughts off themselves.

Over against such pathological egoism put another sort of character altogether, Thomas Bridges. An unwanted babe, he was found by a riverside. They picked him up at a bridge; that is why they called him Bridges. They discovered him on St. Thomas' Day; that is why they called him Thomas. He did not have a chance. But for all that, Thomas Bridges found the secret of a healthy and a happy life—something to stand for. He picked out about the hardest thing that could be found to do—working with the aborigines of Tierra del Fuego, at the desolate southern end of the Western Hemisphere. Even Charles Darwin paid tribute to his work. For Darwin turned up in that forlorn locality on his famous scientific voyage on the steamship Beagle, and afterwards sent a financial contribution, saying in effect that at first he had seen little use in missions among the aborigines but now, having learned of the transformation wrought at Tierra del Fuego, he was glad to have a hand in it.

Do you, then, pity Bridges in Tierra del Fuego? Spare your pity for those who need it, the well-educated, well-to-do, parasitic, uninterested people who never have found anything to take them out of themselves. After all, a man like Bridges does find the secret of health and happiness—something worth while standing for.

Could there ever have been a generation with more worthwhile things to stand for than today? To be sure, one need not head in toward Tierra del Fuego or enterprise any public or picturesque adventure like it. I have a friend who is facing death, not an easy death either—two operations already past and now the recurrent trouble inoperable. All the doctors agree six months will finish the matter. Six months more and she must say good-bye to a husband who adores her and lovely children who need her. But she is one of the most radiant and triumphant spirits I have met in many a year.

She is standing for something—the power of a deep religious faith to create a victorious life in a difficult situation. As the New Testament says about Jesus, death hath no dominion over her.

Any way you look at life, what magnificent things there are to stand for, to remind people of when they think of you!

Especially if one is well and strong, young and able, what things there are to stand for! There is honesty—plain, everyday, ordinary honesty—in business and in politics. There is decency in private morals. There is a better economic system, more beneficial for all the people. There are international causes that work for peace. What things there are to stand for!

Let one say this in particular about New York City. One hears, till one is weary, about the temptations of New York. I celebrate them. With joy I celebrate the temptations of New York: temptations to music, to art, to social service, to the support of interracial goodwill and international concord. Here where the currents of the world flow through, how can men and women live thinking only of temptations downward when there are so many alluring temptations upward?

Well, what are we standing for? What do people think of when they think of us?

The second application is no less important. What are we standing for in religion? I know well what some young men and women here are tempted to feel in this regard. They are tempted to be rebellious about religion. In particular, they are tempted to be in revolt against the church, and so they are not standing for much of anything in this great realm, recognized as the source of their deepest inspiration by the early saints, and as a social necessity by such modern radicals as Havelock Ellis, who says, "People without religion are always dangerous."

Let me talk to you for a moment as an individual. You are in revolt against the narrow, cramping, trivial ideas and attitudes in religion which you have often heard expressed, and in that you are right. In a generation such as this, with weighty matters afoot, when you read in the papers of religious men in controversy about apostolic succession, as though the tactual laying on of bishops' hands across the centuries could somehow validate a Christian ministry, you can hardly restrain your impatience with such credulous belief in ecclesiastical magic. Or when, in a time like this, when education has gotten so far afield, you hear men still appealing to Genesis against evolution, or in this law-abiding world trying to run their minds into the molds of ancient miracle narratives as though our spiritual life were somehow dependent on credence in old miracles, belief in the like of which in our day would justify an alienist's examination, you are up in mental arms against it. And when, in a generation like this with real causes afoot, you see people bothered over trivial sectarian affairs, it makes you almost ill.

But, my friends, do you not see that there are two ways in which these old, trivial, petty religious attitudes can ruin you? First, if you try to accept them and believe them yourself, that will ruin you. But second, if you let them negatively determine your religious thinking, if you hold them so in the forefront of your mind that you are always fighting them, hating them, revolting against them, that will ruin you too. Forget them! The real questions of religious faith and spiritual life today are not related to them. The fundamentalist-modernist controversy is now no better than kicking a dead lion. The real questions of religious faith and spiritual life are out ahead where scientists like Jeans and Eddington, or philosophers like Whitehead, Hocking, and Montague, or great issues about Christianizing the economic and international order, are putting them. To accept this new world of ours with its new knowledge and its fresh situations but still to keep spiritual life high, beautiful, effective, and creative—that is the real problem.

What, then, are we standing for in religion? For myself, I shall try to stand for Jesus Christ as the interpreter of spiritual life. In this world with its cynicism, its disillusionment, often its disheartenment, how men and women are needed to stand for him with the intellectual, personal, and social implications of his gospel! And it is going to be serious business standing for him in this generation.

It is said that a man once came to Whistler, the artist, and asked his help in hanging a new and beautiful picture. The man complained that he could not make the picture fit the room and Whistler, looking over the matter, said, "Man, you're beginning at the wrong end. You can't make that painting fit the room. You will have to make the room fit the painting." So when we carry into this modern world the picture of spiritual life that Jesus Christ brought, we cannot make it fit the room. Put it over against our private morals, our disintergrating family life, our economic system, our international order, and it will not fit the room. We must change the room to fit the picture. That is serious business. Will you stand for it?

If a man does stand for that, he makes a contribution to the world's life of a quality impossible if he stands for anything beside. For, after all, we men and women are much like flagstaffs. Some flagstaffs are very tall and prominent and some are small, but the glory of a flagstaff is not its size but the colors that it flies. A very small flagstaff flying the right colors is far more valuable than a very tall one with the wrong flag. When a man is altogether done with life, I should suppose that the most satisfying thing would be the ability to say, I am ashamed that I was not a better, taller, straighter flagstaff, but I am not ashamed of the colors that I flew.

Are We Part of the Problem or of the Answer?

EVERYWHERE today the word "problem" confronts us. Listening to the radio or reading the morning paper we face a jungle of huge and complicated difficulties involving all mankind, and in comparison our small lives appear impotent, no bulldozers to clear jungles with but feeling rather lucky if we have a fairly comfortable corner of the jungle to settle down in. Each of us is tempted so to feel, but there must be a healthier way than that to face this generation.

Suppose there were no problems in the world. God might have made this universe like Aladdin's palace, all complete for our lazy occupancy, no difficulty to face, nothing new to discover, nothing puzzling to solve, nothing required but to settle down and luxuriate. After even a few weeks of that, can you imagine anything more boring? Instead, God has introduced us into this wild, raw, unfinished world to bear a hand in its completion—which means that human life's very essence is facing problems, being waked up by their demands, and that only so has mankind's growth in intellect and character been possible. To be sure, I often want to tell God now that it is being overdone, with difficulties so huge they frighten rather than stimulate, but in wiser hours, even in a generation such as this, one feels the challenge and the stir, so that an older man like myself understands what that editor about to be beheaded in the French Revolution meant when he said, "It is too bad to take off my head. I wanted to see how all this is coming out." That, at least, is the starting point of a healthy attitude.

One cannot stop there, however. We as individuals, small though we are, are not outside the world like spectators on the bleachers watching a game. Willy-nilly, we are all in the thick of the world's game, participants in its winning or its loss, with this question rising for each of us: Am I myself part of the problem, or part of the answer?

We have a traffic problem on our American highways, for example, where millions of automobiles run, where death and worse than death, a dreadful toll of maimed and mutilated lives constitutes a cruel and needless sacrifice of health and happiness. Well, you drive an automobile—are you part of the problem or of the answer?

We have a family problem in this nation, broken homes a public menace, with moral standards cracking and marital infidelity a national disgrace, yet made a joke of in popular movies and best-selling novels. Well, are we part of the problem or of the answer?

Our theme ranges far this morning and goes deep, and here is a text for it. One full moonlight night in Palestine I stood on the summit of Mt. Tabor and, looking fifteen miles across the plain to the dim shadow of Mt. Gilboa, thought of the ancient days when Saul was King of Israel and when, perhaps on such a night, he slipped away from his army and sought the Witch of Endor in her cave, there on Little Hermon far below me. Note this: in the twenty-eighth chapter of First Samuel we read, "Now Saul had cleared the mediums and wizards out of the country." So, he recognized witchcraft as a public evil, and had issued an edict against it—all witches and wizards, begone! But four verses afterward we read this: "Saul said to his courtiers, 'Find me a witch, that I may go and consult her'." That is one of the most human passages in the Bible—a man recognizing a public evil as evil, but when the pinch came becoming himself part of the problem. All witches begone! but four verses afterward, Seek me a witch!

We all behave like that. Nothing would be much easier than to stir this congregation with a moving sense of the evil of race prejudice. In our time have we not seen an exhibition of it so barbaric that it leaves us turbulent with indignation? In our own country who of us does not regard the Ku Klux Klan as a public menace and disgrace? But when all of us are thus unanimously stirred by recognition of this cruel public evil, let each of us turn inward to himself and see what secret racial antipathies he harbors, what primitive shrinking at the color line he feels, what irrational discrimination against some other race he practices. Even in so obvious a matter, are we part of the problem or of the answer?

In a deep sense no man can help being part of the world's problem. "All we like sheep have gone astray." "All have sinned, and fall short of the glory of God." There is no avoiding that. Do our best, we still are sinners, participants in the world's evil. Our modern thought has belittled sin, made game of it, called those who stress its dreadfulness puritanical, and has even laughed morality off as a mere changing fashion. That is cheap thinking. See what sin really is! In a world with difficulties enough already, with the fortunes of our children dependent on their solution, sin takes us one by one and makes us part of the problem. That is not a little matter, but treachery against mankind, and we are all involved in it.

Nevertheless, once in awhile we do see someone concerning whose character we feel, That is the answer! Given enough such quality, such spirit and behavior, and the world's problems could be solved. It is for that we plead today, and sinners though we are, by God's grace every one of us can in some degree attain to it—not so much part of the problem as the solution.

Considering this theme, let us first face our powerful temptation to make exceptions of ourselves. Saul did that, and who doesn't? Witchcraft a public evil—he saw that. But when his own bad days closed in, the old superstition resurged in him and he made an exception of himself: "Find me a witch, that I may consult her."

In this congregation that kind of thing is surely going on. About the church, for example! You would not bring up your children, would you, in a community where there were no Christian churches? You recognize that the church problem in this country is of deep public concern, and that to have the right kind of churches in our American communities, powerhouses of inspiration for private character and social service, is of first-rate importance. You see that the surrender of the churches to unintelligent leadership, their desertion by those who might have been expected to stand by them and the consequent lapse of those faiths that produce character and that perpetuate the great spiritual heritage of our race, is a public peril.

Almost everyone, of whatever religious background, grants that. Yet in New York City there are over a million Protestants unassociated with any church. Well, I am asking some of you, are you part of the problem or part of the answer?

One of the noblest statements of the moral law ever made was phrased by Immanuel Kant: "So act that thou canst will the principle of thine act to be law universal." That is to say, so live that if everybody acted on the same principle it would be well with the world. But, alas! seeing objectively the principles whose universal application would be well for the world, how commonly we subjectively make exceptions of ourselves! The black market a social peril, but we patronize it. Drunkenness a public menace, but we drink too much. Honesty basic to all business, but we try an undercover deal. Bad temper one of the most damning evils in a home, but we let ourselves be the terrible tempered Mr. Bang. The religious education of our children a national need, but with our children we let it slide. In one realm after another, All witches begone! but then, we say, Seek me a witch! Or as modern psychology puts it, we rationalize, with endless excuses dispensing ourselves from obligations that we wish all others would observe. That everybody should side-step responsibility for the church, Oh, no, not that! but then we do. Longfellow went to church once and wrote in his diary when he came home, "John Ware, of Cambridge, preached a good sermon." And then he added these five unusual words, "I applied it to myself." So may God grant this morning!

One reason why we thus throw off the sense of personal responsibility is that the public difficulties are so huge that what a man does with his own life seems of small account. No matter what he does, still like glaciers the world's affairs move on their relentless way. What does his life matter? That is a familiar defense mechanism now.

When I began my ministry the situation was reversed. Then it was difficult to get Christians interested in public problems, and we who believed in the social gospel had to shout to make ourselves heard. You there! we said, trying to save your own souls, come out of your absorption in your individual faith and salvation and see the application of Christian principles to the world at large! Now, however, in intelligent circles at least, times have changed. We are all interested in public problems—how can we help it? They are immense, spectacular, obsessing. Our own and our children's destiny depend on their outcome. We live and move and have our being in an atmosphere of anxious concern about huge problems.

So today the Christian minister finds himself changing his tune. You, so concerned about the world's situation, he says, it is downright hypocrisy in one area after another to cry aloud that we must cure mankind's evils when our own lives are part of the evil to be cured. This, at least, is a man's responsibility—to move his own life over so that he is part of the solution. And what a godsend a man is who does it, so that seeing him our hearts cry, That kind of living is the answer!

Let me speak for a moment especially to you young people, growing up in a generation when the idea of moral law as something objectively and eternally there—some things everlastingly right and some things everlastingly wrong—has so largely broken down, the great standards of right and wrong no longer recognized and morality made a matter of as you like it, of what you as an individual can find pleasure in, and can get away with. How prevalent that idea is everyone must see. The way I behave is my private business, a youth says. To which I answer, The way you behave is most certainly not your private business; it is the world's business. From this dilemma no man can escape: he is either part of the world's problem, or part of the answer, and that is not just your private business or mine. In this country now it is estimated that some four million people drink far, far too much, to the obvious hurt of themselves and all around them, and that hundreds of thousands of them are chronic alcoholics. That is a national menace, affecting the whole country's life. What an individual does, therefore, in that regard, is not his private affair alone. Am I part of the problem, or of the answer?

As a preacher I worry because so much of our preaching is like lightning; it is general; it concerns the great evils of the world and the great ideals we should pursue. This morning I wanted to bring some forked lightning in that would hit something, as though one talked to the Prodigal Son in the Far Country and found him, as might well be the case, quite worked up about the world's moral evil and the ill consequence it resulted in, and as though one said to him, Son, you are right about the world's evil, but just now you are part of it. What about solving that much of the problem? What about your saying, I will arise and go unto my Father?

This leads us to the most positive and constructive aspect of our theme, namely, the inspiring effect of even one life that does that, concerning which we feel, That kind of living is the answer. A youth recently came to see me all down in the dumps because this is so vile and ugly a world. I said to him, "You are a youngster. You don't half know how vile and ugly the world is. Do you know, for example, that today there are ten million people in India totally blind, and thirty million more partially blind?" "Good heavens," he said, "I didn't know it was as bad as that!" "Well," I answered, "it is as bad as that. No youngster like you can half know how bad the world is. But listen! Those people do not need to be blind; the causes are all known—vitamin deficiencies and the rest. And a Christian missionary physician, Dr. Victor Rambo, has gone into India with the answer that in widening areas is redeeming, and if he is properly backed will redeem the Indian people from blindness. He says it can be done, and he is starting on it. Now which are you going to bet on, in the long run—the evil, or the solution, when already the solution is visibly at work?" Well, even that down-in-the-dumps youth could not resist the pressure that moved him over from being aghast at ten million blind people in India, to being excited by a person who incarnated the solution. That youth started by saying, How awful! He ended by saying, How marvelous, to be in a game like that!

Friends, that's life in this wild world—vast problems, and then someone comes, seeing whom, we cry, That's the answer!

Is not this one of the central meanings of Jesus to the world? Born in a manger, died on a cross, no wealth, no prestige, nothing to count on except those intangibles of character that cynics belittle, and yet across the centuries towering still, the life concerning whom more and more people know that he is the answer. Where his spirit comes, that is the solution, and just as in science, though all mankind thinks a disease incurable and only one man has found the remedy, a new era has dawned, so Christian faith is sure about Christ in the long run against all the world's evil. As one troubled soul said, "Son of Man, whenever I doubt of life, I think of Thee."

Today we are saying that each of us in his own degree can thus be part not of the problem but of the solution, and that kind of person is about the most inspiriting sight we see. I thank God for some I know. They keep me going.

To be sure, there are some people here who, I fear, may be hurt by this sermon. The burden of their life is that they do feel themselves part of the problem—economically dependent, ill, handicapped, stopped in their tracks by physical disablement so that they feel themselves leaners, not lifters. To some such person here this sermon so far may have been like a stinging whip. I am part of the problem, he may be saying, part of the world's burden, and I cannot help it.

Friend, listen! Nothing in this world is more inspiriting than a soul up against crippling circumstance who carries it off with courage and faith and undefeated character—nothing! You too can be part of the solution. Mr. Newton Baker, Secretary of War in President Wilson's cabinet, told me that after World War I he used to visit in the Federal hospitals the worst casualties of the American Army. One of the very worst was a man with both legs gone, one arm gone, both eyes gone, his face terribly mutilated, who was wheeled around the grounds of the hospital in a perambulator by a nurse, but who still was radiant and full of spirit. Nobody expected him to live. When later Mr. Baker met somebody from the hospital he said, "Did that young man live?" And the answer was, "Did he live? I'll say he did! He married his nurse!" Marveling at the capacity of women to love, Mr. Baker put the matter by, until a few years later as trustee of Johns Hopkins University he received a letter from the president. They wished, said the president, to do an unusual thing, to hold a midsemester convocation to bestow the degree of Doctor of Philosophy upon a young man who, though heavily handicapped, had done one of the most brilliant pieces of work ever done at the University. His name was that of the crippled veteran. Mr. Baker, quite incredulous that it could be the same man, but struck with that phrase "heavily handicapped" made inquiries. Sure enough, it was he! Both legs gone, one arm gone, both eyes gone, but still, not part of the world's problem but part of the answer.

Not every handicapped person can win through to so conspicuous a result, but the spirit—the spirit that stays undefeated in spite of everything—is part of the solution, and those of us still strong and well who see it take another notch in our belts and go to our tasks again with fresh courage.

As for the moral and spiritual realm, what we have been talking about this morning is personal conversion—by God's grace to be so inwardly changed that a man passes over from being part of mankind's disease to being part of the cure. Whenever that happens it makes a difference to the whole race. No little thing that Prodigal did when he came home, not little for himself nor for his father, nor for the world. That event is still one of mankind's unforgettables. God grant that it may happen here today, for in the long run everything depends on enough people who are part of the answer.

Six Ways to Tell Right from Wrong

OUR thought starts with the plain fact that it is not always easy to tell the difference between right and wrong. Any pulpit, therefore, which keeps up the traditional exhortation, Do right! Do right! as though, with a consensus of popular opinion as to what right is, all that the world needs is to be urged to do it, is indulging in a futile kind of preaching. Behind a great deal of our modern immoralism is not so much downright badness as sincere confusion as to what is right. In many a dubious situation how we wish that some one would tell us that!

The factors that enter into this condition must be obvious to anybody.

For one thing, change of circumstances. Old customs and old codes of behavior in family life or in the relationships between men and women, let us say, undertake to tell us how to act, but the circumstances in which those codes and customs are supposed here to function are radically different from the circumstances in which they first emerged, so that although their basic principles may be valid their applications are endlessly perplexing. In consequence, old patterns of behavior smash up and old prescriptions for right and wrong do not seem pertinent, and every day human beings, who always like to have their roadways plainly marked, go astray, not because they deliberately want to but because they are honestly confused about which the right road is.

Again, our cosmopolitanism, pouring all the cultures of the earth into one melting pot, has, among other consequences, resulted in ethical confusion. Our Pilgrim forefathers, with a wilderness on one side and a sea on the other, in their comparatively isolated community and with their comparatively homogeneous population, could reach a popular consensus of moral judgment or even a dogmatic certainty as to how men ought to act. But in a city like this most of the ways of behaving known on earth are poured together, so that the issue is not a single clear right against a single clear wrong, but such diverse and competing ideas of right as to befuddle the minds even of the elect.

The upshot of all this is that conscience is not enough. Of course, conscience never has been enough. Many of the most terriffic deeds in history, from the crucifixion of our Lord down, were conscientiously done. Listen even to Paul in his first letter to Timothy: "I was before a blasphemer, and a persecutor, and injurious: howbeit I obtained mercy, because I did it ignorantly in unbelief." Paul throughout his life had been conscientious. Toward the end of it he could say to his Jewish brethren, "I have lived before God in all good conscience until this day." That did not mean, however, that as he looked back over his life all the things he had conscientiously done seemed to him to have been right. Upon the contrary, he confessed: a blasphemer, a persecutor, an injurious person, such was I, conscientiously but ignorantly.

Today I propose talking about this matter with homely practicality to my own soul and to yours. We may take it for granted that we would not be here in a Christian church if in general we did not desire to do right. We may even take it for granted that if, as in Shakespeare's "As You Like It," some one should ask us Touchstone's question, "Hast any philosophy in thee, shepherd?" we would say, Yes indeed, we have; we believe the basic ideas of Christianity about life's meaning—that is our philosophy. But we had better take it for granted also that this general desire to do right and this general acceptance of the Christian philosophy of life do not solve our problem. So as automobilists our problem is not solved when we desire to take the right road or when we hold a true cosmology about the solar relationships of the earth on which the right road runs. Oh, for a homely sign-post now and then, some practical, directive help amid the confusion of competing ways to tell us where to turn! So this morning I invite you to no airplane trip into the lofty blue but to a practical land journey as we set up six homely guide-posts to the good life.

In the first place, if a man is sincerely perplexed about a question of right and wrong, he might well submit it to the test of common sense. Suppose that some one should challenge you to a duel. What would you say? I would advise you to say, Don't be silly! As a matter of historic fact, dueling, which was once a serious point of conscientious honor, was not so much argued out of existence as laughed out. The common sense of mankind rose up against it, saying, Don't be silly! So Cervantes in *Don Quixote* finished off the ridiculous left-overs of the old knighthood, saying, Don't be silly! So Jesus, in his parable of the rich man who accumulated outward things but cared nothing for the inward wealth of the spiritual life, did not say, Sinner! but Fool!—"Thou fool, this night thy soul shall be required of thee: then whose shall those things be, which thou hast provided?"

So, too, more intimately, here is a youth whom you may know, whose behavior burdens with anxiety his family, his teachers, and his friends. They argue with him; they exhort him; they penalize him to no effect. But some day a fine girl for whom he cares says to him, it may be no more than three words, Don't be silly! and lo, something happens in that boy that home and school and church together could not achieve.

What we are saying now is that this is a healthy thing for a man to say to his own soul before somebody else has to say it to him. One wonders how many here would be affected by it. You do not really care anything about drink, and left to yourself you would not drink at all, but it is so commonly offered to one nowadays and is so generally taken as a matter of course, that you are drinking too much. Don't be silly! Or you may have in your hands today a choice between promiscuous sexual liaisons and a real home where two people love each other so much that they do not care to love anybody else in the same way at all; where romance deepens into friendship and overflows into children; where, as the sun grows westerly, the family life becomes every year more beautiful. And with that choice in your hands you are playing with promiscuity. Don't be silly!

Or it may be that you have a good set of brains and real ability so that if you wanted to you could prepare yourself for some worthwhile work in the world, and just because you are financially able you are trying to be aimlessly happy, not going anywhere,—just meandering,—endeavoring to pick up all the sensations that you can accumulate. I should not think it worth while to call you first of all bad, but I am sure it would be true to call you silly.

That is the first test and, alas! twenty years from now somebody here this morning, listening to this and paying no heed to it, will be looking back on life and saying that bitter thing, "God be merciful to me, a fool!"

In the second place, if a man is sincerely perplexed about a question of right and wrong, he may well submit it to the test of sportsmanship. Now the essence of sportsmanship is that in a game we do not take for ourselves special favors which we deny to other players but, making the rules equal for all, abide by them. In daily life that means that a man should always question concerning his conduct whether, if everybody acted on the same principle, it would be well for all. There is no doubt, then, why it is wrong to crowd in ahead of your turn in a line at a ticket office. Play the game! There is no doubt why it is wrong to cheat the government with petty smuggling or to join whispering campaigns about people when you do not know the facts, or to treat contemptuously a person of another race or color. Play the game! In all such cases we know well that we would not wish to be treated ourselves as we are treating others and that if everybody acted on that principle it would not be well for all. Sometimes one thinks that half the evil in the world is simply cheating. People do not play the game.

Do not, I beg of you, restrict the application of this test within the limits of individual behavior. There are ways of making money in our economic system, not simply illegal but legal, speculative gambling with the securities of the people, using public utilities as a football to be kicked all over the financial field in hope of making a goal of private profit with it, or betting day after day on stocks that represent genuine values which honest business once created but which now can be used merely for a gambler's chance without creating anything. If everybody acted like that there would be no values even to gamble with and no welfare for any one. Be sure of this, that this rising tide of public indignation against the economic wrongs has this much justification: we have a right at least to ordinary sportsmanship and in wide areas we have not been getting it. The Golden Rule, my friends, is a grand test. Husband and wife, parents and children, employers and employees, black and white, prosperous and poor, Occident and Orient—what if we did not cheat! what if we did as we would be done by! what if we played the game!

In the third place, if a man is sincerely perplexed about a question of right and wrong, he may well submit it to the test of his best self. Notice, I do not say to his conscience, for the conscience merely urges us to do right without telling us what the right is, but deeper than conscience and more comprehensive is this other matter, a man's best self. For, of course, no one of us is a single self. How much simpler life would be if we only were! There is a passionate self, reaching out hungrily for importunate sensations, good, bad, and indifferent. There is the careless self taking anything that comes along, excellent and vulgar, fine and cheap. There is the greedy self in whose eyes an egoistic want blots out all the wide horizons of humanity beside. But deeper than all these is that inner self where dwells the light that, as the Fourth Gospel says, lighteth every man coming into the world.

Let us illustrate it from biography. You know the story of Pasteur, great scientist, devout Christian, builder of modern medicine. In 1870, when the Germans invaded France, he already had had a paralytic stroke and was a cripple. He could not help repel the invaders. His friends urged him out of Paris that he might not be "a useless mouth" to be fed through the siege. His biographer tells us that sometimes when he was sitting quietly with his wife and daughter, in the little village of Arbois, the crier's trumpet would sound, and forgetting all else, he would go out of doors, mix with the groups standing on the bridge, listen to the latest news of disaster, and creep like a dumb, hurt animal back to his room. What could he do? What ought he to do? "Unhappy France," he wrote to a friend, "dear country, if I could only assist in raising thee from thy disasters!" Then something happened inside Pasteur that has changed the world. He, half paralyzed, a man already warned of his end, determined that he would raise France again to glory by a work of pure beneficence, that he would erect a monument to his country's honor that would make the military monuments of the conquerors seem puerile. In his biography you can read it all, how by years of inspired and sacrificial labor he at last fulfilled his purpose. So Pasteur, wondering what he ought to do, what he could do in a perplexing situation, carried the decision up to that finest self.

Sometimes when I preach here I wonder if there may not be in this congregation a youth who, so choosing his vocation, so testing his ambition, so dedicating his intelligence, will not help to raise America again. She needs it, unhappy country!

Be sure of this, that if, in large ways or small, any one of us does help to ennoble our society and build a better nation for our children and their children to be born into, it will be because we have taken our secret ambitions up to the tribunal of our finest self. There *is* something in us like a musician's taste, which discriminates harmony from discord. There *is* something in us like a bank teller's fingers, which distinguish true money from counterfeit:

> . . . To thine own self be true,
> And it must follow, as the night the day,
> Thou canst not then be false to any man.

In the fourth place, if a man is sincerely perplexed over a matter of right and wrong he may well submit the question to the test of publicity. What if everybody knew what we are proposing to do? Strip it of secrecy and furtiveness. Carry it out into the open air, this conduct we are unsure about. Suppose our family and friends knew about it. Imagine it publicly talked of whenever our name is mentioned. Picture it written in the story of our life for our children afterwards to read. Submit it to the test of publicity. Anybody who knows human life with its clandestine behavior understands what a searching and healthy test this is.

How often in politics, in church life, in business, in personal character we see things that remind us of a claque at the theater hired to applaud a play! They can get away with it as long as the public does not know it is a claque. It depends on secrecy for its success. What a test publicity is!

Do you remember how Phillips Brooks put it?

> To keep clear of concealment, to keep clear of the need of concealment, to do nothing which he might not do out on the middle of Boston Common at noonday,—I cannot say how more and more that seems to me to be the glory of a young man's life. It is an awful hour when the first necessity of hiding anything comes. The whole life is different thenceforth. When there are questions to be feared and eyes to be avoided and subjects which must not be touched, then the bloom of life is gone. Put off that day as long as possible. Put it off forever if you can.

I know one business firm in this city which in a few weeks will crash into a receivership under the tremendous blow of a righteous court decision. Ten years ago that firm did a secret thing which would not stand the test of open knowledge. For ten years those men have lived in deadly fear that it might be known. And now the light has fallen.

Yes, and just the other day in personal conference I talked with an individual on the ragged edge of nervous prostration because in the secret furtiveness of private life something was afoot which it would be disastrous to have known.

Things that cannot stand sunlight are not healthful. There is a test for a perplexed conscience. How many here do you suppose would be affected by it? Imagine your behavior public.

In the fifth place, if a man is perplexed about a question of right and wrong he may well submit it to the test of his most admired personality. Carry it up into the light of the life which you esteem most and test it there. Why is it that some of us do not like cheap jazz? It is because we have known and loved another kind of music. Why is it that some of us do not think that Coney Island is a beautiful place? It is because on autumn days when the artistry of heaven has been poured out in lavish loveliness upon the trees we have walked in the spacious woods alone with our own souls and God. Why is it that some of us regard with a deep distaste all this promiscuous sexuality? It is because we have lived in homes where love was deep and lasting and dependable.

My friends, it is the beauties and the personalities that we positively have loved that set for us the tests and standards of our lives. Why is it, then, that conduct which seems to some people right seems to some of us cheap and vulgar, selfish and wrong? It is because for years we have known and adored the Christ. There is a test for a perplexed conscience. Carry your behavior up into the presence of the Galilean and judge it there.

If some one protests that he does not propose to subjugate his independence of moral judgment to any authority, not even Christ's, I answer, What do you mean by authority? There are all kinds of authorities—ecclesiastical, creedal, external, artificial—against the imposition of whose control on mind and conscience I would as vigorously fight as you. But there is one kind of authority for which I hunger, the insight of the seers. In science, in philosophy, in literature, in art, in music, not simply in morals and religion, I would, if I might, enrich my soul with the insights of the seers. A modern essayist says of Wordsworth, the poet, that he "saw things that other people do not see, and that he saw with quite unique clearness and frequency things which they see at most rarely and dimly." Aye! More than once some of us have carried our perplexed consciences up into the presence of the Christ and have made a saving use of his eyes.

In the sixth place, if a man is perplexed about a question of right and wrong, he may well submit it to the test of foresight. Where is this course of behavior coming out? All good life, my friends, depends upon the disciplining of clamorous and importunate desires in the light of a long look. We Christians who are trying to be intelligent long since gave up our belief in hell, but one suspects that many of us, throwing over the incredible and picturesque impossibilities of that belief, have dropped also a basic truth which our forefathers carried along in it. Every man who picks up one end of a stick picks up the other. Aye! Every man who chooses one end of a road is choosing the other. Aye! Every course of behavior has not only a place where it begins but a place where it comes out.

Life is like a game of chess. Some youth is here this morning with all his pieces on the board and freedom to commence. They tell me, however, that when a man has once played his opening, he is not so free thereafter. His moves must conform to the plan he has adopted. He has to follow the lead with which he has begun. The consequence of his opening closes in on him until at last, when checkmate is called, See! says the expert, when you chose those first moves you decided the end. Well, with what gambit are we opening our game?

We really do not need to be so perplexed about right and wrong as we sometimes are. To be sure, there is nothing infallible about all this. Goodness is an adventure and "Time makes ancient good uncouth." Nevertheless, the test of common sense, of sportsmanship, of the best self, the test of publicity, of our most admired personality, of foresight,—these are sensible, practical, high-minded ways to tell right from wrong. I call you to witness that in all this I have not been imposing on you a code of conduct; I have been appealing to your own best moral judgment. Alas for a man who neglects that! For though, as in Paul's case, one may come out at last to a good life, it is a bitter thing to have to look back and say, A blasphemer, and a persecutor, and injurious—such was I—ignorantly.

The Practical Use of Faith

ONE of the most powerful influences in the world for good or for evil is faith. For faith primarily is a practical power to be used or misused. A strange misunderstanding obsesses many minds to the effect that faith first of all is a speculative problem to be discussed, whereas the substance of the matter is that the faculty of faith is one of the constituent elements of human nature, like the power to think or the power to love, to be used or misused.

When, for example, a religious exhorter urges us to have faith, he mistakes the state of the case. We have faith already; we would not be human beings without it; we never have existed an hour without exercising it; we have our being by virtue of our capacity to believe in something, and, using it, we make of life a heaven or a hell. Just as we have a love-life, we have a faith-faculty; no normal person needs to be urged to have it, but we all need to learn how to handle it.

Or when the so-called unbeliever questions our right to have faith, he too mistakes the case. Indeed, there is no such person as an unbeliever, if by that we mean a person who lacks faith. He may use his faith-faculty for this or that, believe in war or peace, monogamy or promiscuity, God or materialism, but all the time this faculty of faith is at work within him, involved in every vital activity of mind and life.

This matter demands attention because many of us now are facing situations, environmental in this chaotic generation, personal in problems that make carrying on hard, where the use of faith is a matter of life and death. Said a stalwart specimen of American manhood recently, "Without faith I could never get through what I am facing now." To that man faith was no longer first of all a problem to be discussed. He confronted a situation which demanded the marshaling of his interior resources. He had been compelled to go down into the armory of his soul to find weapons of the spirit with which to face antagonistic days, and there he had rediscovered faith, not as a problem but as a power. When a man does that, he is getting back to the New Testament in general and to Jesus in particular: "If ye have faith as a grain of mustard seed, ye shall say unto this mountain, Remove hence to yonder place; and it shall remove." *There* is faith, not at all bristling with speculative difficulties but rather exhibiting power to move mountainous obstacles.

Let us at the start face one difficulty certain to be in many minds: the supposed conflict between faith and intelligence. Intelligence has so continually to fight popular beliefs that the predisposition of many minds is habitually to set over against each other intelligence and faith. When Galileo grasped the new astronomy, he had to fight old beliefs. When Harvey knew that the blood did circulate he faced opposing beliefs that it did not. So we have come to say, Give us intelligence but beware of this vice of the mind, this impediment to progress, faith. To this, of course, the answer is clear. Granted that faith is one of the most dangerous forces in the world! Men even have faith in war as a way of settling international difficulties, and from such major faiths, bringing ruin on whole civilizations, to individual beliefs—in rabbits' feet and astrology, fake medicines and demonology, incredible ideas about the world and obsolete creeds in religion—faith can debauch life, corrupt the mind, and impede progress.

That is precisely what we are driving at. Faith is a prodigious power, to be used or misused; the fate of mankind depends largely on what is done with it. We never can solve the problem by eliminating faith. Of all mad faiths the maddest is the faith that we can get rid of faith. A human being is essentially a creature who necessarily and forever believes in something. The only cure in this world for the wrong use of faith is the right use of it. Deep at the center of every personality, where we handle our own solitariness, we are working out success or failure, salvation or destruction, by our use of this perilous power.

Positively, then, let us consider some of the wholesome and saving uses of it. In particular, note four mortal enemies of the soul: aimlessness, feebleness, fear, and cynicism. If ever there was a time when these mortal enemies went up and down the earth seeking whom they might devour, it is today.

Aimlessness, then. Whatever else a strong faith does, it certainly gathers up the life, pulls it together, and gives it direction. Even a bad faith does that. One of the basic facts about human life, commonly forgotten by those who depreciate the need of faith, is that man is a creature who looks in three directions. He looks back and has a past. He looks in and has a present. He looks ahead and has a future. No man would be a man without that last, but what that last means to him depends on what it is out there, ahead, in which he verily has faith. If some one says that we cannot prove what lies ahead, just so! That is where demonstrable knowledge breaks down every day in every life, and so the direction of our going depends largely on what it is ahead there in which we verily believe. Lacking that, every one of us, as some one has said of our modern civilization, is "like an engine running without a headlight."

Here is the real answer to those who are predisposed to set faith and intelligence over against each other. Far from its being true that faith and intelligence are in conflict, we habitually mass our intellectual activity around the things in which we have faith. Did not the Wright brothers use their intellects upon their airplanes? I should say they did! And they did so because first of all they had believed in flying long before it was here. Did not we in this church use whatever intelligence we could conjure up in building an institution with doors wide open across all sectarian boundaries? Indeed we did, and often wistfully wished we had more intelligence at our disposal. And behind that was our faith in the possibilities of a non-sectarian church before it was here. All the intellect any man has is marshaled around the things he believes.

The conflicts, therefore, between intellect and faith are incidental, but the necessity of faith to intelligence is essential. Faith blazes the trail; intelligence builds the avenue. Faith pioneers new country; intelligence settles it. If in this congregation now there is a mind alert and eager, trying to see something clearly, think it through rightly, implement it successfully, we may be sure that such intellectual activity is centered in something that person believes.

Often Christian ministers urge faith in Christ. More than once, it may be, that appeal has seemed to you weak and insignificant. Who can blame you? Christian preachers commonly caricature faith in Christ and make it little more than passive acceptance of somebody else's opinions concerning him. But some of us from boyhood have seen the spirit of Christ reproduced in those who influenced us most, so that he has become the object of our faith and, despite our lamentable waywardness, has set the direction of our going. That experience is real and the consequence in life is inevitable. Life is not aimless; it gets concentration, integration, direction, aim. A strong faith can do that for a man and nothing else in this world can.

Another mortal enemy of our lives to be handled only by an intelligent use of faith is *feebleness*. In Bunyan's *Pilgrim's Progress* we are told that Doubting Castle was kept by Giant Despair and his wife Diffidence. Auybody might have thought of Giant Despair but it was a stroke of genius to put in his wife. For it is true that, when faith fails, diffidence, incertitude, insecurity, feebleness arrive with all their debilitated family.

Despite our boasted modern knowledge, many people still feel the deep need of inward power but do not know how to get it. First they try their wills. They strain their volition. But often that is like blowing with full cheeks upon our own sails to make the ship go; it does not release the winds of power. Then they try their minds. They say they will think the situation clearly through. But often, when they have thought the situation clearly through, it seems much worse than it did before. They have not released power. Then, in some fortunate and unexpected hour, an experience may come which renews their faith in life and, lo! something strong stands up in them that might move mountains.

I do not wish simply to discuss this. I wish I could help create it in all of us. We cannot produce power. No, but we can release it, and the greatest releaser of power in life is faith. Happy the man, then, who knows where to turn for those experiences which restore his faith in life. Sometimes beauty does it. Fed up with life, fatigued, done in, saying as one man said to me recently, Nothing left to believe in! we keep a tryst with nature or with music and come back, as the psalmist said, as one who has walked in green pastures and beside the still waters, restoring his soul. What has happened is a vision of another world above this world and interpenetrating it, which has renewed our faith in life and so brought back our power.

Or, it may be, in a dark hour finding life ugly, sordid, brutal, and feeling sick of this "dirty decade," where much of our literature has been "an explosion in a cesspool," to use a critic's phrase, we see, it may be, no more than a single deed, courageous, sacrificial, high-minded, beautiful, and lo! all that day, our faith in life restored, we walk with power.

Of course our friends do this for us. Walt Whitman said once, "I no doubt deserved my enemies, but I don't believe I deserved my friends." Just so! And what friends do for us is to lift us up from our collapsed moods, renew our faith in life, and so restore our power.

All experiences of released power are associated with renewed faith in life. And faith in life is not an accident. There are places where it comes. Alas for the man who does not know them and has no well-trodden pathway beaten to their doors! Especially unhappy is the man who has no deep, inner sanctuary of his own where his soul stands in the presence of the Over-Soul and is assured again that life as a whole "means intensely, and means good." That is personal religon at its center. The deepest difference between Christianity and irreligion is this: irreligion is a declaration of lost faith in life, that it came from nowhere save the dust, that it goes nowhither save back to it again, and that in the end it means nothing; and Christianity is a declaration of undiscourageable faith in life, its spiritual origin, its endless possibilities, its eternal meaning. When deep in the center of his personality a man has that perennial spring of faith's renewal, he possesses the fountains of power.

Another peril to life, *fear*, no man ever yet succeeded in handling well without a strong, intelligent faith. To be sure, if faith is used wrongly it produces fear. A man can believe in hell and be scared to death of it. He can believe in ghosts and by them be haunted. He can believe that he is sick until he is frightened into sickness. Faith wrongly used peoples the world with dread, but if, instead, a man learns the high art of intelligently using faith, he is done with obsessing fear.

We have lighted here upon a significant matter. Hitherto we have been talking about faith as though it were a way of laying hold on things already in existence; now we have to say that faith is one of the most creative forces in our lives and that continually it brings into existence something which was not there before.

So does fear. If you fear some things enough, you will produce them, and, by the same sign, if you have faith in some things enough, you will create them.

Few things need more to be said than this on the matter of peace and war. Many in this discouraged time talk as though the age-long war system were a static fact and the embryonic peace system were another static fact, and the issue were the analytical appraisal of their comparative strength, with prophecies about the probable outcome. But such a static approach leaves out altogether the creative element. If enough people keep on believing in the war system, nothing can stop war. But if enough people would verily believe in the peace system, then the war system would prove as vulnerable as many another ancient curse. Edmund Burke, English statesman of the first magnitude, at one time regarded slavery as an incurable evil that never could be stopped. Fourscore years afterward, Lincoln wrote the Emancipation Proclamation. So, today, when the peace movement is hard-bestead, I for that very reason give my faith to it. Now is the time to mass around the peace system the creative faith of those who, before God and their consciences, have lost faith in the war system.

As human beings we are so made that we cannot help living in two worlds, the 'is' and the 'ought,' the actual and the possible, the factual and the ideal. Now the power which reaches out into the 'ought' and transforms it into the 'is,' which lays hold upon the possible and of it makes the actual, is creative faith. When such faith stands up, fear falls down.

The fourth enemy is *cynicism*. Nobody needs a description of that. It knocks at the doors; it taps on the windows of every personality here. As one of our modern writers sums life up:

> . . . It's all Nothing.
> It's all a world where bugs and emperors
> Go singularly back to the same dust.

Some of us, surely, came here feeling that, and if we are to surmount that feeling, it will be only by a strong faith. Without faith we inevitably exist within the boundaries of sight. But nobody ever yet succeeded in living within the boundaries of sight. Always, just over the border of sight, we have to live by insight. That is faith. As another has put it, faith is "veracity of insight."

Do not make this matter so mysterious that it ceases to be real and practical. It is as true in science as anywhere else. Lightning was a matter of sight for ages until one day insight came with such tremendous consequence as all our modern world bears witness to. As the Benéts say,

> Ben Franklin made a pretty kite and flew it in the air
> To call upon a thunderstorm that happened to be there,
> —And all our humming dynamos and our electric light
> Go back to what Ben Franklin found, the day he flew his kite.

Indeed, Sir Oliver Lodge, speaking of Isaac Newton, praised "his extraordinary instinct for guessing right." Guessing right? The discovery of the law of gravitation came from veracity of insight.

Recently a brilliant student of the new generation, so equipped in intellect and character that he will go far before he is through, and specializing in economics and government so that he is living and thinking in the most disturbed area in modern life, said to me quite out of the blue, "After all, everything I do or ever shall do is motivated by religious faith." That encouraged me, coming naturally and spontaneously from the lips of a brilliant and unconventional youth. I think I see what was in his mind. Always beyond the barriers of sight runs insight. This universe is not simply what on the surface it seems to be. Nothing that we can catch in testtubes or measure with yardsticks or reduce to mathematical formulas goes to the bottom of reality. The invisible world of spiritual values is real. All that is best in us is the revelation of something eternal behind and ahead of us. This universe is infinitely more marvelous and meaningful than irreligion thinks. So Phœnician sailors once told Herodotus that they had voyaged out through the Straits of Gibraltar and, turning south, had come to the place where the shadows fell the wrong way. Herodotus was incredulous. He thought they were trying to fool an old man. He was incredulous too soon. Even this earth was more marvelous and meaningful than he had dreamed. So is this spiritual universe with its endless possibilities and its living God. Around that conviction the profoundest thinking of man's mind has gathered in support, but all such philosophy is only partial confirmation of something which preceded it: a leap of faith, a venture of intuition, a discovery of veracious insight.

Well, we have only one life to live. To live it aimlessly, feebly, fearfully, cynically is to be a total loss. "And this is the victory that hath overcome the world, even our faith."

Family Religion

OUR subject suggests at once a verse in the Epistle to the Colossians which I should suppose would haunt any one deeply concerned over the present posture of events in our American homes. "The church that is in their house," says Paul.

The phrase goes back to the time before there were special buildings called churches. The only place where worship could be held under cover was in a house, and there in some home in Colossæ the little company of Christians habitually gathered and worshiped. While, however, this is the bare meaning of the phrase, it is obvious that when they chose the house in Colassæ where the church was to meet they must have selected one representing the best they knew in family relationships. They could not have carried the church into a wrangling, unhappy home. The phrase, therefore, becomes symbolical of something permanently true in a Christian family. We desperately need to think about it in America today—the church that is in your house.

Religion moves in different areas and organizes itself around different centers. There is personal religion, which we carry around with us and live by in the inner regions of our personalities. There is ecclesiastical religion, institutionalized in churches, with their traditions, polities, rituals, and rubrics. And there is family religion which, when it is at its best, floods a home with light and makes the relationships therein sacred and beautiful. It creates a church within a house.

We are all concerned with this last area of religious life. We came from homes, we live in homes, we plain to have homes—nowhere are our deepest personal interests more involved than in the problem of the family. And when we step outside our individual concerns and consider the nation, it grows daily more obvious that the real battleground for the moral life of America is the family. We may multiply our inventions and raise to its pinnacle the highly articulated, mechanized miracle of a civilization which we have started here; we may increase our industries and accumulate wealth; we may even build great temples dedicated to public worship and great schools dedicated to public education; but, after all, what this country will amount to in the end depends upon what happens to its homes. There is no substitute for parents.

Moreover, religion has a tremendous stake in the home. All our Christian ideas are home ideas and all our Christian language is home language, whether we call God our Father or ourselves his children, or define our social ideal in terms of human brotherhood. One cannot think or talk Christianity without the atmosphere and terminology of the family. Christianity is not simply religion; it is religion saturated with family life until it means fatherhood, sonship, brotherhood, love. So the fortunes of Christianity and of the home are inseparable. What happens to one inevitably happens to the other. Let the family life of this nation decay and there is no magic by which the Christian religion can be maintained. When we think of the family, then, we are at the center of things as individuals, as citizens, and as Christians.

In the first place, many people run upon the need of a church in their house when they have children of their own. An all-too-typical mother came to me in poignant distress about her religious life. She had received a traditional religious training in childhood, had surrendered her faith during college and had graduated as an agnostic, had moved out into a fortunate marriage, been blessed with a large family of children, and had been so busy and happy that for personal purposes she had not missed religion. What worried her was her children. Said she, 'I have friends who also are without religious faith whose children are being brought up as mine are and I cannot endure the consequence. They are all little pagans. I would not for anything have my children grow up so. I must have some religion to give them. I do not feel the crucial need of it myself but I must have some for my children."

That mother's case represents a situation increasingly common. Parents in shoals have been abandoning the religious training offered by the churches. Fathers have preferred the automobile or the golf course to the sanctuary, and mothers have followed them, or, becoming modern on their own account, have espoused some 'ism,' from positive atheism to general indifferentism. One way or another, a large proportion of the children of the United States today are being reared without any religious training worthy of the name.

When, however, the pendulum swings far one way, it is likely soon to swing the other. Things are not going well with the moral character of America on the basis of irreligious family life and irreligious education. Many fathers who are not particularly worried about themselves, although probably they ought to be, are deeply worried about their sons. One hears parents lamenting in their children the lack of something—they are not quite sure what—which they had in their youth, something stabilizing and directive that produced quality in character and purposefulness in life. They vaguely suspect that it may have been the religious influence of their homes. They wish that their children had something like it. They are certain that their children need it. Sometimes, as in the anxious woman's case, they make up their minds that their children must have it.

It is not possible to exaggerate the stake which we all have in this matter. When a man reaches the vicinity of fifty years of age, he begins to understand how much everything he has cared about depends on the children. Death in itself is not undesirable. Death, when it cuts athwart our personal affections and our plans can be terrible enough but, for all that, when a wise man stands back from life and looks at the matter objectively, he thanks God for death. Thank God that we do not live to the reputed age of Methuselah, that "The days of our years are threescore years and ten, or even by reason of strength fourscore years," and that then we stop and do not go on weighing down the race longer with our accumulated conservatisms! Thank God for the world's new chance with the children! Each generation comes up fresh from the gates of the dawn and in a sense the world can start over and try again. But while this rhythm of birth and death is advantageous, what a responsibility it entails! Everything depends upon the training of the children.

We want a new international spirit issuing in a new construing of international life, and the world organized for peace instead of war.

But when we have made our last plan about external arrangements, the issue will depend upon the training of the children.

We want a united Christianity. Sick to death are we with these futilely divided churches that cannot even take the Lord's Supper together. But when we have made all our arguments and devised all our schemes, the ultimate problem is the training of the children.

We want religion, pure and undefiled, as an effective force in the character of our nation. Indeed we do. Some in the invisible congregation may be listening in who have not been in church for a quarter of a century, but that would be true for you too. You know that more genuine, character-producing religion is needed in this nation. It was a financial journal—not a preacher—which said that what we need most of all is some of the religion that mother used to make. But whether in the end we are going to get it depends upon the training of the children. What about the church in your house?

We may say that the ecclesiastical church ought to help. Of course it ought! We may say that the church school has here its responsibility and opportunity. Indeed, it has! But, after all, what can be done in the religious training of the children in the church on Sunday is only accessory to the home. There are no substitutes for parents.

In the second place, the importance of the church that is in the home is accentuated by the fact that, after all, religion is something we catch rather than learn. There are many things even more prosaic than religion which thus are caught rather than taught. In high school I hated mathematics and, like many another boy, looked forward with eagerness to the millennium when I should have passed my last examination in the abominable subject and would never have to look at it again. Then, going to college, I fell under the influence of one of the most inspiriting personalities I ever met. He was a professor of mathematics. I was always going to drop mathematics in college but I never did—went straight through my course with it, elected everything he gave, did not so much learn it as absorb it. He performed the incredible miracle of making even mathematics contagious. If that can be done with mathematics, what shall we say about other more obviously personal, intimate, spiritual things, like poetry, for example. One can teach a child many things about poetry—meter, rhythm, scansion, and the rest—but if ever you find a youth who loves poetry you may be sure that he caught that from somebody. The love of poetry is handed down by contagion.

So is religion. It is a fire that is passed from one life to another, not primarily by instruction, but by kindling.

Take as a sample only one doctrine of Jesus, the sacredness of personality. All personality is sacred, Jesus said, whether in man or woman, king or slave, saint or sinner. The most sacred thing in this universe is personality, and it never is to be scorned or wronged, but helped. Whatever is most distinctive and original in Jesus' message radiates from that center and one cannot understand his conception of God, his ethical teachings, or his practical program of life unless one understands that.

Nevertheless, set a little child down before that statement as a doctrine and try to teach it to him. Get the matter logically set out: all personality is sacred. Arrange the corollaries and make a neat, dogmatic lesson of it. How much will the child really learn that way? What a child gets about the sacredness of personality he chiefly absorbs from the way his parents live with each other, with the household servants, with their friends and their enemies, with folks of other colors, other races, other classes. If you see a child to whom personality really is sacred across the lines that divide us prejudicially from one another, so that he counts nothing human alien to himself, you may be sure he caught that from somebody. My friends, the only religious *teaching* that amounts to much consists in explaining to a child the history, meaning, and reasonableness of something which he already has caught.

Suppose it were not religion that we are talking of but a poem on the love of nature, like Wordsworth's:

> . . . How oft—
> In darkness and amid the many shapes
> Of joyless daylight; when the fretful stir
> Unprofitable, and the fever of the world,
> Have hung upon the beatings of my heart—
> How oft, in spirit, have I turned to thee,
> O sylvan Wye! thou wanderer thro' the woods,
> How often has my spirit turned to thee!

One can make a doctrine out of that. What is the meter? What is the scansion? What is the rhythm? What is the geography of the Wye? Some of us recall that way of introducing children to literature. In the Scotch comedy, "Bunty Pulls the Strings," a youth protests against learning the catechism on the ground that he does not understand it, to whom the father indignantly replies, "Who's expecting you to understand it—learn it." We all know that method of teaching subjects.

But when a teacher does for a boy what one did for me in my high school days—takes him up into his room week after week and reads to him the loveliest things in English speech until he catches the flavor and fragrance of them, joins in appreciation of them, and falls in love with them—then to explain why they are beautiful becomes almost a painless process. One likes to understand what one loves.

If religion, like other fine things, has to be caught, the home is the place for it. We are all the time trying to load off upon some other organization the responsibility of our homes. As another has rephrased the ancient saying, When my father and my mother forsake me, then the Boy Scouts will take me up. We may well be grateful for the Boy Scouts, and for all the religion that can come into a child's life from the church, the church school, the day school, and every other agency interested in the welfare of children. But, after all, it is the life that the child catches at home that goes deepest and lasts longest. What about the church in your house?

In the third place, the importance of this matter is accentuated by the fact that, willy-nilly, in the home we are teaching our children religion of some sort. Once in a while one hears parents say that they do not intend to teach religion to their children. Religion is an intimate, personal matter which every child has a right to choose for himself, and they propose to leave the child neutral while he is growing up and then let him freely select religion for himself. How plausible and liberal that sounds! But anybody who knows child psychology at all knows how absurd the proposition is. Even if we wish to, we cannot keep a child religiously neutral. What do we think religion is—a bay window put on the side of a house after it is finished? Do we suppose we can build the entire house and then add religion as an afterthought? Religion is not thus an addendum appended to life but the spiritual atmosphere pervading the whole establishment, and as soon as a child is born the home begins creating in him a spiritual climate, teaching him basic reactions to life, attitudes toward life, feelings about life, which inevitably enter into the very substance of any religion which he ever will possess.

Suppose, for example, that some parents should say what, alas, many parents do say in effect, that sex is a very intimate, personal matter and that they are not going to teach their children anything about it but let them be neutral until, of age, they choose for themselves what sex shall mean. You see at once how mistaken and dangerous that would be. Sex is not merely a side show in life; it is so central that our reactions to it color the whole of life for good or ill, for beauty or ugliness. Just because it is so intimate and personal, not even a child can be neutral. Be sure of this: if we do not shoulder our responsibilities as parents and teach our children what sex means at its best they will pick up attitudes on that matter somewhere else, the more's the pity! So it is with religion. No child remains neutral. One of our leading psychologists, investigating the nature of school children's thinking, found that two little souls had already gotten some major religious ideas from the pictures of Satan on tins of deviled ham upon the pantry shelves.

Some time ago a young woman came to my confessional who, having discovered that her supposed husband was a bigamist, had left him and, undertaking the support of herself and her child, was finding life not only practically hard but spiritually forlorn. She needed religion and she knew it, but all the truth and warmth of it eluded her. The reason was not far to seek. Her childhood home had been a domestic hell, with habitual quarreling, profanity, drunkenness, and dreariness. She had become so habituated to fear, suspicion, distrust, and hopelessness that to rise into confidence, faith, and hope, the climate and atmosphere where religion dwells, seemed to her almost impossible. Those profane and contentious parents would probably have laughed at the idea that they were giving instruction to their child in the field of religion, but they were—a very dastardly course of lessons, which made faith in God for her a psychological exploit of the first magnitude.

Our homes run the gamut from such an abysmal pit to lovely and radiant households of the kind some of us have known, where faith in God and goodness was as natural as breathing. What about the church that is in thy house?

Finally, the importance of this matter is accentuated by the crucial need of our young people themselves. What are you training your children for? What objective have you in mind in your rearing of them? I can answer for our household. We are trying to train our children for independence. We are sure that today children need primarily to be trained for independence.

What some will think of that is easily imaginable. To train children for independence, they will say, is the last thing wanted; children are too independent now; they begin even in early adolescence to refuse the bridle and harness, and one has only to watch them anywhere to see them jumping fences and making the wide world their race course. Train them for obedience. Teach them the meaning of authority. Bring them under restraint. Does one throw kerosene on fire to quench it, that you talk about training youth for independence?

The reasons for such an outburst are obvious enough, but for all that, the outburst misses the point. The children of today are independent and nothing can keep them from being so. The more vigorous and worth while they are the more independent they will be, *but they are not being trained for it.* They are going out as though independence were an easy matter to handle, whereas of all fine arts it is the finest and most difficult. Life is like a tree—every time new branches come there must be stronger roots. And youth in our generation has branched out—one can fairly lie awake at night and hear it branch out—into new liberties, new responsibilities, new self-expressions beyond the power of any to prevent.

People sometimes talk as though this expansion of life into new liberties were a substitute for religion and made it less necessary. One might as well talk about branches being a substitute for roots. Branches *require* roots. How can we drive that lesson home on our young people and on their parents? There never could have been a generation before which more specifically and crucially needed training in the meaning and handling of independence.

Every summer when I go up to my Maine island I find some trees that have blown down—too many branches above ground and not enough rootage below ground. And every fall when I come back to New York I find some lives that have broken down for the same reason—too much strain, not enough staunchness; too much modern life, not enough deep religion. Some of you who are not conventionally religious but who do care about the moral welfare of this nation may well listen to John Ruskin on the downfall of Venice. "The decline," he says, "of her political prosperity was exactly coincident with that of domestic and individual religion." Just so! What about the church in your house?

Mankind's Deep Need—the Sense of Community

A SINGLE look at the world reveals how deplorably we are split up into fragmentary and conflicting individuals and groups. We often say that this is a crazy world, and in the literal meaning of that word it is true, for crazy comes from the French, *écrasé*, which means broken and shattered. We human beings ought to be a co-operative community, using the resources of this planet for the common good, and we are not.

In practically every service of public worship in the church we employ the Lord's Prayer, but how many have clearly noted one of its most outstanding characteristics: "When ye pray," say, "Our." "Our Father . . . our daily bread . . . our debts . . . our debtors." If one supposes that that communal emphasis is due to Jesus' intention that the prayer should be used only in public when the disciples were together, recall, upon the contrary, that he just had said to them: "When thou prayest, enter into thy closet, and when thou hast shut thy door, pray to thy Father which is in secret." Even there, where each was alone, each was to say not simply I, and mine, but our.

No more vital problem confronts humanity today than learning to say *that*. Human life is caught now between two contending currents—on the one side, the unifying forces that create proximity; on the other, the disruptive forces that prevent community. Is there any greater tragedy in life, whether in a family or in a world, than thus to have proximity without community? Sometimes on the Maine Coast the stormy wind blows in from the open sea at the same time that the tide flows out from the great tidal rivers that indent the shore. Then let the boatmen look to themselves! There is tumult in the waters when those contending forces meet.

So today from one side come the countless agencies that produce proximity. Once Daniel Boone, the Western frontiersman, saw new settlers passing near his isolated cabin, and he asked the travelers where they were living. When the answer came that they were about seventy miles away, Boone turned to his wife and said: "Old woman, we must move; they are crowding us." As for nations, how great the distances once seemed, but now see how inextricably intertangled all peoples are! Proximity confronts the world. While, however, countless forces thus crowd us together, many tear us apart: economic forces, breaking us up into angry and competing groups; specializations, disrupting us into countless fragmentary tasks; racial antipathies, making us hate one another; national hostilities, making us fight one another; and through all these the moral factors, envy, covetousness, prejudice, and all uncharitableness, that prevent community.

In this situation, thrown together by some forces and disrupted by others, one thing is obvious. We cannot unscramble ourselves. We cannot go back to the old days of isolation. When a river has flowed down from the Adirondacks to Poughkeepsie, it cannot flow back again. There is only one way out of the situation—forward, through proximity into community. Moreover, at our best we ought not to want to go back. The most desirable blessings in human life come from fellowship, from beautifully putting things together with a right sense of their community. God cried to hydrogen and oxygen, Say our! and when they learned aright the principle of community, water came, and rain, and dew, and the sea, and the Yosemite. Creation itself, whether in God's nature or in man's art, consists in putting things together in a community. They say that in Wagner's opera *Die Walküre* there are a million notes, but what makes the opera great is the way the artist combined these isolated items into a community and cried, Say our! What thus is true in nature and in art is true in human life. The loveliest fellowship man knows is a good home, and there we say not I, and you, but we, and our. From a solar system or an elm tree to a symphony or a stained glass window, or from these to a lovely family or a fraternal world, putting things beautifully together is the essence of creation and the glory of life.

Let us throw the light of this truth upon certain areas in our experience today, and first of all upon the discouraged mood of many who feel that human nature is so essentially selfish that we never can build a communal life. It is natural, they think, for man to say I, and my. Self-preservation is the basic instinct, they say; and to teach men on a large scale to say we, and our, is artificial, like teaching gorillas to eat at table with a knife and fork; you can do that with a few gorillas, but it does not go deep—still, they are gorillas. So man, behind his superficial co-operation, they say, is still an egocentric animal, saying I, and my! To which I answer, Do you really think that that is a complete statement? One need not minimize the power of egocentricity in human nature to think that statement unbalanced. Alongside this deep-seated selfishness in man, just as deep-seated and original is something else—the need of comradeship. A lonely child, wanting companions, said once to his mother: "Mother, I wish that I were two little puppies, so that I could play together." That childish remark is, nonetheless, psychologically profound. Said the old Latin proverb: "One man is no man at all."

What, for example, is the basic element from which, so the anthropologists say, stems out practically every characteristic factor in human life? Language. This it is, they say, which marked evolving man off from the animals and blazed the trail of his ascending life. And what is language? It is man's persistent endeavor to escape from his solitariness, to discover a world of companions, to create a device of communication so that he may have comrades with whom he can think together, speak together, play together, plan together, and build a communal life. That instinct of comradeship is as deep-seated and original in man as is his selfishness.

Indeed, before man, it began among the animals. Listen superficially to the animals, and you might suppose that they were saying, There is barely enough food to go around; what I get you lose; what you get I lose; there is between us an unavoidable antipathy; we are natural enemies. But lift your thought even a little, and it is as though the animals were saying, It may be we were mistaken; it may be that our mutual antagonisms are superficial and our common interests profound; it may be that if you and I were blended into we, we could do more for all of us together than either you or I could do for each of us alone. So bees hive, and ants build colonies, and birds flock, and wolves hunt in packs. The solitary ichthyosaurs, the giants of the primeval slime, have perished, but the birds, the bees, the ants, have survived—the co-operators, who learned to say Our.

Shall we human beings, then, say that we are so selfish we cannot build a communal life? Shall we not rather say that selfishness itself leads us to a communal life? We want physical health for ourselves, but that is no longer an individual matter alone but a communal matter. Epidemics know no boundary lines. We can have health only if the community shares it. Our deepest needs are of that quality. From good drinking water, which is not a matter of our individual wells but of the communal reservoir, to the morals of our children, which are not the fruit of our influence alone but of the whole bent and trend of the community's life, our self-interest and our sense of community involve each other. We want peace; our individual lives are torn by war, and our children's world is threatened by its impending consequence; but we cannot get that alone as individuals or as nations—that is a matter of building a world community. Let no man say we are too selfish to get a communal life! Let him say, rather, that if our selfishness has any intelligent understanding of the realistic facts, it will lead us to a communal life. We cannot have anything we want most unless we share it. We cannot be saved at all unless we are saved together. We are one body with many members. We had better say Our!

Let us throw the light of this truth upon another area of our experience—our religion. For here is a major shame, of which we Christians ought to repent: Whereas religion ought to help unify men, it divides them instead. An honest preacher would not wish to go further with this subject without facing that fact. Someone, hearing this plea for community against human alienations and estrangements, may well be saying, So! but what the preacher represents—religion—is one of the worst causes of discord in the world. "Physician, heal thyself!" Have not the worst wars been religious wars? Remember the Irishman, weary of the long feud between Catholics and Protestants in his country, who cried: "Would that all Irishmen were atheists so that we could live together like Christians." As for America, look at our religious divisions spoiling fraternity. Wanted: a religion that will stop accentuating human alienations, and help the world say Our! "Our Father . . . our daily bread . . . our trespasses"!

How familiar is the kind of person in whom religion instinctively results in his saying I, and my—*my* church, *my* doctrines, *my* prejudices—and then, looking across the boundary to folk of another tradition, he says They—*they* with their mistakes and falsehoods. But once in a while we meet a man whose religion is of another quality and consequence, who, dealing with any human life, Catholic, Protestant, Jew, Hindu, or Moslem, shows an inclusive spirit that says Our.

Commonly when this plea is made for magnanimity, inclusiveness, generosity in religion, some think that it is a plea for a thinned-out faith of surrendered personal convictions. Upon the contrary, it is a plea to get down to the two basic convictions of all great religion. What are they?

First, one God! Sometimes I think I will stop preaching about everything except monotheism. It is basic. Everybody says he believes it, and practically nobody does—not really. Most people seem to think that monotheism moves chiefly in the intellectual realm—that it is a philosophy. But that is historically false as to its origin, and morally shallow as to its consequence. Monotheism came up in the Old Testament out of social struggle, racial antipathy, and war. It was the insight of great prophets proclaiming that across all human alienations there was *one* God, and every son of man his child. "Have we not all one father?" cried the prophet. "Hath not one God created us? why do we deal treacherously every man against his brother?" That is monotheism. Across all lines that men have drawn, it goes, saying first of all and deepest of all: "Have we not all one father?"

The other basic conviction in great religion is the value of every personality. Some kinds of individualism break life up into fragments, but not this kind of individualism, Jesus' kind, which reaches beneath all divisions and lifts up every life, whether Jew or Greek, Scythian, barbarian, bond or free, saying, You are a child of God, a person of infinite value. That breaks down all boundaries and opens the door to a universal humanity. How desperately we need that kind of religion now. Almost every other influence in life makes us think of people in fragmentary groups. The two sexes, old and young, employer and employee, white and black, rich and poor, educated and uneducated—how split up we are! And then, to have a religion that not only accentuates these differences but furnishes a whole new category of sectarianisms and partisanships is tragic. Great religion goes down beneath all these divisions, lifts up every man into the light, saying, You are a son of the one God, and a brother in the one family.

When we plead for that kind of religion, we are not pleading for a thinned-out and washed-down faith of surrendered convictions. We are pleading for a religion that has gotten itself grounded on a firm foundation, sustained by the two pillars that upheld the whole structure of Christ's life—one God, our Father; every man sacred, our brother.

Let us turn the light of this truth upon another area of our experience—democracy. Democracy consists in saying Our. That is what it is. Autocracy says, My government; democracy consists in all the populace saying, Our government. The despot says, My people; democracy says, Our people. Today we are seeing democracy assailed by powerful enemies from without, but still I suspect the graver dangers are within. Our democracy is deplorably broken up into competing and estranged groups—economic, social, racial, industrial, religious. The splintering forces are dominant. One feels the granulation of American life. No attack on American democracy from without can ever wreck it unless within we forget how to say Our!

If within our democracy we are going to save ourselves from this peril, there must be some major shifts of emphasis in our American life in these years ahead.

For one thing, concerning the family. It is in a good home that we human beings first of all learn to say Our. A family does not start with an individual but with a trinity—father, mother, child—each one saying not so much I, and they, but we, and our. We cannot have a nation of communally minded men and women, taking within the compass of their care the needs of others as though they were their own, unless we have a nation of good homes, where that spirit gets its initial start and its vital nurture. I sometimes wonder whether we are not going to see a movement of reaction on the part of womanhood against some of the major trends of this last generation that have carried many women far away from home-making, in one of the most significant migrations in all history. I would not surrender a single gain of all the many that have been won this last century by woman's strike for freedom to enter every realm of human endeavor and prove her mettle. But today the deep necessities of our social life, and the profound, inalienable needs and aptitudes of womanhood itself, suggest a compensating movement of balance and counterpoise. One way or another, we must exalt the home—the most indispensable unit in our society. For everybody who ever has learned really to say Our, learned it in the first place as Jesus did in Nazareth, in the holy family.

If we are to save our democracy from this inner granulation, we must have another shift of emphasis, from a too great content with the motive of private profit, to a more inclusive care for the economic well-being of the whole community. How terribly our financial inequalities split us up into antagonistic groups! Sometimes I think it sheer hypocrisy on Sunday morning to repeat the Lord's Prayer here—"Our daily bread." Every significant economic movement in the world today is dealing, one way or another, with this problem—how to escape the old, out-dated, too-individualistic, *laissez faire* economy, every man for himself and the devil take the hindmost, which splits us up into angry groups—how to find a way to meet our common needs together. Communism is about that, and socialism, and the cooperatives, yes, and corporate capitalism itself, gathering together industry in great units and distributing ownership. One way or another, economic proximity forces on us all the problem of economic community. Just because we hate communism, rightly fear it as a false and perilous solution, let us not forget the towering problem itself. Our democracy never will be safe until it is economic as well as political, until our daily business draws us together around common interests instead of splitting us apart, until all the people can really pray: "Our daily bread."

Whatever we do with our homes and our economics, there is still another area where we need a shift of emphasis. We must exalt at the heart of this nation a unifying spiritual tradition. Democracy can survive powerful centrifugal pulls, if it has the centripetal pull of a unifying spiritual tradition—speaking the same language, loving the same great literature, holding memories of the same past, believing in the same God, cherishing the same scale of moral values. My fellow citizens, look to that, if you wish to keep our democracy together.

When in the last century de Tocqueville, the French aristocrat, visited us, he expected to see democracy a failure, and to his amazement he found it working. He put his finger on this central cause. These Americans, he said in effect, amid all the things that divide and estrange them, have great areas in common—a common spiritual tradition, a common faith, a common scale of moral values—and when they debate their differences, they debate them within the area of an undergirding and inclusive community of ideas and ideals.

When the assault of communism and naziism on democracy from without is spent, still these problems will be left. O America, look to the things you have in common. You can be strong only as you learn how to say Our!

Finally, throw the light of this truth upon our private lives. We as individuals never can deeply help anybody unless we say Our. A mother smitten with blindness, appreciating the goodness of her son, phrased her gratitude thus: "It is not so much that he does things for me, as that he fixes things so that we can do them together." No deep personal need is ever met with less than that.

That is one reason why trouble often leaves a life more useful than it was before, for after facing hardship a man can lay his life alongside another life and say We, and our. A man in great despair came to see me some time since, and as he started on his story I recognized my own great despair, the deepest trouble that I ever met, suffered years ago. So, as he began to tell me how he felt, I said: "Don't you tell me how you feel; let me tell you!" So I drew for him a blueprint of all that was going on in his mind and heart. In amazement he looked at me and said: "My God, how did you know that?" So he and I were on common ground, and I could help him, saying, We, and our. Among your personal relationships are some people whom you so could help. They are on your wave length, friend! *They are on your wave length!* You could say Our, with them, if you would.

Some years ago a young man went down to Panama with a business group, fell into bad habits, drank too much, until his derelictions become too obvious to be winked at and the chief summoned him to an interview. The youth went up trembling. He had a wife and children back home here. He knew he well deserved to be fired. He was frightened. But someone who chanced to hear the conclusion of the conversation says it ran like this: "Son," said the chief, "we are not going to drink any more, are we?" "No sir," said the youth, "we are not." "And each week we are going to send so much money back to the wife and children, aren't we?" "By heaven, sir," said the boy, "we will!"

You can tell how fine a thing is by the qualities that it requires. What does it take in a man to say I, and they? Pride, conceit, vanity, callousness, selfishness—such qualities can say I, and they. What does it take to say Our? Humility, magnanimity, generosity, kindness, humaneness, unselfishness. You never meet a finer thing on earth than a person who thus incarnates the Lord's Prayer: "Our Father . . . our daily bread . . . our debts . . . our debtors . . . lead us not into temptation . . . deliver us from evil."

Modern Civilization's Crucial Problem

THE life of each one of us is divided into two factors—the means by which we live and the ends for which we live—and nothing enters much more deeply into determining the quality of a man or an era than the handling of those two factors. This is easily illustrated in terms of the generation as a whole. The fact distinguishing our day from previous times is obviously our mastery over the scientific means of life. One after another the forces of the universe, from steam to the impalpable vibrations of the ether, have been harnessed for our service, until we possess, as no previous age even in its dreams possessed, the means of living. But when we turn our thought from the means by which we live to the ends for which we live, are we so sure that we are on a correspondingly higher level than our fathers?

One remembers the Periclean Age in Greece, when around the Acropolis a people small in numbers but great in mind first created and then preserved from the impinging barbarism a culture that ever since has been an inexhaustible treasury for the Western world. When we think of the means by which they lived, they were crudely primitive, but when we think of the things for which they lived—Praxiteles and Phidias, Æschylus and Sophocles and Plato—Athens moves up into a position in the spiritual history of man that New York and Chicago may never achieve.

Or one remembers a little group of disciples around a Teacher in Galilee. The means by which they lived were crude indeed. A donkey provided the swiftest method of travel that they ever tried. Their houses of one room with two small windows and probably no chimney, where the family slept on an upper platform and the beasts slept on the floor, were roughed out of native stone or sun-dried brick

—hovels to live in, poverty-stricken conditions to live under. But when one thinks of the ends for which they lived, ah, my soul!

Everywhere, when we compare ourselves with previous generations with reference to our means for living, we are supreme, but whenever we turn our attention to the ends for which we live, a different picture presents itself. "Improved means to an unimproved end"—how much of our modern life is summarized in that shrewd phrase of Thoreau! We often jestingly recognize this contrast between means and ends as when, for example, we laughed at Voliva of Zion City using the radio to tell the world that the earth is flat. So when the Atlantic cable first was laid, Thoreau, in protest against the popular enthusiasm, said that probably the first use made of it would be to let us know that Princess Adelaide had whooping cough. We do jokingly recognize the contrast between amazing instruments and the trivial uses to which they can be put. How many of us, however, have dropped our plummets deeper into this important matter, improved means to an unimproved end?

The movies, for example, are a marvelous invention and sometimes they are beautifully used. They could be very beautifully used. Yet we all know into what crass, commercialized, conscienceless hands a wide area of movie production has fallen, so that this amazing instrument, teaching boys and girls through their eyes, the swiftest way by which any of us learns anything, is being deliberately used to make vice attractive and dress licentiousness in charm—improved means to an unimproved end.

In our campaign for disarmament, we often remind ourselves how very crude and primitive ancient battles were. The Greeks won Marathon with ten thousand men and lost only one hundred and ninety of them; the charge of the Light Brigade involved only six hundred cavalry; even Napoleon at Austerlitz led seventy thousand French and lost but eight thousand. Now, however, forces are in the hands of military power that in a few hours could depopulate London and Paris of their millions, and the next war, if it comes, will no longer see champion against champion or mere army against army, but whole populations against whole populations—improved means to an unimproved end.

That phrase comes as near as any I know to stating the crucial problem of modern civilization. Ever since James Watt made his steam engine and the era of scientific inventiveness got well under way, we have been absorbing ourselves in the creation, accumulation, elaboration, multiplication of the means of living. But that second matter cannot longer be kept in the background. It crowds up into the front. It is the crux of the situation today. Unless we can reestablish the spiritual ends of living in personal character and social justice, our civilization will ruin itself with the misuse of its own instruments. And just as soon as we begin thinking about the spiritual ends of life we are thinking of religion.

Why is it, indeed, that in this last generation so many people have supposed that they could get on without religion? It is because this last generation has been absorbed in the provision of more means by which to live and that is not religion's realm. When some one says today that the dominant interest of our time is not religion but science, he speaks the truth. That is the fact, and it is the fact because the dominant interest of our time has been the provision of more means by which to live, which is the realm of science. But it is not the function of science to provide the ends for which we live. That is another matter. That is a man's philosophy of life, his spiritual ideals, his religion. What is a generation profited if it gains the whole world of means by which to live and loses its soul, the spiritual ends for which to live?

That is the text we are talking on. That is the voice of religion as it was the voice of Christ. And, mark it! this generation cannot dodge that question. Everywhere we turn, it faces us. Every road we travel on, it meets us. It besets us before and behind and lays its hand upon us. What is a man profited if he gain the whole world and lose the end, the soul?

Before we are through answering that question, we shall have a revival of spiritual life. It is coming. We may hasten it; we may delay it; but no group of men, and I think no set of ideas, can permanently stop it. We shall have a revival of religion.

Of course, I can imagine objectors who will protest against this statement. Let us consider them.

One person, for example, may say, There is going to be no revival of religion; no likelihood exists that this generation will ask searching questions about the spiritual ends of life, because we are too satisfied with the enjoyment of these new and fascinating means of living. To this I answer, Not so satisfied as on the surface might appear. No city was ever so richly equipped with the scientific means of living as New York. Does it strike you as preëminently happy and satisfied? Upon the contrary!

If you should hear about some individual man that he had a million dollars a year and could buy what he wanted, what is the first question that would rise in your mind? I know the first question that would rise in mine: I wonder if he is happy. Suppose we heard that he had a town house and a country house, a yacht, a fleet of automobiles, and was served by all the ingenuities that science has devised; I still would wonder—Is he happy?

But if you should hear about some man that he had found his work and loved it, that he was creating some beauty, doing something useful, and would rather put himself into that than anything else in the world, you would not wonder. You know that *is* happiness. Happiness is not primarily a matter of the means by which we live; it is a matter of the spiritual end for which we live.

If you should hear even about a humble man that he loved people, that like Peter he had a healing shadow, that like a river he had found his channel, like a garden the fruit that he could grow, like a lantern the dark places of the earth where his light was needed, you would know that he was happy. You do not wonder whether Jesus was happy; you can see he was.

Consider, then, our generation as a whole—long on the means of living, it may be, but short on happiness. For we are not dogs to be satisfied when a few bones are flung to us, though they be automobiles and subways, electric lights and airplanes. There is something else in us that makes the very essence of our humanity; we have to live *for* something. The deepest hell that some of us could ever fall into would be to have everything to live with and nothing to live for.

If this is the law of our being, one by one, do you suppose that the generation is under another law? Statisticians have estimated that a century ago the average man had 72 wants, of which 16 were regarded as necessities, but that today the average man has 484 wants, 94 of which are regarded as necessities, and that, moreover, whereas a century ago 200 articles were urged upon the average man by salesmanship, now 32,000 articles are urged on us. I do not belittle all that. The means by which we live is the underpinning of existence, but it is not the secret of happiness. That is a matter of finding something worth while to live for.

I appeal to your experience. Have you found something worth living for, some beauty to create, some goodness to achieve, some truth to discover, some spiritual aim to give yourself to? If not, you are not happy and not all the accumulation of the means of life can make you happy. What profit, even in happiness, if a man gain this whole modern world of means and lose the soul? The discovery of that fact means a revival of spiritual life.

In the second place, I can imagine a man saying, No, we are not going to have anything like a revival of religion; the materialistic philosophy was never more in the saddle than it is today; what Russia is doing officially against religion millions are doing personally; the atheistic philosophy has swept the intelligentsia along and carried in its wake wide sections of popular opinion. Just so, I answer. That is one reason why we are going to have a revival of religion. For in any generation when a few people merely play with the materialistic philosophy of life, it can remain attractive, but when multitudes go after it, when it is so successful that it begins to reveal, as it does now, all that it thinks, and to show just where it leads, then a reaction is due.

The great triumphs of materialism have been Pyrrhic victories; they defeated themselves. If, therefore, you say that in this last generation the materialistic philosophy has carried off a resounding victory, I answer, That is what is going to ruin it, for when the materialistic philosophy has its swing and goes its limit, it carries us out into a senseless world, full, it may be, of means to live by, but with nothing much in it worth living for.

It carries one out, for example, into an intellectually senseless world. You would not take a billion cards and put a letter on each and throw them up into the northwest wind, expecting them to fall together so as to make sense. You would not expect out of all those billion cards even ten to fall together to make a sentence like "This is a cat." The chance of that happening would be negligible; yet they try to tell us that protons and electrons, by themselves, fortuitously have fallen together into law-abiding stellar systems, into human personality and social progress. That is believing in sheer magic. As Professor Montague of the Department of Philosophy in Columbia says, the chance of that being true would have to be represented by a fraction with 1 for the numerator and a denominator that would extend from here to one of the fixed stars. Give it enough rope and the materialistic philosophy hangs itself, for it leads out into an intellectually senseless world.

Worse than that, however, it leads out into a spiritually senseless world. Life it not mostly theory; it is mostly something else. For one thing, it is hardship. Not only do troubles come very deep, but love comes also, deeper yet, binding us up into one bundle of life with other people so that what happens to them happens to us, and

> . . . he who lives more lives than one
> More deaths than one must die.

How often a man wishes he had genuine spiritual life, not so much for his own sake as for the sake of another for whom he cares!

> Old Mother Hubbard,
> Went to the cupboard,
> To get her poor Dog a bone,
> But when she came there,
> The cupboard was bare,
> And so the poor Dog had none.

Queer nursery jingle, but there is depth in it, for even when a man cares about a poor dog, he does want a bone in his cupboard. And when it is not a poor dog but a child, a boy or girl going out to live in this difficult generation, how a man does hate that bare cupboard of his own soul, empty of the spiritual life which comes alone from high things to live for! For what can you give a child worth giving to a child at all if you cannot give something beautiful to live for?

See, then, this cycle that humanity is traveling around, which it has traveled more than once before. A generation starts doubting, doubts the church and the creeds, doubts God and immortality, doubts that there is any purpose in the universe at all or any goal ahead, doubts all the bases of idealistic living, and then, having stripped life of spiritual significance, it begins to doubt its doubts. Like the fabled serpent, disbelief turns and eats itself. The generation cannot even have faith in its own lack of faith. Then the reaction is due. When a materialistic age gets a materialistic philosophy, though it be fabulously rich in the means by which to live, it begins to say, What profit!

Nevertheless, I can imagine one more objector saying, No, nothing like a revival of religion is coming; look at the moral situation—to which I answer, Look at it. War always brings a long aftermath of moral looseness. We might suppose that war would sober people, and war does sober some. That English mother who had three sons fighting on three fronts and on the same day received from the British War Office three letters telling her that all her sons were dead was probably sobered.

After the first world war the Prince of Wales went into one of those hospitals where they keep the utter wrecks—one whole ward filled with men whose faces had been shot away. They begged the Prince not to look at the six worst cases, and when he had seen five of them they fairly insisted that he should not see the last, but he did—nothing left of the man's face except a bit of the forehead—and, white as a sheet, the Prince bowed down and kissed all that remained of the brow. There are sobering things about war.

But the total effect of war is not sobering. Only sentimentalists with no knowledge of the rudiments of psychology suppose it is. People as a whole when they face a terrific situation flee from it psychologically into excitement, wildness, hectic sensuality, drunkenness—anything to make an emotional escape from the pressure of an intolerable situation. Then, when millions of people are making a flight into excitement and wildness, millions of others flock after them and the inevitable next step comes on apace: a philosophy, namely, to rationalize it all—sex-mad psychoanalytic theories, supposedly learned books about the glories of extra-marital relationships and the general advisability of moral looseness and the appalling danger of being decent and self-controlled.

Do not suppose that because on Sunday you see a minister in a black gown perched in the carved pulpit of a Gothic church, that he does not know. A working minister can sometimes see more of the seamy side of life in a week than a roué sees in a month, for the roué may see only his own rottenness, but the minister in intimate disclosure will see the deep and varied iniquity of many.

If, therefore, you say, Look at the moral situation! I answer, Look at it. What do you argue from it? If you argue that it is going on and on from bad to worse you have all history against you. Inevitably the pendulum swings. Did you happen to see that recent cartoon—a mother with all the obvious signs of flapperishness from indecent dress up, the very picture of emancipated modernity, and beside her a daughter looking demure, decent, and sensible? The daughter is saying, Mother, do stop trying to be so modern, it is all out of date! Just so!

The dean of one of our foremost colleges recently said that the tide already had turned and in place of the sophistication, the blasé cynicism, the wild experimentation of these recent years, there was coming a renaissance of natural eagerness, earnestness, and idealism. I am not half so anxious about some of this younger generation, in which I think are many of the finest youths this world has ever had, as I am about some of you older ones, the left-overs and relics of the war psychology.

All around us in New York we see families where, if the fathers and mothers would straighten up, aye, if they would sober up, there would be little to worry about among the children.

My friends, this generation is not going to escape the question of our Lord. We may make money and become rich, multiply our means of pleasure, grow wild, tear self-control from the throne and put license there, but up from the gates of the dawn there comes another generation to assess us with discerning eyes. What profit if we lose the soul?

If a genuine revival of spiritual life should really come, what could we not do with this world? When I say a revival of religion, of course I do not mean emotionalism, ecclesiasticism, creedalism—God forbid!

I mean a revival of ethical Christianity that will lay its hand on these amazing modern means and dedicate them to human good. There never was such a chance in history. Our ancient forefathers were in comparison poverty-stricken. They always lived under the fear of penury and famine. They never had the means to carry through their dreams, but we have. Our hands are full of scientific means, and see what we are doing with them! The trouble is not with our means; it is with our ends—and there is no cure for that difficulty except the revival of genuine Christianity with effective intellect to make it work.

For this is the conclusion of the matter. Those who are saying that Jesus is done for, that he is going, not coming, that he is a first-century Palestinian and outgrown, face the surprise of their lives if they live long enough to see it. What has Jesus to do, they say, with an age of subways, airplanes, electric lights, and automobiles? What can he tell us about right and wrong in a machine age that he could not even dream? To this I answer, In so far true! Jesus has no direct contribution to make to the means by which we live, but I should be doing a great piece of business in some consciences here, if I could make them listen to Jesus about the ends of life. That is his realm. What are you living *for*? What profit if a man gain this whole modern world of means and lose the soul?

How Believe in a Good God in a World Like This?

WE FACE an old question this morning: How can we believe in a good God in a world like this? Job confronted it ages ago, and Sophocles wondered how the gods could look complacently down on so much suffering and pain. Our generation feels afresh what Keats called "the giant agony of the world." How shall we reconcile an all-good and all-powerful God with earthquakes and cyclones, cholera and cancer, the long ruthlessness of the evolutionary process, ills like insanity that fall on individuals even at their birth, and all the welter of lust, poverty, and war, that human life involves? We come to church to sing the praises of the all-great and all-good God, but in how many hearts the question rises, How can he be all-good and all-great if he made a world like this?

Our difficulty in dealing with this problem is accentuated by the fact that the higher our concept of God, the more perplexity we face. If we could be polytheists, believing in many gods, then we could blame life's good and evil on the various deities. If we could be Zoroastrians and believe in two gods, one of light and one of darkness, one all benevolence and one all malice, then we could blame life's evil on the evil god. When, however, we believe in one God, our Father, all-powerful and all-good, we face perplexity. Arson is a crime among men, but the Creator habitually looses lightning and volcanoes that burn up men's habitations. Murder is a crime among men, but the Creator habitually looses earthquakes that slay multitudes. Poisoning is a crime among men, but the Creator makes the cobra and viper. As has often been noted, the Creator habitually does on a vast scale things for which men are sent to prison or executed. The first effect of Christian faith in a God of love is not to solve this problem but to state it in its most difficult form. To believe in one God, all-good and all-powerful, makes the cruelty of life hard to understand.

No easy escape from this problem is possible by blaming the evil on man's sin. Man's sin is responsible for many evils, and if man could be redeemed to decency this world would be a far happier place; but man is not responsible for the long ruthlessness of the evolutionary process, or for lightning, volcanoes, earthquakes, or for disease germs, or for the planetary setting of human life with the inevitable struggle that it involves. The Creator must bear his heavy share of responsibility. Why, then, we do believe in a good God?

Of course, one reason is that when we decide not to believe in a good God because of the world's evil, we discover that far from solving any problem we have merely jumped from the frying pan into the fire. It is difficult to explain the presence of evil in the world of a good God, but to some of us it is impossible to explain the goodness in the world on the basis of no God. One, for example, looking at Calvary, may center his attention on the cross alone, saying, There can be no good God in a world where such unjust cruelty befalls; or he may center his attention on Christ upon the cross, saying, There must be a good God in a world that produces him. There is more than the mystery of evil here to explain—there is the mystery of good.

Once I decided that I could not believe in the goodness of God in the presence of the world's evil, and then discovered that I had run headlong into another and even more difficult problem: What to do about all the world's goodness on the basis of no God? Sunsets and symphonies, mothers, music, and the laughter of children at play, great books, great art, great science, great personalities, victories of goodness over evil, the long, hard-won ascent from the Stone Age up, and all the friendly spirits that are to other souls a "cup of strength in some great agony"—how can we, thinking of these on the basis of no God, explain them as the casual, accidental by-products of physical forces going it blind? I think it cannot be done. The mystery of evil is very great upon the basis of a good God, but the mystery of goodness is impossible upon the basis of no God.

Most of us have seen the Great Stone Face on the New Hampshire mountain, that Nathaniel Hawthorne made famous, carved by cosmic weathering. That face came as the accidental by-product of physical forces going it blind. But we have known other faces—in our families, and among our friends, and others still—that, like the Christ, have revealed to us divinity itself, and for which that explanation is inadequate. To say that those faces came from casual cosmic weathering, that they are the accidental by-products of aimless atoms, presents us with a sheer absurdity in comparison with which the problem of evil pales.

Our ultimate decision in this matter depends largely on where we center our emphasis. Blindness and deafness fall upon a little child, and we instinctively cry, No good God would allow a thing like that! But then we shift our emphasis to Helen Keller herself, upon whom the blindness and the deafness fell, her spirit, her faith, her courage, her victory, standing a few years ago in the University of Glasgow to receive an honorary degree, and saying of the honor: "It is a sign that darkness and silence need not bar the progress of the immortal spirit." Some people center their attention on the physical affliction, and say, There can be no good God! Some of us cannot lose sight of Helen Keller herself, and say, There must be a good God! Moreover, when you ask Helen Keller—as so often happens when you think not of sympathetic spectators who look on trouble, but of those who bear it—that is what she says too.

This, then, is the first reason why some of us believe in the good God. The problem of evil is very difficult when we believe in a good God, but the problem of goodness seems to us impossible when we do not.

Another reason encourages us to believe in the good God, namely, that as we have grown older, we have come to take mystery for granted, not to resent it as much as we used to, and not to expect to crowd the explanation of an infinite universe within the confines of a limited mind. Listen to this from a contemporary scientist: "At the present day the scientific universe is more mysterious than it has ever been before in the history of thought." To be sure it is! And if that is true of the physical cosmos, how much more true of this realm where our thought is moving.

If a man lays it down as a precondition of his believing in the good God that he must get an explanation that will answer all questions and solve all problems, he might as well stop where he is, for there is no such explanation, theistic or atheistic.

I can remember in my early years bitterly resenting this mystery of evil, this weird, uncanny, cruel incidence of unexplained suffering. It still troubles me. I have no formula that solves it all. My father used to say that the chief reason why he wanted to go to heaven was that he might get God off in a corner and ask him some questions. I agree! Still, I do not resent the mystery as I once did. Any way you take it, this is a mysterious universe. Always it presents itself to us in terms of a strange dualism—light and darkness, right and wrong, good and evil, happiness and pain, life and death. Everything comes in opposites. All the great religions have so pictured life in terms of conflict. Hinduism called it a conflict between reality and illusion; Zoroastrianism a conflict between light and darkness; Platonism a conflict between spirit and matter; traditional Judaism and Christianity a conflict between God and Satan. Behind this dualism we believe that somehow there is monism, that this is a *uni*verse, springing from one power; but in actual experience it presents itself as a dualism.

If, in that dualism, a man starts by believing that the basic and creative element is evil, how does he explain good? How did such goodness as we know ever come to pass in a world where the basic element is evil? But if a man starts with the conviction that the basic and creative element is good, then, while he faces the mystery of evil, it still may be true that good can yet surmount it, rise above it, transmute its lead into gold—yes, more than that, use it until as from some travail shall come a birth worth all that it has cost. This is what faith in the good God means. Cried Paul: "The whole creation groaneth and travaileth in pain together until now." Paul knew *that* as well as any evolutionary scientist. Creation is travail, he said, but it is waiting for a birth, the "revealing of the sons of God." Faith in the good God means this daring confidence. It is no neat, slick, varnished creed, as it sometimes seems to be when it is repeated in a church. It is a great venture of faith in a universe deeply mysterious, whose basic element is not evil but good.

For still another reason some of us are encouraged to believe in the good God, namely, that what we call evil, pain, tragedy, plays a positive role in life. There may be more sense in it than at first we think. When we complain against the tragedy of life, what are we asking for? A world that shall be all ease, pleasure, and happiness? There are hours when we would welcome that. We are fed up with trouble. We have seen too many tragedies that crush the lives and souls of men with no conceivable good consequence. Yet if even in such indignant and rebellious hours I were offered a chance to go to the traditional heaven, all pearly gates and golden streets, endless idleness and singing, nothing hard to undertake or difficult to do, I should shrink back. I should be dead sick of that within a week. Everybody knows that strange factor in human nature that made MacMillan, the explorer, say after a terrific twelvemonth with Peary in the Arctic: "This has been the grandest year of my life." Everything most worth-while in our living has come out of a background of struggle against obstacles.

Look again, then, at this tragic world about which we complain. All the suffering we bear comes from four factors. Out of four factors, singly or conjointly working, comes every ill that falls on human life.

First, the law-abidingness of the universe. How much trouble comes from that! If we break the law of gravitation, we suffer. No cosmic law ever slips its leash.

Second, the evolutionary nature of the world. Life always starts us in a low and ill estate, and makes us fight our way up toward a better. We are introduced into an unfinished world, and called on painfully to help complete it. We are started with animal nature, ignorance, superstition, poverty, war, and with faith and valor have to struggle out toward something better. How much suffering comes from that!

Third, the power of moral choice. It is not unlimited, but it is real. We are not mere automata. We can choose. And that power of initiative can be misused. How much trouble comes from that!

Fourth, the intermeshed relationships of human life. We are not set like bottles in the rain in solitary endurance of our fate. We are interrelated. We flow into one another. We are members one of another, and as individuals and nations our woes, problems, and tragedies spill over from one into the other's life. We are intermeshed in an inescapable mutuality. How much of human tragedy comes from that!

Every suffering that falls on man comes from the single or conjoint operation of those four factors. The law-abiding universe, the progressiveness of human society, the individual power of choice, the intermeshed mutuality of living—there is no tragedy that does not spring from them. Yet if you had omnipotence for an hour, would you eliminate from the universe a single one of them? Would you make this universe whimsical and capricious and not law-abiding? Would you make it static, like Aladdin's palace, made by magic for lazy occupancy, and not progressive? Would you make human beings mechanical automata with no power to choose? Would you tear us apart from our relationships and leave us like bottles in the rain, freed from those ties that make life beautiful? Everything worth-while in life also comes from these same four factors whence its tragedies spring.

We are not pretending that this is a complete theoretical explanation of the problem of evil. There is no such explanation that we can grasp. But considering that if we were granted omnipotence, we would not dare abstract from the structure of the universe a single one of the major factors from which human tragedy comes, we may well look with fresh eyes of hope and courage on this strange, mysterious scene. Maybe it is travail for a birth, vaster in significance than we think—the whole creation groaning and travailing in pain together until now, but with a consequence that shall be worthy of the struggle.

Once more some of us believe in a good God because we long since have given up early childish, naïve ideas of God that once we held. An almighty carpenter, making this world just as he wants it, an omnipotent monarch, sitting on a throne and ruling this world just as he pleases—those are childish pictures of God. If God is an omnipotent monarch who can do anything he pleases, he has no business to please to do some things he does, and permit some things that he allows.

I could not believe in the good God unless I had another way of conceiving him. Deep at the heart of this universe there is a constructive, creative Spirit not ourselves. He has made a cosmos here vast and orderly, whose laws never slip, so unified that they say that even if one lifts one's finger the very stars feel the impulse, so simple that it is all made up of less than a hundred elements, and so intelligible that it fits into mind, and mind fits into it. A constructive, creative power is here, not so much like matter as like mind.

Moreover, that creative power comes to spiritual consequence. He makes not stars alone but souls, not rocks alone but minds. Man is not self-created, but with his spiritual life he too came up out of the source of all things. Einstein's intellect, Shakespeare's genius, Beethoven's beauty, Christ's character—they too are the overflow and consequence of the creative power, and they reveal his quality.

Moreover, this constructive and creative power works out to moral victories. Across the long ages he swings up a spiral, so that for all our low estate one would be a fool who would choose to go back to live in the Stone Age. Again and again in history great evils have won great triumphs, only in the end to find themselves undone and made fools of. Pilate sat in judgment on Jesus, but now Jesus sits in judgment on Pilate. Such strange reversals are the commonplace of history. Countless incidents illustrate Lowell's lines:

Though the cause of Evil prosper, yet 't is Truth alone is strong,

. . . .

Truth forever on the scaffold, Wrong forever on the throne,—
Yet that scaffold sways the future, and, behind the dim unknown,
Standeth God within the shadow, keeping watch above his own.

Moreover, in this vast, creative process, pain is not an accident. It is indispensable. Ever as one moves up in the scale of life, sensitivity increases. No creativity without sensitivity! No music, no art, no sympathy, no character, no social hope, without increased sensitivity. But all increase of sensitivity means increase of capacity for pain. Pain, therefore, is not an intruder in the universe; it is part of the warp and woof of life. No pains, no gains.

When I believe in the good God I believe in that creative, constructive Spirit not ourselves, who makes for righteousness. He is not omnipotent in any popular sense of that word. He cannot make a triangle, the sum of whose angles is not equal to two right angles. He cannot make wrong right, or truth false. He cannot even do with us what he wants to do, if we inwardly and stubbornly resist him. God too has a fight on his hands. He is up against something. We may not phrase his antagonist in terms of the traditional devil, but God is still up against something, in the universe and in ourselves. He has a struggle on his hands. And to believe in him is no neat and finished creed. It is betting one's life on the constructive forces of goodness in this universe against all the evils that sometimes seem to win the victory.

This, then, is the conclusion of the matter. The contribution of Christian faith to the problem of evil has lain not so much in supplying a theory to explain it as in furnishing power to surmount it. Our English friend Maude Royden even says: "I never try to explain evil. If anybody asks me to explain suffering, I say I can't. I say I have a power that can surmount it." Jesus himself never said, I have explained the world, but he did say, I have overcome it.

Early Christianity certainly did not dodge trouble. It started with tragedy in its darkest form. It began with a cross, and a man hanging on it, saying, "My God, my God, why—why hast thou forsaken me?" There never has been an adequate answer to that question. But one thing the cross made plain—that in this world now, and in ourselves if we will have it so, there is a power that can surmount such evil, rise above its tragedy, carry off a victory in the face of it, use it, transmute the symbol of the cruelest punishment the ancient world knew into the symbol of salvation, until the miracle happens of multitudes singing:

> In the cross of Christ I glory,
> Towering o'er the wrecks of time.

The Greatness of God

OUR inherited idea of Deity, it is commonly insisted today, goes back to old Hebrew conceptions born in an ancient land where men still thought the earth flat, with Sheol, the place of the dead, a little way below and the heavens a few miles above. If in our modern world, the complainants say, God is to be credible and intelligible, we must grasp a new and more adequate conception of him, starting from different premises and scaled to different dimensions.

This demand for a more worthy and adequate conception of God has struck many people as news and shocking news at that. As a matter of fact, achieving a worthier idea of God has always been the problem of religion. Only a dead religion can escape it. Every living religion grows and, growing, seeks more adequate conceptions of the Eternal. Indeed, the glory of the Hebrew-Christian tradition lies in having done that—its history can be told in terms of that. Moreover, so far from condescending to the ancient Hebrews, we shall be fortunate if we handle our problem in this realm as courageously and fruitfully as they handled theirs. "The Lord is a great God," said the psalmist. That sounds as though even then they were reaching out for a larger idea of God. Of course they were!

Let us briefly summarize the amazing story of the development of the idea of God in the Hebrew-Christian tradition. Go back to the earliest stages of Hebrew thought, and Jehovah, the God of the Hebrews, is associated with a mountain, Sinai. I have been on top of that mountain, where Jehovah was once supposed to have talked personally with Moses. Sometime I hope to climb Mount Olympus, on whose summit Zeus, the God of the Greeks, was supposed to dwell. The idea is precisely the same. Many a people had a mountain god. So Jehovah on Sinai's top could hide Moses in the cleft of a rock, forbidding him to see his face but allowing him to seek his back.

In such primitive fashion the Hebrews began their idea of God. They even pictured him walking in the garden in the cool of the day and hunting for Adam beneath the trees. But the centuries passed. The Hebrews were in Palestine, which, although it is no larger than Vermont, seemed to them a great land. No longer were they thinking of Jehovah as living on top of distant Sinai. He was with them in Palestine. They worshiped him on every high hill. He filled Canaan. Their idea of him had expanded and grown, and as they thought of that and then thought back to the old conception of God upon Sinai, they said, "The Lord is a great God."

Nevertheless, they did not conceive him as outside of Canaan. No people at that stage of mankind's development supposed that a people's god could be found outside of that people's land—all gods were geographically limited. That is what David meant when, driven out by Saul to the Philistine cities, he said, "They have driven me out this day that I could not cleave unto the inheritance of Jehovah, saying, Go, serve other gods." The Hebrews then did not dream that you could worship Jehovah except on Jehovah's ground. Other countries, other gods!

That is what the memorable words of Ruth meant when, coming across the Jordan gorge from the land of Moab, where she had always worshiped Moab's god, Chemosh, she accompanied Naomi to Bethlehem, where Jehovah was God. "Entreat me not to leave thee, and to return from following after thee; for whither thou goest, I will go; and where thou lodgest, I will lodge; thy people shall be my people, and thy God my God." Change countries, change gods!

Centuries passed. World-wide lines of communication opened up. People could not keep their gods geographically limited. In the apprehension of the Hebrew people, Jehovah had expanded now to be the God of all the earth. "It is he that sitteth above the circle of the earth," said the Great Isaiah, "and the inhabitants thereof are as grasshoppers." And as they thought of that they said, "The Lord is a great God."

Still there was heaven above and Sheol, the place of the dead, beneath. Did God have anything to do with those? When we think about working out a new and larger idea of God, let us go back and see what they did, laying the foundations of anything we shall ever do in that respect! They would not let God stay little. That is what the psalm means:

> If I ascend up into heaven, thou art there:
> If I make my bed in Sheol, behold, thou art there.
> If I take the wings of the morning,
> And dwell in the uttermost parts of the sea;
> Even there shall thy hand lead me.

That psalm represents one of the most magnificent enlargements of the idea of God in the history of human thought. He was God, not simply of the earth, but of the sky and of the abode of the dead, and as they thought of it they said, "The Lord is a great God."

Then, after centuries, the Hebrew-Christian tradition moved out into the Greek world. That presented a serious problem. Hellenism impregnated the minds of that ancient world into which young Christianity went so venturesomely forth. No problem do we face in trying to adapt the gospel to a new world-view which those Christians did not face when they went out into that amazing world of Greek philosophy. But they did not give up God; they deepened their idea of God. "He is not far from each one of us: for in him we live, and move, and have our being"; "God is love; and he that abideth in love abideth in God, and God abideth in him"; "In the beginning was the Logos, and the Logos was with God, and the Logos was God." God spiritualized! And as they reached out to grasp this deeper thought, they cried, "The Lord is a great God."

Still, however, they had the earth in the center, with the sun, moon, and stars going round it, a cozy place without great distances. Then the crucial hour struck, and Copernicus, Galileo, and Kepler came, and men moved out into an incredibly vast universe. They did not, however, give up God. Multitudes thought they would have to. That is why they fought the new view so. They were afraid man would have to give up God. But he did not. He did what he has always done when he has faced a situation like that—enlarged and deepened his conception of God. That is what Addison's hymn means, written in 1712, when the new world-view was coming to its full flower and man was facing the incredible distances and mechanical regularities of the heliocentric universe:

In Reason's ear they all rejoice,
And utter forth a glorious voice;
For ever singing as they shine,
'The Hand that made us is divine.'

That is to say, "The Lord is a great God."

Today we face the same situation again: a new revelation about the universe—law-abiding beyond our power previously to think, a world infinite and infinitesimal, physical and psychological, such as never dawned on the imaginations of our forefathers. In June, 1918, a new star blazed in the sky. A new star? No, that star blazed in the days of Alfred the Great, but the light just reached us. A great new universe is here, and in consequence the demand grows vocal that we must have a new idea of God—if, say some, we need any idea of God at all. There's the rub. Perhaps now we shall have to surrender God. Perhaps now, they fear, in this universe so new we cannot maintain any idea of God.

That fear fails to take into account the nature and history of human thought. Repeatedly in the Hebrew-Christian tradition, to which we belong, we have faced this issue, where we had either to grasp a deeper conception of God or else give up God altogether, and we have never given him up yet. Neither will we surrender God now. We will grasp a worthier idea of him. That thing is happening with us which has happened ever since our thought of God started with stories of Sinai and the Garden of Eden. Some people stand looking back and saying, God is gone! but the rest of us are standing in reverence before a vaster universe and are saying, The Lord is a great God.

If this is the story of the development of the idea of God in our own tradition so that that tradition can say about itself what Paul said about himself, "When I was a child, I spake as a child, I understood as a child, I thought as a child; but when I became a man, I put away childish things," let us try to help ourselves in dealing with this present confusion about God.

In the first place, we should not be upset by religion's 'growing pains.' To be sure, the discomfort is irritating. In particular, mankind is incorrigibly lazy, would like to stop progressing, and especially would always prefer to stop thinking. Who is it said that no human being ever did any thinking unless he absolutely had to? The hardest work in the world is thinking, and especially getting larger thoughts. It would be comfortable, then, if we could say about God, that is the final thought of him; that finishes our concept of Deity, and we shall never have to think about it again. But, after all, is there any one of us who would choose that? Just where would we stop in this long story of man's developing conception of the Eternal? With Sinai? With the geographically limited god? With the god of the old astronomy? We know we are unpayably indebted to those forefathers of ours who went through the discomfort of expanding religious experience and thought, and came forth with a guerdon and reward to show for it, "a great God."

Experts have estimated that a pound of honey may cost forty thousand miles of flying on the part of the bees. A family may eat a pound of honey on its griddle cakes for breakfast as a matter of course, but what it meant to the bees! So every beautiful thing in our idea of God has had its cost—its forty thousand miles of flying. As we look back upon our forefathers, thankful for the contribution which they have made to our idea of God, so will our children look back on this generation and estimate our worth in part by what we do now, when once more religion reaches out for a more adequate conception of the Eternal.

To be sure, this process is confusing and always has been. They called Socrates an atheist. They made him drink the hemlock as an atheist. Socrates an atheist! Of course, what that meant was that he denied the contemporary ideas of God, the pantheon of the Greek deities on Olympus, with their battles and amours. But he was no atheist. He had so splendid an idea of God, as Plato interprets him, that centuries after his martyrdom his name was often coupled with Christ's by the Christian fathers of the church, and his sayings were quoted as though from the Bible itself.

Many people do not know that the early Christians were themselves called atheists. They were hated all up and down the Roman Empire and were flung to the lions as atheists. Of course, what that meant was that they denied the current ideas of the pagan gods, but in fact they were working out an idea of God, in terms of spirit and love, to which the future belonged. This fact applies even to men like Voltaire. It is amazing to note how a bad name clings to a dog, as the proverb says, or to a man like Voltaire.

Multitudes of people think Voltaire an atheist. Voltaire did not come within reaching distance of being an atheist. What he denied was current ideas of God. The Roman Catholic idea of God in the France of his day, an intolerant god who wished all non-Catholics banished or burnt—in him Voltaire disbelieved. The god of the Calvinists in his day, who foreordained unborn babes by the million to eternal damnation—in him Voltaire disbelieved. Voltaire was one of the greatest humanitarians of history. He had in him many things both lovely and unlovely, but he cared about people, especially people whom other people had wronged, and the only God he could believe in was a God who loved people.

When Voltaire was an old man, Benjamin Franklin called on him in Paris. Franklin had with him his seventeen-year-old grandson, and when they parted the American philosopher asked the French philosopher to give the boy a blessing. The chronicler says it was a solemn moment for the spectators as Voltaire stretched his lean fingers over the boy's head and said, "My child, God and Liberty, remember those two words!"

We need not be upset by religion's 'growing pains.' This generation will not give up God.

In the second place, we should recognize frankly that to our limited and partial minds the real God is incomprehensible. We, with our minds that have been developing for a few millennia upon this wandering planet in the sky, cannot adequately and literally grasp the compass of the Eternal.

The immediate result of the fact that the real God is always to us incomprehensible is that we must think of him in terms of symbolism. Whenever anybody thinks of anything universal he has to think in symbolic terms. The mathematicians know that even mathematical formulas are symbolic. I have an engineer friend who is trying to make relativity real to my poor mind by picturing a shuffleboard game on a ship's deck, with the stick relative to the player's posture, and the player's posture relative to the deck's slope, and the deck's slope relative to the pitch of the sea, and the pitch of the sea relative to the earth's rotation, and the earth's rotation relative to the solar universe—so on *ad infinitum*. It is a somewhat desperate endeavor to make a large idea real to a small mind, with a picture.

Yet when we come to think of the great God, what else can we do? Sometimes I think it would be worth while to preach a series of sermons on symbols, because we use them constantly and so many people do not know what they are doing when they do use them. We go to one of Wagner's operas, and it is all symbolic. Remember the Rhinegold and the Rhinemaidens singing in the river! Now, if there is anything absurd it is three girls singing at the top of their voices under water. When we hear the opera, however, it is not absurd. The maidens are a symbol of the innocence of gold before it was perverted by the greed of men.

All life is full of symbols. A handshake is a symbol, a lifted hat is a symbol, a kiss is a symbol, the country's flag is a symbol. What is that keepsake in your pocketbook? It is a little thing, but it reminds you; it has associations; it makes you think of somebody. What is that wedding ring upon your finger? I well remember when my mother lost her wedding ring. I remember how we all searched for it and how she wept. It was not the marriage, but it was the symbol. What is the cross in the chancel? That is Christianity's keepsake. That is Christianity's wedding ring. That is Christianity's flag.

When, now, we think of the great God, we have to use symbols. We take some element within our experience and lift it up as far as we can reach and use it to help us think about him. We call him a rock, and a fortress, and a high tower. We call him father, and mother, and husband, and friend. We call him Ancient of Days and the Hound of Heaven. Men call him the eternal lotus flower and the rose of Sharon and the bright and morning star. And Christians say they see the light of the knowledge of the glory of God in the face of Jesus Christ. These are all symbols of the great God.

Long ago Verazzano, one of the early explorers, landed upon the Accomac Peninsula and, looking out across Chesapeake Bay, thought it was the Pacific. Would you laugh at him? I would not. In how many particulars he was right! First, there is a Pacific Ocean; it does exist. Second, in general he had the right direction; to be sure, the ocean was twenty-five hundred miles farther on, but he was headed right. And third, Chesapeake Bay has the same kind of water in it that the Pacific has. It is far truer to think of the Pacific Ocean in terms of Chesapeake Bay than it is to deny the Pacific Ocean altogether.

That fact needs to be faced today by some of our too-impatient minds. Recognizing that all our thoughts of God are inadequate, sometimes even childish, seeing that we cannot with our partial thought grasp the full compass of the Eternal, we are tempted to give up God altogether. But this is the wrong approach. It is far truer to think of God in terms of an inadequate symbol than not to think of him at all. The great God is; our partial ideas of him are partly true.

The first consequence of this is to make a man temperate and tolerant toward other people's ways of thinking about God. Here is my friend, for example, bowing before the image of his saint. I cannot do that, but I am not scornful. I see what he is doing. He is thinking of the Pacific Ocean in terms of Chesapeake Bay. And what is more, he gets more out of that and thinks more truly than some of our too-hasty minds denying that there is any Pacific Ocean at all.

Or here is another man who says, I am an atheist. And after talking with him I see that he is not an atheist. What he is denying is not God, but some popular picture of God. That is what most atheism is. There is very little of the Simon-pure article, and sometimes one can help a man like that by making him see that when the little gods go, the great God comes. One can send him out saying: The gods are dead! Long live God!

Nevertheless, we should not leave the matter there. What we have said about symbolic thinking concerning God seems to me true and important, but it is not the end of the matter, and if one takes it for the end one leaves God too vague to do business with. Let us, therefore, say this further thing: God is very great, but he has a near end where he literally touches us. How important are the consequences from that fact—God has a near end!

Recently I visited once more my island off the coast of Maine and fell in love again with the sea. Now, I do not know the whole sea. It is very great. I never sailed the tropic ocean where the Orinoco and the Amazon pour out their floods through primeval woods. I never watched the Antarctic sea where today pioneers press their perilous journies over the polar ice pack. Wide areas of the sea are to me unknown, but I know the sea. It has a near end. It washes my island. I can sit beside it and bathe in it and sail over it, and be sung to sleep by the music of it.

So is God. He is so great that in his vastness we can think of him only in symbolic terms, but he has a near end. Indeed, the nub of the whole inquiry about the nature of Deity lies in the answer to this question: Where do we think in our experience we touch the near end of God? Do we think that only matter is the near end of him and that all the God there is is simply physical, or do we think that in spiritual life at its best we have touched the near end of Deity, and that when we start with that and think out through that as far as we can go, we are thinking most truly about him?

To believe in the Christian God is to believe that in spiritual life at its best we have touched the hither side of God. Whatever more he may be, he is that. Ask the New Testament what God is, and the New Testament says, "God is love." Say to the New Testament, then, Where do we reach him? and it answers, "He that abideth in love abideth in God, and God abideth in him." That is God's near end.

Of course, this is what the 'divinity of Jesus' means. Many people are troubled because they cannot believe that all of the great God was in Jesus. Of course, all of the great God was not in Jesus. The omnipresence of the great God was not in Jesus. The omnipotence of the great God, swinging the eternal stars, was not in Jesus. No intelligent theology ever meant by the 'divinity of Jesus' what some people think is implied in it, but this it does mean, that in the spiritual life and character of Christ we touch the near end of God. There God reaches us. There he washes our island.

This puts vitality into our dealing with the Divine. I know a man against whom enemies rose up, and he was tempted to vindictiveness, but when the hour struck for his possible revenge he held his hand because the magnanimity of Christ was in him. That was the near end of God. I know a man before whose desirous eyes the gains of unjust industry were stretched out, and he held his hand. That was the near end of God. There is beauty in this world, from sunrise in the desert to a poem or a symphony, that touches our spirits to finer issues and the love of which differentiates us from the beasts. That is the near end of God. There are social movements across the centuries that weave individuals into families and families into tribes and tribes into nations and nations into empires, which having long stood embattled, with fratricidal hatred in their hearts, now begin to say, though stammeringly, what once only the greatest of the prophets said, We will learn war no more. That is the near end of God.

Go out, then, into this generation so confused about God. If they say to us, We need a larger idea of him, let us answer, Yes. May we be forgiven because so often we mistake the Chesapeake for the Pacific! But say this other thing also: God has a near end; in everything that we call beautiful or good or true he touches us; there we do business with him. "Know ye not that ye are a temple of God, and that the Spirit of God dwelleth in you?"

What Does the Divinity of Jesus Mean?

THIS sermon springs from endless inquiries sent me by radio listeners. They want to know what the "divinity" or "deity" of Jesus means. They have heard about it all their lives in the church's creeds, hymns, and sermons. Some believe it but are not quite sure what they are believing. Some disbelieve it but are not sure what they are disbelieving. What does it mean? they ask.

The reply to this question, if it is to be vital, must be personal. What does the divinity of Jesus mean to us in the actual practice of our daily lives? Monogamy, for example, is an abstract word, in discussing which men can lose themselves in labyrinthine arguments until someone breaks through, saying, What is monogamy? It is the kind of home I had, where my father and mother loved each other so deeply that they did not care to love anyone else in the same way at all, and so, across the years, threw around their children the security of a lovely and dependable home. That is monogamy. That is what it means. That is why I believe in it. Similarly, the divinity of Jesus has often been discussed as an abstract theological concept until someone has said, The divinity of Jesus was not at first an abstraction at all; it was a fresh insight into life's significance; it was far more nearly poetry than theology, something to sing about, rejoice in, and live by; it was a new and exhilarating message about God and man.

Let us see it in such terms of daily living if we are to know its meaning.

To help clear the air of some prevalent misconceptions, let us say at the start that the divinity of Jesus certainly does not mean that Jesus was not human. Of course he was human. The first disciples did not start by thinking of him as divine but by taking him for granted as obviously human. He was to them, as he must be to us, first of all man, and then divine in what sense he can be divine, being unquestionably human.

The Master's body was a normal human body like our own, familiar with weariness, hunger, thirst, pleasure, suffering, and death. The Master's emotional life was normally human like our own—sometimes astonished as at the centurion's excess of faith; sometimes compassionate as when he looked on the unshepherded multitudes; sometimes indignant as when he saw his Father's house made a den of thieves; sometimes rejoicing; and sometimes so cast down that he cried: "My soul is exceeding sorrowful, even unto death."

Moreover, Jesus' mental life was normally human like our own. It developed like any youth's. As Luke says, "Jesus advanced in wisdom and stature." He went to the synagogue school in Nazareth, and, sitting on the floor with his fellow pupils, recited in unison the lessons the rabbi dictated. He learned, as we all do, from what he saw, and his teaching everywhere reflects the recollections of his boyhood's home —the sound of wind down the village street, the cost of sparrows in the market place, putting patches on old garments, the working of leaven in the dough, hens gathering chickens under their wings. As for his major teaching, everywhere one catches the accents of the psalmists and the prophets, on whose writings he had been reared.

More particularly to our purpose is the humanness of Jesus' spiritual life. He prayed, not as though he were God, but as though he were man. Sometimes he prayed in triumph, as on the Transfiguration Mountain, when his face shone; sometimes he prayed in grief, as in Gethsemane, when it is written: "Being in an agony he prayed more earnestly." All his life he lived in such humble, filial dependence on God, and when fulsomely praised he retorted: "Why callest thou me good? none is good, save one, even God." So his life was lived, his work done, his sorrows borne, his temptations faced, in the spirit of simple, childlike dependence on God. Of course he was human, and he must be divine in what sense he can be divine, being assuredly human.

With this clear assertion of the humanity of Jesus in the Gospels, modern Christians are familiar. But many moderns do not know that throughout its early history the church fought some of its most serious theological battles to maintain its hold on this humanness of Jesus. Suppose I should say that Docetism was an early heresy that nearly tore the church asunder and that it concerned who Jesus was. Would you not naturally suppose that the Docetists must have doubted his deity? Upon the contrary, they asserted that he was God but they did not believe that he was man. They said that he only seemed to be born with a body, to possess flesh and blood, to suffer and to die. And the church fought the Docetists tooth and nail and drove them out. Were I to say that a heretic, Apollinaris, convulsed the church with his idea of Jesus' nature, would you not suppose that he must have doubted his deity? Upon the contrary, he asserted that, but he denied that Jesus had a human soul and a human will, and the church withstood him and cast him out. Throughout the early centuries some of the most serious battles in the church were fought in the endeavor to keep a firm hold on the real humanity of the Master.

We start then with this truth, that Jesus was human and that he must be divine in what sense he can be divine, being assuredly human. What, then, does the divinity of Jesus mean?

In the first place, it is an assertion primarily not about Jesus but about God. Everything else, I think, is seen awry unless that is clear. The divinity of Jesus is primarily an affirmation about God. Isaac Newton looked at the falling apple in the orchard until he overpassed looking at it and looked through it into a universal law. The astronomer looks at the star until he overpasses looking at it and looks through it into a cosmic truth. Those first disciples looked at Jesus until they overpassed looking at him and looked through him into a revelation of something eternally true about God. That is the way all universal truth is discovered, by looking at something significant until one looks through it and sees an eternal matter. So the disciples looked at Jesus until, as Paul said, they saw "the light of the knowledge of the glory of God" in his face.

Most of us here believe in God but how diverse the meanings of such faith! This diversity springs from the variety of answers we give to one central question: Where is God—not What, or Who, is God?

as so commonly the question is put, but Where is God? That is the crucial inquiry. Where do we look for him?

In response to that question some say we find God in the universe at large. The profoundest cosmic fact that science gets its eyes upon is not matter—if indeed, modern science knows what matter means—but a mathematical equation, and that is mental. God, says Jeans, the physicist, is like a great mathematician. So, in the organizing mind at the heart of the universe, we see God. Well, I agree. But is that all?

Others say we find God in the beauty of the world. More than a mathematician is at work here—an artist too, to whom symmetry, proportion, harmony, balance, color, are so real that, from microscopic creatures, invisible to unaided eyes, to the stars above, there is a beauty in the world where we find God. I agree. But is that all?

Others say they find God in the moral order of the world. This is a spiritually creative universe. It produces personality. It insists on obedience to moral law as the price of personal and social peace. It brings its heavy judgments down on human sin. It says that we must live co-operatively if we are to live well. There, in that moral order of the world, we see God, some say. To that also I agree. But is that all?

To find God in the organization of the cosmos, in the beauty of creation, in the moral order of the world, is good. But as some of us know well, all *that* can leave a man untouched in the personal depths of his life. What happened to the disciples, however, cannot leave a man untouched in the depths of his life. For there swam into their ken the strongest, loveliest personality the world has known, and they looked at him until they began to look through him and to see the most significant thing ever seen in the religious history of man—God there. The best life we know, they said, is supremely the place where we can see God. Not simply in the organization of the cosmos, the beauty of creation, the moral order of the world but here, in the mercy, saviorhood, love, and will of Christ, here—though it be the most daring assertion ever made about deity—is revealed God. What is highest in human life, revealed in Christ, they said, is deeply grounded in the universe; God is like *that*.

If we do not so see Jesus when we look at him, what do we make of him? I am taking it for granted that we recognize in him a transcendent quality. What, then, do we make of this most amazing, potent, spiritual life that has visited the world? In the long run we make of him one of two things: either an accident or a revelation—one or the other. He might be an accident, a fortuity in a materialistic world, the chance product of blind forces that never purposed him and never cared. He might just have happened. Or it might be that those first disciples were on the trail of the everlasting truth when they looked at him until they looked through him and saw in him the revelation of the Eternal. That is the great question about Christ. Is he an accident or a revelation?

In every realm one runs upon that kind of question. When men first picked up magnetized iron, they faced it. What was this extra quality, this strange power which made iron more than iron, iron plus, so that it exercised a potency that ordinary iron did not possess? Was this strange extra an accident, or a revelation of something profound in the constitution of the cosmos? As always happens, it turned out to be a revelation. If we cannot avoid such questions even about magnetized iron, we cannot avoid them about the quality of Christ. To call him an accident in the universe seems to me preposterous. At any rate, I personally must range myself with those first disciples who looked at him until they looked through him and saw in him "the light of the knowledge of the glory of God." They went out into the Roman Empire with this thrilling message to deliver, that God was like Christ.

In the second place, however, while the divinity of Jesus is primarily an assertion about God, it is also an affirmation about Jesus. It does put him in a unique place. Once after an appreciative paper on Shelley's poetry had been read, one member of the group arose in the discussion, saying rather truculently that he could not see anything in Shelley, to which the reader of the paper, replying later, simply remarked: "Mr. So-and-So says that he does not see anything in Shelley. Poor devil!" If a man can see nothing special in Jesus, that, I suspect, is the answer: Poor devil. Most of us, however, do not belong in that class. We can feel the transcendent quality of Jesus' life and understand at least a little the experience the disciples must have had with him.

First, of course, came a recognition of his spiritual superiority. A visitor at one of the services of Frederick Denison Maurice in Cambridge, England, when that preacher was at the height of his power, came out completely subdued and awed, saying, "There was something divine there not of this world." So from the beginning the disciples must have felt about Jesus.

Then, I suppose, came the sense of moral challenge in his presence. He was not easy to face. You recall what Iago said about Cassio:

> He hath a daily beauty in his life
> That makes me ugly.

With shame and contrition the disciples felt that. The Master was not easy to live with. Peter's first reaction was not comfortable: "Depart from me; for I am a sinful man, O Lord." He had a daily beauty in his life that made them ugly.

Then, I suspect, there grew in them a strange sense of the Master's rightful authority over their lives. He taught them, said Matthew, as one having sovereignty. Make no mistake about this. His authority did not mean regimentation. He never made James like John or John like Peter. His authority, as with all spiritual excellence, issued not in regimentation but in stimulation. Under his sway qualities and powers began coming out in them unguessed before, qualities and powers original, individual, creative, each man becoming more truly himself, the more he became Christ's.

As this kind of experience, which no one can adequately put into words, progressed, see how inevitably the disciples moved up from one stage to another in their thought of him. At first they may have said, God sent him. After a while that sounded too cold, as though God were a bow and Jesus the arrow. That would not do. God did more than send him. So I suspect they went on to say, God is with him. That went deeper. Yet, as their experience with him progressed, it was not adequate. God was more than with him. So at last we catch the reverent accents of a new conviction, God came in him. That was not so much theology at first as poetry. It was an exhilarating insight and its natural expression was a song. God can come into human life! they cried; God has come into human life! Divinity and humanity are not so separate that the visitations of the Eternal are impossible. "God is love; and he that abideth in love abideth in God, and God abideth in him"; "Know ye not that ye are a temple of God, and that the Spirit of God dwelleth in you?" "In the beginning was Mind and the Mind was with God, and the Mind was God. . . . And the Mind became flesh, and dwelt among us (and we beheld his glory, glory as of the only begotten from the Father), full of grace and truth." So they sang it. God can come into human life because God has come into human life.

At its best, that is what the church has always meant by the divinity of Jesus. Do not, I beg of you, tie this great affirmation up with miraculous accompaniments, such as the virgin birth. I am not deeply concerned whether you believe the virgin birth as a historic fact or not, although, as you know, I cannot believe it. But I am concerned that no one should tie up in one bundle the virgin birth and the divinity of Jesus. The divinity of Jesus was not physical. That is absurd. It was spiritual. It was the inner quality of his life in which his divinity consisted. The two great protagonists for his divinity in the New Testament were John and Paul and neither directly nor indirectly did they ever allude to the virgin birth. No, the divinity of Jesus was a convinced and singing faith that God can come into human life because God had come into human life.

Take even the old creeds, the Nicene, for example, greatest of them all. We repeat no creeds in this church. We require no subscription to them. I would not use them as the natural phrasing of my faith. But all the more I am sometimes jealous that we should not misunderstand them. A modern liberal Christian hears the Nicene Creed calling Jesus "very God of very God," and says, I cannot believe that. I too should not naturally use the Nicene language, but yet see what the Creed was really trying to say! That Creed was formulated in a time when the contemporary philosophy had torn God and man completely asunder. On the one side was God, pure Being, utterly incapable of coming into contact with human life, and on the other side was man, sunk in the darkness of matter, utterly incapable of touching God. This was the prevalent philosophy. And this idea was so affecting Christian thought that even Christians were tempted to say that if Jesus were human he could not be divine and if divine he could not be human. So utterly diverse and separate were divinity and humanity that God himself could never come into human life. It was against this idea that the Nicene Creed rose magnificently up with its affirmation: God can come into human life; very God can come into human life; the divine and the human are not irreconcilable, like oil and water, which cannot be mixed. It never would occur to me to use the Nicene language as the natural expression of my faith, but what the Nicene Creed was driving at in the terms of its own day is my faith. Say it until it becomes real to your thought and living: God did not simply send Jesus; he was not simply with Jesus; he came in Jesus. God can come into human life because he has come into human life, and what the Fourth Gospel pictures the Master as saying is true: "He that hath seen me hath seen the Father."

Finally, the divinity of Jesus is an affirmation not only about God and about Jesus but about man. Have you ever seen a precious stone in the rough, carried out of the dark, where it seemed dull and dingy, into the light where the sunshine could break through it and in lustrous radiance reveal beauties no one could have guessed? So in Jesus human nature was carried out of the dark into the light, and from that day to this no one who has really known him has been able to think of human nature as necessarily dull and dingy. See, they have cried, what it can become when the Divine is released through it!

In this realm lies one of the common fallacies of those who refuse to see any meaning in Jesus' divinity. They say: Jesus is a good man, and simply because he is a good man he can be our ideal, for we can imitate him, but if he were divine we could not imitate him, for that would put him out of our class and spoil him as our ideal; let him be to us simply a good man!

I never heard an argument that seemed to me so to stand the truth upon its head. I should say in answer, Jesus is, indeed, an extraordinarily good man. His goodness was the only thing he had with which to make an impress on the world— no wealth, no prestige, no worldly learning, nothing but his goodness! And every year that goodness looms so much the higher that millions of us are sure its chief influence lies not behind but ahead. He was a marvelously good man. And now do you seriously mean that, being a good man like that, we can cheerfully and hopefully set out to imitate him? Upon the contrary, if Jesus is only a good man, he towers there, solitary and alone, an isolated phenomenon in human history.

If, however, that is not all the truth, if he is not simply a good man, if it was God in him who created his quality, and if the same God is seeking entrance to our lives, trying to live out in us, according to our capacity, the same spirit, then we may hope. Let us say it abruptly: It is not so much the humanity of Jesus that makes him imitable; it is his divinity. If he be only a good man, he is an isolated phenomenon like Shakespeare or Napoleon in other realms. How can I, pulling on my own bootstraps, set out to lift myself by imitation to the stature of such? But if Jesus is divine and if divinity is in each of us, like the vital forces which in winter wait in the frozen ground until the spring comes, that is a gospel! While the trees of the wood are still bare the crocuses bloom, but if they were only crocuses, that would be no good news. If, however, they reveal the vibrant life that runs through all the arteries of the waiting world, such news should make all the trees of the wood rejoice before the Lord; for he cometh in the springtime to redeem them all.

Such is the gospel of the New Testament about Jesus and his relationship with our lives. He is not an isolated phenomenon; he is "the firstborn among many brethren"; "till we all attain unto the unity of the faith, and of the knowledge of the Son of God, unto a fullgrown man, unto the measure of the stature of the fulness of Christ."

If one says that still his divinity in scope and compass far overarches ours, surely that is obvious. As Emerson says: "A drop of water has the properties of the sea, but cannot exhibit a storm." So we reveal God without the deeps and tides and currents which Jesus knew, without the relationships with the world's life which his influence has sustained. Yet the God who was in Jesus is the same God who is in us; you cannot have one God and two kinds of divinity. It was one of the supreme days in man's spiritual history when human nature in Jesus was carried out from the dark into the light and men saw as never before what could happen to it when the divine life was released through it.

Of all foolish things, I can think of nothing more foolish, when looking back over our race's history and discerning amid its tragedy and trouble this loveliest, strongest, spiritual life that has visited the earth, than to try to minimize him. Upon the contrary, exalt him! If you cannot discover the Divine in that life, then I do not see how you can vitally discover it anywhere. And if you do find the Divine in him, then that is indeed a great affirmation about God and about Christ himself. But last, and most practically of all, it is an affirmation about human nature that in these desperate days I need constantly to have refreshed—an assertion about the possibilities of human nature when the divine Life is released through man.

Hospitality to the Highest*

EVERY biographer delights to discover in the infancy or childhood of his hero some event which may be a symbol and foregleam of the hero's subsequent career. But did ever a single incident in any one's infancy suggest so much as is summed up in Luke's saying about Jesus' nativity at Bethlehem: "There was no room for them in the inn"?

As one reads the words now, there is foreboding in them. *That* was to be the Master's experience throughout his ministry—no room for his teachings in the minds of men or for his quality of spirit in their lives, no room in the synagogue for his reforming zeal or in the nation for his prophetic message. The crucial difficulty of his life which denied him the service he longed to render, closed to him the hearts he longed to change, and brought him at last to Calvary, was something so simple, so familiar, so little recognized as a tragic evil, and so universal among us all, that one almost hesitates to name it—inhospitality.

In a picture of Jesus' boyhood in Nazareth, he runs to his mother with outstretched arms and his cruciform shadow falls on the ground before him. So in imagination men long have dwelt upon the premonitions of tragedy which the Master's childhood may have known. Crucifixion, however, is a form of cruelty too extreme to be familiar. We do not readily picture ourselves crucifying Jesus. But this other element in the Christmas story is well known to all of us; we may not disclaim our share in his rejection through finding no room for him. Yet, familiar as it is, such inhospitality was the central tragedy of Jesus' life. A century after Bethlehem, in far-off Ephesus a loyal disciple wrote the Fourth Gospel, and still the tragedy was the same:

* A Christmas Sermon.

"He came unto his own, and they that were his own received him not." And today, from how many preoccupied lives and embittered human relationships does the Master hear the ancient words, "No room"!

One does not mean simply that we lead practically overcrowded lives, cluttered with such preoccupying business that from our limited time and attention the highest is shut out. Of course it is true that the loveliest things in life, which, hospitably welcomed, would enrich us all, are commonly excluded by such preoccupation. Great books are not read, great music is not heard; we are too busy. There are beauties in nature whose enjoyment "redeems from decay the visitations of the divinity" within us; but we are too busy. We miss enriching friendships and possibilities of happiness in our family life; we are preoccupied. No room—of how much sorry loss of priceless opportunity is not that the explanation!

So, too, the major enemy of Christianity itself is not atheism but secularism, not the theoretical denial of Christ but the practical crowding out of Christ and everything he stands for. When the hall is filled with immediate and temporal concerns, when every seat is taken and even standing room is crowded, how can anything else get in? It is this which makes difficult the task of all teachers of spiritual life, whether in the realm of beauty or of religious faith. One does not mind so much those who carefully and deliberately cry, I do not believe. They are not many and they at least are serious. But the dull, impenetrable, stolid, overfull lives that can say nothing, even when the Christ comes to them, except, No room for him—that is the tragedy.

Behind such practical crowding out of the highest, however, is a deeper matter. Spiritual inhospitality to the best, whether in music or books or friendship, or in dealing with Christ himself, is not mainly due to our being too preoccupied. If at the inn they had known what the Christ Child would become in the world, some of them at least would have found a place for him. We find places for the things we really care about. They crowded Christ completely out because they never guessed who he would be. How could they? But we know. We have no such excuse. It was nearly two thousand years ago that the hostler at Bethlehem

. . . opened up the stable
The night Our Lady came.

We know Jesus. Have we not come from homes where his spirit made a radiance in the faces we loved best and a fragrance in their lives? Are we not sprung from a civilization where artists like Raphael have glorified him and musicians like Bach have written their noblest compositions in his praise? Has not even an agnostic historian, Lecky, said that "the simple record of three short years of active life has done more to regenerate and to soften mankind than all the disquisitions of philosophers, and all the exhortations of moralists"? We cannot plead that we do not know Jesus. There are many questions about Christianity and about Christ which we cannot answer. But Jesus himself, the essence of his character, the quality of his spirit, the core of his teaching, we do know. And we know that those areas of life where his spirit has been welcomed and enthroned, as we have seen it in some genuinely Christian friendships and families and in some genuinely Christian social attitudes, are the loveliest results our civilization has to show for its centuries of struggle. So when we cry, No room for him! it is not so much because we are practically preoccupied as because our souls are of such a quality that they are hospitable to something quite different from Christ.

On Christmas Sunday morning, therefore, as in imagination we stand at Bethlehem's inn and see how easily the highest can be shut out by a little inhospitality, we well may say to ourselves that to be hospitable is about as important and as self-revealing an act as any we perform.

Consider, for one thing, how much of the richness of our lives comes not from our outward strenuousness but from our inward hospitality. When we hear a famous American described, as one was described, as "a steam engine in trousers," how clearly the type of character suggested by that stands out. Vigor, energy, drive, strenuousness—such valuable qualities are there, without which no continent like ours could have been subdued. But if a man is merely a steam engine in trousers, how much less than a man he is!

Upon the other side, suppose we had never heard of Wordsworth, knew nothing concerning him save, it may be, his lines beginning:

> . . . Therefore am I still
> A lover of the meadows and the woods,
> And mountains; and of all that we behold
> From this green earth.

How instinctively our estimate of him would rise! We should know at least that he was not merely a steam engine in trousers. He had an interior hospitality to some lovely things. There were times when beauty came to his door and he made room for it. And we should expect in such a life some richness, some radiance and fragrance, some charm and winsomeness which no trousered steam engine can ever know.

One goes to Dresden and finds it a busy town. Its streets are thronged, its markets populous, its industry manifold; one can spend there laborious and animated days. Some of us remember most clearly, however, not our strenuous expeditions there but a quiet room where Raphael's Sistine Madonna is and where we sat silent and absorbed trying hospitably to understand. That memory goes deeper, reaches higher, lasts longer, is more significant than anything else we brought from Dresden. Life is like that. Our enrichment comes from our hospitalities.

Far from being sentimental, this is as true of the mind as of the spirit. How full our American universities are of strenuous minds and how poor they are in rich minds! The strenuous mind can do many things—amass facts, learn techniques, develop skills, teach classes, give examinations, write books, and make speeches. As Stephen Leacock says, it is the business of the American professor to chase his students "over a prescribed ground at a prescribed pace, like a flock of sheep. They all go humping together over the hurdles, with the professor chasing them with a set of 'tests' and 'recitations,' 'marks' and 'attendances,' the whole apparatus obviously copied from the time clock of the business man's factory." "This process," adds Leacock, "is what is called 'showing results.'" How much of our so-called educational life is thus strenuous but how little of it is rich! For to possess richness of mind one must be more than strenuous, one must be hospitable. A wealthy mind cannot always be vehemently adoing but must sometimes be entertaining guests. No one can be mentally rich who does not know what Browning meant when he made his Cleon say:

> I have not chanted verse like Homer, no—
> Nor swept string like Terpander, no—nor carved
> And painted men like Phidias and his friend:
> I am not great as they are, point by point.
> But I have entered into sympathy
> With these four, running these into one soul,
> Who, separate, ignored each other's art.
> Say, is it nothing that I know them all?

This world is bad enough, my friends, but at Christmas time we may be forgiven for saying our best about it. There are lovely things here after all. Not only has Christ come and found some lives with room to take him in, but in our Western tradition at its best and in our personal lives at their best, even in a troubled time like this, there are such opportunities for hospitality as most of our forefathers never dreamed. And these gracious and beautiful things come asking of us only a welcome. It seems so small a thing to ask! Beethoven's symphonies and Shakespeare's sonnets, flowers in the woods and Christ in the heart—they come seeking hospitality. Well, then, how much of all that is best in the world belongs to us? I press that home upon our consciences. How much of the best in the world belongs to us? That surely is measured by our hospitality. Poverty-stricken in spirit and poor in mind, some may blame their impoverished estate on circumstance, but most of us cannot. We have had homes too fine, friends too loyal, opportunities too rich to make that excuse. The reason we are poor is pictured in the story of Bethlehem's inn—the star over it, the angels singing about it, the Wise Men from afar seeking it, but, as for the inn itself, no room for him there.

How magical a change a little hospitality can make! A youth turns, as it were, the corner of a street and, running into a new idea, makes room for it, and lo! his life is utterly transformed. Hoping for the return of his stolen gold, Silas Marner, the crusty miser in George Eliot's novel, opens his door as a neighbor bids him and in an unexpected moment of hospitality welcomes the little child who creeps to his hearthside, and lo! his whole character is reoriented and redeemed. Peter meets Jesus by the lakeside and, though ashamed to welcome so great a spirit into so unworthy a life, saying at first, "Depart from me; for I am a sinful man, O Lord," he makes room for him at last and by that not only he but all the world is altered. One of the mysteries of life is a man surprised into unsuspected greatness by a momentary hospitality, like Paul's on the Damascus Road, so that afterward he says, "It is no longer I that live, but Christ liveth in me." And the thrill of preaching lies in the knowledge that this can still happen. For Bethlehem is not historic merely. The ancient scene is reproduced in many a life today. Still Christ comes to the inn. Only, we can change the outcome. Room for him! Room for him there!

Were we to say nothing more, however, our Christmas message might seem private and subjective, as though in a troubled generation we were content merely to make our personal lives like oases in the midst of a barren land. But our truth goes far beyond that. One cannot understand aright the whole world's trouble unless one sees it in terms of inhospitality.

What if mankind did not so habitually repeat the scene of Bethlehem! What if, when saviors come in any realm, we did not meet them with this obdurate, impassive refusal of a welcome! Thales first foretold a solar eclipse, the one in 585 B.C., and the ancient Greeks at Alexandria knew that the earth was round. Why did the facts about our solar universe have to wait long, dull centuries and man live still in a meager world before the truth shone out? When we furnish our houses, we put 'Welcome' on the very doormat, but when we furnish our minds we do not. Has ever a new and saving idea come to the race without hearing the cry, "No room"?

The tragedy of mankind is this impassive, obdurate refusal to welcome the saviors of the world. For the saviors have not been lacking—not in science, not in music, not in spiritual faith and life. They have come, but whether it be Galileo or Wagner or our Lord himself, with what impenetrable inhospitality has the race refused them! This puts the world's salvation squarely up to us, the common men and women.

The saviors come—God sends them; it is we, the masses of the people, who cry, No room! Sometimes in retrospect this unreceptive inertia of mankind seems ridiculous to the point of laughter. Said a school board in an American town a hundred years ago, "You are welcome to use the school house to debate all proper questions in, but such things as railroads and telegraphs are impossibilities and rank infidelity. There is nothing in the Word of God about them." That is ludicrous, we think. When, however, one considers humanity's estate today, this shutting of the doors to new ideas is no laughing matter. We are moving out into situations in economic life and international relationships so unprecedented that old formulas are as inadequate to save the day as old ox-carts are to handle modern transportation. Inhospitality of mind and spirit to new ways of dealing with our economic life, to new ways of thinking about international relationships, can utterly ruin us. Granted that 'Welcome' on the mind's doormat is too promiscuous and indiscriminate. Hospitality of mind is too important to be loosely given. But when I think of you and of myself, in these dangerous years ahead, what most of all I fear is this, that in our times new ideas will come, new social outlooks to which the future of mankind belongs, and, because our minds are filled with old ideas, old prejudices, old mental habits, old class interests, old forms of patriotism, we will cry, No room!

You see, at first hospitality seems merely a gracious virtue. Strenuousness may be difficult but hospitality is lovely. My friends, a mind and spirit that can recognize and welcome the highest when it comes is one of the supreme gifts of man. It is indeed true that, next to genius, what is most like it is the power to know and admire it. Next to being creatively great oneself is the capacity to recognize greatness when one sees it, and make room.

True in the realm of mind, this certainly is true in the realm of character. Can you imagine Pilate being inwardly hospitable to Jesus? How could he be? Cynical and crafty Roman, habituated to Cæsar's service, sophisticated in his thinking and hard as nails in his life, what could he have done with the Man of Nazareth wandering at liberty through the rooms of his soul? Is any discomfort worse than to entertain a guest day after day in your home when you are alien to him at every point and what he wants forces the suspension or suppression of your main desires? Or can we imagine Caiaphas, the High Priest, being spiritually hospitable to Jesus? Shrewd, cagy old ecclesiastic, with a stereotyped religion and a crabbed mind—what had he in common with this "young Prince of Glory" whose religion was as fresh as the flowers on his Galilean hillsides and whose good-will was as spontaneous as the affection of the children whom he loved? What could Caiaphas have done entertaining him? Indeed, if one thinks hospitality easy, let him watch Judas Iscariot trying to be hospitable to Jesus. I think he really tried. But there was something else in him—the love of money, was it?—that filled the inn at last so that the end of Jesus' life, like the beginning, heard the cry, this time with tragic consequence, No room!

We are not proposing, then, this Christmas Sunday morning, an easy thing—to let him in, to make room for him—but we are proposing a glorious thing. A man's best memories, when life is closing, I think, will be his finest spiritual hospitalities and what came of them.

Imagine, for example, some one here—a hard-headed man, analytical of mind, a little proud of his freedom from sentiment—looking now, it may be, upon this Christmas festival with shrewd, appraising eyes. How valuable such a cautious and analytical attitude can be, and yet, if that is all, how utterly impoverishing! I have seen Yosemite Falls in the springtime leaping from its great height in a diaphanous tracery of spray and mist. Now, the analyst is right—that waterfall is H_2O. That is important truth. But something else is there, not to be gotten at and inwardly possessed by analysis but by receptivity, appreciation, insight, responsiveness, hospitality. With only one life here on earth to live, it is a pity, because of an inhospitable mind, to miss the spiritual values which mean most, reach highest, last longest, and in the end make life rememberable. Above all, make room for *him*, fairest among ten thousand and the one altogether beautiful.

One suspects, however, that the real barrier to our welcoming of Christ is not a sophisticated mind but an unworthy life. Sin is the obstacle. There are things in our lives which will have to leave if Christ comes in. That is why the world as a whole rejects him. If he came in, war and greed, and many a social evil they have produced, would have to go. So he is still "despised, and rejected of men." That too is why some here today are saying, even though the words do not take audible form upon their lips, No room. If some one says that, with vehement determination barring the door against him and choosing to live with the company which would have to leave were he to enter, how can a preacher's words melt that deliberate refusal? But if some are saying, No room, humbly, because their lives seem too soiled to welcome so great a guest, then there is hope. Friend, he did not come in the first place to a palace, but to an inn. And through the centuries since he never has despised the common, vulgar, soiled, and humble dwelling places. Such are his specialties. He seeks them out. What huts has he not entered! At what dilapidated hovels has he not knocked, seeking their hospitality! And what amazing consequence has come to those who welcomed him! Good news, indeed! "Good tidings of great joy which shall be to all the people"—if there is room for him in the inn.

Taking Jesus Seriously

LUKE'S Gospel tells us that after Simon Peter had come to know Jesus, had had Jesus in his own home, had been welcomed by him to discipleship, and had begun to see the kind of person he was and the work he did, he "fell down at Jesus' knees, saying, Depart from me; for I am a sinful man, O Lord."

At first sight that seems a strange response to make to the Master. To become acquainted with the most glorious character that ever came to earth and then to cry, as Dr. Moffatt translates it, "Lord, leave me; I am a sinful man"—what kind of response is that to the beauty and strength of Jesus? But on second thought that is taking Jesus seriously, and without that there is no such thing as taking him seriously. Simon Peter was right—when in any earnest fashion a man sees Christ, if he knows himself at all and with any reality apprehends the transcendent personality of the Master, his first response is not a satisfied admiration, adoration, worship, but a cry from the depths of conscience: Go away from me; you disturb me; I do not belong to your scale of life; I cannot rise to what you ask; leave me, for I am a sinful man, O Lord! That is taking Jesus in earnest.

Anyone acquainted with Christian thought during the last generation knows that at this point we are saying something that needs to be said. Many people have pretty much reduced their Christianity to admiration of Jesus—an admiration taken for granted as easy, natural, and to be expected. Of course, we admire Jesus—almost everyone says that. I have no use for your Christian doctrine, says one; I will have nothing to do with your Christian churches, says another, but of course, I admire Jesus.

You recall Sidney Lanier's poem in which, reviewing the great characters of history, he finds in every one of them something that needs to be forgiven. But when he thinks of Jesus, he says,

> What *if* or *yet*, what mole, what flaw, what lapse,
> What least defect or shadow of defect,
> What rumor, tattled by an enemy,
> Of inference loose, what lack of grace
> Even in torture's grasp, or sleep's, or death's,—
> Oh, what amiss may I forgive in Thee,
> Jesus, good Paragon, thou Crystal Christ?

Many consent to that. They admire Jesus' character—that is about all the Christianity they have. But in these desperate days I should suppose it evident that that is not enough. Admire Christ? But Christ is no beautiful sunset concerning which it is sufficient to say, How lovely it is! Look at our generation, outdoing the beasts in beastliness, and at our own lives, stained by all the outward evil we deplore, and then look at Christ! Simon Peter was right—he is not simply admirable but terrible. He is the most disturbing personality we ever face. We do not instinctively run to him. Instinctively we try to escape him. Give him his way and it means the upset of our world, and as for our own lives, we cannot live with ourselves and with him at the same time. Anyone who takes Christ in earnest begins where Simon Peter began, "Lord, leave me; I am a sinful man."

Start, for example, with Christ's teaching. It is difficult to find anyone who does not admire it. One of the easiest ways to get applause in America is to praise the Sermon on the Mount. Much of our preaching has consisted in that—how noble Jesus' ethical precepts are; who does not admire them? For myself, however, I could not preach a sermon like that to save my life. To be sure, the Sermon on the Mount is noble. That is the trouble. Reading it, one sometimes feels as a moron might feel reading a university catalogue. Of course, that catalogue is marvelous, offering all this wealth of opportunity, but a moron would want most of all to throw it away and never think of it again. Something drastic and miraculous must happen to him before the transcendent privileges of the university are within his dimension. Well, look at our world and at our lives in comparison with the ethical precepts of the Master: the contrast and disproportion are appalling. A man who has not so felt about the Sermon on the Mount has never taken it seriously.

Or, consider Jesus as a personal example. To be a Christian, we say—and we often say it smoothly and easily—is to make Jesus our ideal and to follow in his steps. Indeed, that very phrase is Simon Peter's. Long afterwards, when he wrote his Epistle, he said that Christ suffered for us, leaving us an example, that we should follow in his steps. But he did not say that at first. At first he saw too clearly the gulf that separated him from Christ to talk about taking him for an example. He felt like a sick man seeing some magnificent Sandow stalk before him, great in stature, perfect in physique—attractive, yes, but maddening too, making his own weakness odious by comparison. What could he in his frailty have to do with an ideal like that? Leave me alone, he cried!

So, in our day, in words that to some easy-going Christians would seem at first intolerably irreverent, Dorothy Sayers has interpreted this initial response to Jesus:

> Thou liest, Christ, Thou liest; take it hence,
> That mirror of strange glories; I am I;
> What wouldst Thou make of me? O cruel pretence,
> Drive me not mad so with the mockery
> Of that most lovely, unattainable lie!

Someone, however, may be saying that to be a Christian is not so much legalistically to obey Christ's teaching, or imitatively to follow in his steps, as it is to catch his spirit. Often we hear Christianity so described. As though we were simplifying matters, we say that to be a Christian is to catch Christ's spirit. But that is the hardest thing of all. Once Jesus took a towel, and, girding himself, washed his disciples' feet. In Palestine that act was so familiar that the disciples had seen it countless times, but when Jesus did it, a solemn hush fell on them, and in that simple deed a quality and meaning were present that they never could forget. What is this inner radiance, this mystic gift of spiritual grace that illumines common deeds until they become immortal, and turns even the ordinary breaking of bread into an undying sacrament? And now men say that we are to catch that spirit of Jesus and so be Christian. My soul, at that point most of all I understand Simon Peter: O Lord, leave me, for I am a sinful man.

See what we are trying to say! When one really sees Jesus and takes him seriously—his teaching, his example, his spirit—the Master can be the most forbidding and shaming figure that ever walked the earth.

What, then, is the way out, for the New Testament makes it plain that there is a way out. The New Testament is the most triumphant book in man's spiritual history. It starts where Simon Peter started, but it does not stop there. All the way through it are men and women made poignantly aware of their sin and shame, yet all the way through it runs the note of spiritual victory, too, and the reason is not simply emotional but intellectual. This situation we have described drove those first Christians to some profound thinking that we modern Christians, who in easy times have grown superficial, in these serious days need to reproduce.

To begin with, those first Christians thought their problem through until they saw that Jesus is more than Jesus; he is the revelation of the Eternal. How profound a difference it makes in any realm when something is seen as more than itself—the revelation of the Eternal! When some great scientist, a genius unapproachable by us, with brilliant insight beyond our power at first even to understand, discovers some world-transforming truth, he could be thought of only as an individual, utterly shaming and discouraging to us, who, with pedestrian minds can follow him only afar off. But that, thank heaven, is not the whole truth. Galileo, Newton, Watts, and all the rest, are more than individuals. They are revealers of the eternal, opening up new realms of truth and power, which, once opened up, we ordinary folk can enter into and avail ourselves of. So Simon Peter's first revulsion from Christ, impossibly beyond him, turned to hope. Jesus was more than Jesus: he was the revealer of the Eternal Spirit, who could come into our lives, too. "The God of all grace," wrote Peter years afterwards in his Epistle, "who called you unto his eternal glory in Christ . . . shall himself perfect, establish, strengthen you."

When winter gives way to spring, the first sign we see appears in some tree or shrub whose leaves begin to clothe with green the branches that have long been bare. If that tree were merely an individual, how slight its meaning and how disheartening its verdure to other trees still barren! But far from being an individual alone, what we are really seeing in that single tree is a revelation of awakening life, cosmic in its source, universal in its reach, that can come up into all living things and recreate them. That is not discouraging. That is great good news. So to these first Christians Jesus was more than Jesus. He was the Logos, they said, the Word of God, God's expression, the forth-going of the Eternal, revealing himself in one life, that he might make himself available to all.

To be sure, the doctrine of the divinity of Jesus has been grossly mistreated by theology and often put into terms incredible to minds like ours. But it is a pity because of that to miss the tremendous import of its meaning. Jesus' manhood alone, transcendent in quality and unapproachable by us, does call out Simon Peter's first response. But what if Jesus is more than Jesus? What if he reveals the Spirit of the living God, in whom we too live and move and have our being, and who in us can work the miracle of his creative springtime? That is gospel. Peter started by crying in shame before Jesus' human character, Leave me, for I am a sinful man, but he ended by saying in triumph, "Thou art the Christ, the Son of the living God."

So one young man recently said in my presence, "It takes Jesus' godhead to resurrect us from the despair into which his manhood plunges us." There is truth in that. Tell me that Jesus is only an individual man and that I must be like him, and I quit. At that point I know enough about myself to quit, as in Browning's poem, Andrea del Sarto stands before Raphael's painting and cries,

> But all the play, the insight and the stretch—
> Out of me, out of me!

Tell me, however, that Christ is the revelation of the Eternal Spirit, opening up a realm of Divine life and power into which I too can enter, and that is gospel. Then, humbly but really, when I face Christ, I can say, "Spirit of God, descend upon my heart."

Again, those first Christians thought their problem through until they saw that Jesus is more than Jesus—not simply a teacher and a personal ideal but the pioneer of a new age on earth for all mankind. What a difference that makes!

America's first trained nurse, Linda Richards, died in 1930. Only a few years ago the first trained nurse in America was still with us. Now, Linda Richards was important as an individual, but no one who stops with that sees her full significance. She was more than an individual; she was a pioneer, a trail-blazer, the harbinger of a new era in the life of all sick folk in America. She was the beginning of something that is to go on and on beyond herself to greater things. How much more is that true of the Master! Tell us only that he is the perfect man standing there in history, and we shall feel as Simon Peter did at first; but tell us that he is the pioneer of a new age that shall in the end change the quality and transform the relationships of all mankind, and that is not discouraging. That is what the New Testament calls it—news, good news.

The Wright brothers are to us more than individuals. They were pioneers, and while what they did we never could have done, now that they have done it every one of us can share in the new era that they opened up. So the New Testament thinks of Jesus—more than a teacher, more than an example, he opened the gates of a new age, changed B.C. to A.D., introduced into history a new force, let loose in the world a new dynamic that can, and does, and will, change human life and transform human relationships. That is what they meant when they called him the Messiah. Logos—that means that he is the revealer of the Eternal Spirit. Messiah—that means that he is the pioneer of a new age. When Simon Peter saw that truth about him he completely changed his tune. Christ, the Messiah of a new humanity—that was the best news he had ever heard.

Tschaikowsky said that he gave himself to music because of Mozart. "It is thanks to Mozart," he wrote, "that I have devoted my life to music." So Mozart was his messiah, the pioneer for him of a new era in music, and whenever he speaks of Mozart one feels two tones in his voice: first, humility before superior excellence, but second, stimulus, challenge, hope. He could not have introduced the new era, he feels, but Mozart could, and now that it is here he can share it and in it play a part. Well, Christ is much more than Mozart and we much less than Tschaikowsky, but still the truth there lights up our relationship with our Lord. If Christ were only a teacher, telling us what we ought to do, if he were only an individual ideal, telling us to be like himself, then we would be discouraged. But he is more than that. He is, as the New Testament calls him, "the pioneer" of our salvation. What he did we never could have done, but now that he has done it we can share in it and play our part in its coming triumph. That is not discouraging. That is a great gospel.

Again, those first disciples thought their problem through until they saw that Jesus is more than Jesus; not simply teacher and example, he is a savior, too. An immense difference that makes!

One wonders what Jesus said to Simon Peter—beyond the single sentence that the Gospel records—when, penitent, he threw himself at the Master's knees and said, "Depart from me; for I am a sinful man." One can imagine Christ speaking to him thus:

> Simon, it is just because you are a sinful man that I have come to you. That is what I am here for. You tell me to leave you because you are sinful. Man, that is why I came—because men are sinful. I understand why you shrink from me. A sick man is not helped when some paragon of physical perfection stands in his presence, an ideal of health to taunt his weakness, but do not take me so! I am the good physician. Your sickness is the reason I have come, not to taunt you but to heal you. Take me thus, not as teacher and example only but as savior.

Throughout the New Testament that gospel runs. If Jesus is only our ideal, then we are of all men most miserable, but if he is our savior, too, then the doors of hope begin to open.

Who does not feel the need of this today? I do not know that I need any more ideals. The ideals I have for myself and for the world are so tantalizingly beyond reach that they are disheartening, and to tell me worshipfully to admire Jesus as the great ideal, does not help the situation. See what we human brutes are doing to one another on the earth today, all of us involved in the causes, processes, and results of man's diabolical iniquity, and for medicine what if no more can be said than that Jesus is our ideal? What we need is a savior. If Christ is that, if transforming powers are by the grace of God released through him that can remake us men and women, then there is hope. Well, is not that why he came? Is not apprehending that what it means to take him in earnest?

Bishop Booth, of Vermont, lived all too short a life, but while it lasted it was profoundly Christian. After he died his nurse said to a friend, "I know where the Bishop is tonight. His soul has gone to hell." The friend was too shocked to speak, but then the nurse went on, "That's the only place he can be happy; there's such work to do there." That was Jesus' spirit. He sought out hell. He hungered for sinful men. Today in this congregation of supposedly elect spirits he is moving still, saying, "They that are whole have no need of a physican, but they that are sick: I came not to call the righteous, but sinners."

Ah, Christ—our teacher, our example, but more than that: revealer of the eternal grace of God, pioneer of a new humanity, our physician and savior! So there is hope!

Forgiveness of Sins

THE only persons to whom this message is addressed are those conscious of moral wrongdoing. If there is any hearer with no uneasy stirrings of conscience about his attitude toward anything or his relationship with anybody, then this sermon is not for him. For we are going to talk about forgiveness of sins.

Before any make up their minds, however, that they do not come within range of this subject's interest and scope, one would like to be certain that they understand what we mean by 'sin.' So often when we use that word we have in the background of our minds a specific list of gross iniquities—murder, robbery, sensuality, drunkenness. Those plainly are sins. But before any person endeavors to avoid his share in the need of forgiveness, let him add at least three categories more to that carnal list.

Let him add sins of temperament—sullenness, vindictiveness, peevishness, jealousy, bad temper. How much more prevalent they are; how much more harm they do; how much more hidden evil they reveal than even passionate sins! In Jesus' great parable, the Prodigal represents sins of passion, and, ruinous as they are, he did come home again. But the Elder Brother represents sins of temper. With the Prodigal home, the house alight, music playing, dancing on, it is written of the Elder Brother that "he was angry, and would not go in." Bad temper, sullen, envious, bitter—that, as Jesus saw, keeps some people from the Father's house more hopelessly than sins of passion do.

If any one seeks to avoid his share in the need of forgiveness, let him add also sins of social attitude. As one of our leading sociologists has said, "The master iniquities of our time are connected with money-making." When one watches our economic system in operation, one sees how easily a man, friendly enough with individuals whom he meets, can enforce hard practises through a great organization which does more harm, works more misery, ruins more families over a wider area, than he, by his individual friendliness, ever can make up for. Cavour, the statesman, working on the unification of Italy, and using every political trick that he could think of to achieve his ends, said once to his confrères, "If we were to do for ourselves what we are doing for Italy, we should be great rogues." Just so! There are many great and small rogues today who do evil for political and economic organizations that they never would think of doing for themselves.

Nor should any one try to escape his share in the need of forgiveness until he has added to the list sins of neglect. It is not alone the things we do; it is the things we leave undone that haunt us—the letters we did not write, the words we did not speak, the opportunity we did not take. How insistently Jesus stressed the importance of this type of evil! What was the matter with the man who hid his one talent in a napkin? What did he do? That was the trouble—he did nothing; he missed his chance. What was the trouble with the priest and the Levite who left the victim on the road? What did they do? That was the difficulty—they did nothing; they went by on the other side.

Sins of the flesh, sins of temper, sins of social attitude, sins of neglect—I suppose there must be others, but this ought to take in most of us and make us wonder whether, after all, we may not have a share in the need of the gospel of forgiveness.

This morning in particular I stress the difficulty of forgiving sin. So often pardon has been presented as an easy gospel, as though one light-heartedly could cry, Come, everybody, and have your sins forgiven! No, it is hard to forgive sins—hard for us; hard for Christ. "Which is easier," said Jesus in the story of the palsied man, "to say, Thy sins are forgiven thee; or to say, Arise and walk?" You see what the Master implies there. It is easier to tell a palsied man to walk—it is easier to meet any other human need—than to say, Thy sins are forgiven.

At first that sounds strange from Jesus. We should have thought it easy for him to forgive. He said so many glorious words about forgiveness; he exhibited it so marvelously in his life; he made it forever memorable on the cross. One would think forgiveness spontaneously overflowed from him. But no; it was hard for him to forgive, as it always ought to be. And a lesson is there which we modern Christians need to learn.

Why, then, was it hard for Jesus to forgive? In the first place, because he took sin seriously. It is easy to condone sin, to make light of it; but when one takes it seriously, it is hard to forgive. Suppose that some one here were a specialist in tapestries, prized them, loved them; and suppose he saw some ruffians ruining one, ignorantly, brutally ruining a lovely thing that he knew to be worth a king's ransom—would you think it easy for him to forgive that? Another man who could not tell tapestry from cheesecloth would find it easy to condone the deed, make light of it, pass it over. But for the expert to say even about that, Forgive them, for they know not what they do, would not be easy, for he takes tapestries in earnest.

Consider, then, the moral realm. You can go to the theater any night and hear sexual sin made light of, condoned, laughed at. But Frederick W. Robertson, the English preacher, walked down the street in Brighton once with a face terrific as the Furies and grinding his teeth in rage. He had just heard of a man plotting the ruin of a fine girl whom he knew. He took that seriously and it was hard to forgive.

When, therefore, you hear any one talking about forgiveness lightheartedly as an easy matter, you may be sure of this: he is not forgiving sin; he is condoning it, and that is another affair altogether. There is plenty of that without our adding to it. To say that sin does not matter, to make light of it, to take it easily, to be gracious and tolerant about it—there is plenty of that. But that is not forgiveness. That is moral looseness. Sin does matter—tremendously! To condone sin is easy; to forgive it is hard.

Here lies a familiar difference between two kinds of mothers. Some mothers have no moral depth, no moral seriousness. A superficial affectionateness distinguishes their motherhood. They have an instinctive maternity for their offspring, such as bears have for their cubs or birds for their fledglings. When the son of such a mother becomes a prodigal and wallows in vice, she will receive him again—

will receive him, condoning his sin, making light of it, saying that it does not matter, making up more excuses for it than he ever could himself concoct. But some of us had mothers who never would have forgiven us that way. They would have forgiven us, but, alike for them and for us, it would have been serious. They would have borne upon their hearts the outrage of our sin as though they had committed it themselves. They would have gone with vicarious steps to the gateway of any hell we turned our feet toward and stood grief-stricken at the door till we came out. They would have put themselves in our places, lived in our stead, felt upon their innocence the burden of our guilt. They would have forgiven us but it would have turned their hair gray. That is forgiveness. It always means self-substitution. He who gives forgiveness gives himself. And it is not easy.

Of course, all the seers have felt this. If Tennyson in his "Idylls of the King," portraying Arthur standing over Guinevere, fallen in penitent shame before him on the nunnery floor, had made him say some light-hearted thing as though her infidelity did not matter, we would feel the shallowness of that condoning. Moreover Guinevere would have felt it too.

> The sombre close of that voluptuous day,
> Which wrought the ruin of my lord the King—

she knew how serious had been her sin. How then could Tennyson have made Arthur's forgiveness less solemn than this:

> Yet think not that I come to urge thy crimes;
> I did not come to curse thee, Guinevere,
> I, whose vast pity almost makes me die
> To see thee, laying there thy golden head,
>
> My pride in happier summers, at my feet.
> The wrath which forced my thoughts on that fierce law,
> The doom of treason and the flaming death,—
> When first I heard thee hidden here,—is past.
>
> . . . .
>
> And all is past, the sin is sinn'd, and I,
> Lo, I forgive thee, as Eternal God
> Forgives.

That is forgiveness, and it is not easy. "Which is easier, to say, Thy sins are forgiven thee; or to say, Arise and walk?"

In the second place, Jesus found it hard to forgive because he loved people. Ah! you say, the love of people makes it easy to forgive. No, you miss the point. When you love some one deeply and another's sin hurts that person, it is hard to forgive. And sin always does hurt other people. Nobody sins unto himself alone. When, therefore, one cares for people as Jesus did, it is hard to forgive sin.

Joseph's brothers dropped him into a pit, hauled him out again, sold him as a slave to a band of Midianite merchantmen bound for Egypt, dipped his long-sleeved cloak in the blood of a goat and carried it back to the father, Jacob, trying to persuade him that Joseph was dead. Now suppose they had grown conscience-stricken, remorseful, and, unable to stand it any longer, had gone to Jacob, confessing their sin and asking his pardon. Can you not feel the first question that would have risen in the father's heart in a storm of anxious and indignant grief—Where is Joseph? What, then, has become of Joseph? You ask me to forgive you, but your sin is not simply between me and you. Where is Joseph? Somewhere in a distant land, in miserable slavery he may be today. How can I forgive you until I know that all is well with Joseph?

When you love people, it is hard to forgive sin.

So in the Gospels you find it hard for Jesus. He was tremendously severe upon the scribes and Pharisees, you say, and truly he was. But what is the reason? Does it not reveal itself in verses like this, "Beware of the scribes . . . they that devour widows' houses, and for a pretence make long prayers"? Jesus was thinking of the widows and what the rapacity of the rulers did to them. His mother was a widow. We never hear of Joseph after Jesus' early boyhood. He knew what it was for a woman to be left with a family of children. More than once in Jesus' ministry a widow appeared, like the widow of Nain, and always his special gentleness overflowed. When in a parable he wanted to represent need, he pictured a widow pleading with an unjust judge. When, therefore, he was hard on scribes, one surmises the figure of his mother in the background of his mind. "They that devour widows' houses"—that made it hard to forgive.

You say he was tremendously severe on Dives. To be sure he was—picturesquely putting him in Hades with a great gulf fixed between him and paradise. But why? He thought of Lazarus, who had lain at Dives' gate, pitied by the very dogs but unsuccored by the rich man himself. Or you say the Master was hard upon the priest and Levite. So he was. But it was because he was thinking of the victim left on the road, neglected in their selfish haste.

When you care for people, it is hard to forgive sin.

All the seers have felt this. Recall George Eliot's story of *Adam Bede*—Hetty Sorrel, pretty, vain, and superficial; Adam Bede, the stalwart carpenter; Arthur Donnithorne, careless, impulsive, well-meaning, rich. You remember Adam Bede's honest love for Hetty and his wish to marry her, Hetty's ruin at the hands of Donnithorne, her hapless child, her frenzied wanderings. You remember the scene where Donnithorne, having tried desperately to make amends for what never could be mended, goes to Adam Bede and asks forgiveness. Well, Adam gives it, but it is not easy. "There's a sort o' damage, sir," says Adam, "that can't be made up for." Aye, you whose sin hurts other folk, remember that!

Let no one of us evade this principle because our sins may operate in other realms. We all have bad tempers. Out of the charcoal pits of what we are, the fumes arise that blast the flowers of happiness in other lives. We may have even secret infidelities that seep through our cleverest concealments and poison the springs from which other folks must drink. Always our evil involves others.

My friends, forgiveness is the miracle. The first thing that we are sure of in this universe is law. Some one has said that we can no more have sin without punishment than we can have positive electricity at one end of a needle without negative electricity at the other. And it would take more than a light-hearted chatterer condoning sin to convince me that there is anything else here. Too cheap! Too easy! But when I face Christ I face one whose plummet reached to the bottom of sin. Nobody ever took it so seriously; nobody ever hated it so for what it did to people, and yet he taught forgiveness. That is the miracle: that he taught forgiveness, that he practised it so marvelously that no poor human wreck was beyond the reach of its benedictions; and that throughout Christian history the glory of the gospel has been men and women reclaimed by pardon to a reëstablished fellowship with God. It is marvelous good news. There is a merciful side to God and he forgives, but it is a miracle. Never take it lightly. "Which is easier, to say, Thy sins are forgiven thee; or to say, Arise and walk?"

In the third place, Jesus found it hard to forgive because forgiveness is such a terrific experience for the man who is forgiven. Rather, I hear some one saying, it is glorious to be forgiven. My friend, if you say that light-heartedly, I am certain of one thing—you never have been forgiven. To do somebody wrong, to be alienated from him, to be ashamed of yourself, and then by free forgiveness to be restored to the old friendship and trusted again—surely that is the most humiliating experience that a proud man can go through. If there were any other way out of the remorse and guilt of sin, who wouldn't try to find it? For, you see, there is just one thing that forgiveness does—one thing only. Forgiveness does not take away the fact of sin; the Prodigal had still been in the far country. Forgiveness does not take away the memory of sin; the Prodigal never will forget it. Forgiveness does not and cannot take away all the consequences of sin. As Adam Bede, the carpenter, said, "It's like a bit o' bad workmanship—you never see th' end o' th' mischief it'll do." But one thing forgiveness does; it reëstablishes the old personal relationships that have been broken by sin, and makes them deeper and sweeter, it may even be, by awakened love and responsive gratitude. That great thing forgiveness does—and to have been thus alienated and then reconciled through forgiveness is about the most searching experience that the human heart ever goes through.

Is not that what Christians have always meant when they associated forgiveness with the cross of Christ? I do not know what theory of the atonement you may hold, and I might almost say I do not care whether you have any theory at all, but recognize this fact: behind all the explanations of atonement that have arisen and taken form and faded away in the history of Christian thought, this conviction has lain deep—the cross means that it was not easy even for God to forgive. It cost. And that is true to life. If you should grossly wrong your wife and then penitently ask her forgiveness and she should say, "Oh, never mind; it is nothing"—that would solve no problem. It would simply mean that she did not care what you did. A true-hearted woman would go deeper than that. Two things would be in her: first, a love high and deep enough to forgive; but, second, a character, an uprightness that would be wounded and crushed by your sin, and integrity that would find it hard to forgive.

When, therefore, the gospel has invited men to forgiveness, it never has invited them to a light-hearted place where sins are condoned. It has called them to the cross. And they have always heard the cross saying to them that it was hard even for God to forgive. It cost. It cost just what it always costs when men forgive: love putting itself in our place, bearing on its innocence the burden of our guilt. For whether a mother forgives a son or God forgives us, a cross is always at the center of it, and it is not easy.

Everything that we have said this morning has been leading up to this final and climactic matter: no man's sin ever is done with until it has come through this process of forgiveness. Either your sin has been forgiven or else it is yet in you as sin. I think that is about the solemnest fact in human life.

Do not take it from me as a Christian preacher, as though this were especially Christian, or even especially religious. It is universally human. Go back to Æschylus, hundreds of years before Christ, and read his story of Orestes, who sinned and was driven by the Furies over all the earth, finding no peace until he persuaded a jury of his fellow countrymen at Athens to vote forgiveness. Leap the centuries and come down to America. You need not go to church; go to one of the greatest novels yet written in America, *The Scarlet Letter*. See Arthur Dimmesdale, with his unconfessed, unforgiven sin. How shall he be rid of it? He is a man of intellect; he will absorb himself in thought. But that is no way out. He is a minister; he will preach sermons and save souls. But that is no way out. He is a servant and will go from door to door, humbly helping people. But that is no way out. There is only one way—penitence, confession, and forgiveness.

Go even to the psychiatrists, who in more ways than this are saying what Christianity has been saying for centuries. One of the leading psychiatrists in the world said to a personal friend of mine recently, "Most of the cases of mental derangement of a functional type are due to a sense of guilt."

And when, with all this testimony of the seers and scientists, you come to your own life, you know it is true; either your sin has been forgiven or else it is in you still as sin.

We know that most clearly when we are at our best. We have gross, brutal hours, when we forget our unforgiven sins, lock them in the hold, let the roar of the world fill our ears until conscience cannot be heard, but ever and again the finer hours return, when we know that unforgiven sin still is here because unforgiven. Any minister who takes preaching in earnest cannot look out over congregations like this, Sunday after Sunday, without thinking of all the unadvertised needs that must exist beneath our respectable exteriors. Who can sum them up in their infinite variety? But deepest of all, the unforgiven sins! There must be many here this morning. Go down into that secret place. Unlock that hidden door. Take out that unforgiven sin. For your soul's sake, get rid of it! But there is only one way. Whatever theology you hold, it is the way of the cross—penitence, confession, restitution, pardon.

The Inescapable Judgment

OUR forefathers' view of life differed from our own in at least one particular. We moderns characteristically think of ourselves as the arbiters and umpires of life, passing intellectual and moral judgment on it. We see ourselves as the judges. Our forefathers saw themselves standing in the presence of an Eternal Arbiter, who judged them.

To be sure, this contrast can be overstated, but it is real. Some of the most characteristic factors in our modern world, the development of science, the popular trust in intelligence, the spread of education, the exaltation of the free and sovereign individual, all the elements of humanism, issue in this result—that we see ourselves as the judges of life, the umpires of its rights and wrongs, its truths and falsehoods. Is not that what our critical faculties and our consciences are for? Who will pass discriminating sentence on life if we do not? This modern attitude we all must recognize in ourselves. But our forefathers saw themselves not sitting on, but standing before a judgment seat that was infinitely greater than themselves, and listening to sentence passed on them.

Today I raise the question whether in that contrast the truth is all on one side, and especially whether we moderns have not forgotten something. Pilate, for example, was a typical modern at the trial of Jesus. Was he not there to judge the case? Was it not his duty to use such critical intelligence as he had to decide the contentious issue? He was the arbiter and umpire. But now, in retrospect, one sees what was really happening. Jesus, though he said not a word, was sitting in judgment on Pilate. Pilate was not so much judging as he was being judged.

One reason for the fading from our modern religious thought of this idea that we are under judgment is that our forefathers pictured the matter in terms incredible to us. They dramatized it as a cosmic courtroom with an anthropomorphic God upon the judgment seat, and they postponed it, making it a post-morten assize, where some day we all would stand before the judgment seat of God. Alas, how religion suffers from its symbolism! It takes an eternal truth and pictures it in the figures of speech of a generation that understands them. Then centuries pass, and a whole new set of mental categories and cosmic outlooks occupy the minds of men, so that the old pictures are meaningless and incredible. Then out goes the baby with the bath. Men throw away the living truth because the frameworks of thought in which it has been set are no longer at ease in their imaginations. So the abiding fact that we face judgment from an Arbiter infinitely greater than ourselves has largely vanished from our modern Christian message.

Today I confront myself and you with an idea of the divine judgment that seems to me inescapable. John stated the matter in the third chapter of his Gospel, the nineteenth verse: "This is the judgment, that the light is come into the world, and men loved the darkness rather than the light; for their works were evil." So! Who can escape that?

This picture of judgment as light, showing up what cannot stand the light, should appeal to us moderns, if only because it was deliberate modernism when John first wrote it. John's Gospel was addressed to the Greeks. They did not like, any more than we do, the old Hebrew picture of a dramatized, post-mortem, cosmic courtroom and an anthropomorphic judge. They had Plato behind them, and neo-Platonism running through their thought. They needed a new picture of the divine judgment if it was to be real to them, and John, knowing that it is the truth that matters, not the transient frameworks of imagination it is set in, gave it to them. "This is the judgment, that the light is come into the world, and men loved the darkness rather than the light."

At once that begins to hit home on our lives. If a man should say that the earth is flat, or that it was made in six days, or that insanity is caused by devils, what would be his judge? Light has come into the world. When a generation chooses ugliness in music, as though there were nothing better than jungle discords for modern orchestras to imitate, what is its condemnation? That light has come into the world. When homes are rancorous and children mistreated, when vindictiveness consumes a man as though the end of existence were to get even with another, when nations plunge into war, what is the condemnation? That light has come into the world, and men love darkness rather than light.

The inescapable judgment confronts us all. When light comes anywhere it shows things up. Even when we are physically soiled and disheveled, we stick to the shadows if we can. Beautiful, light may be, but it is also a discriminating test. It is always a judge. What got by in the dark, now that the light has come, can get by no longer. Moreover, light has come into the world in one realm after another, so that every one of us is under an inevitable judgment, not outwardly dramatic, as though we stood in a cosmic courtroom, not post-mortem, as though we merely feared a future sentence, but as John pictured it to the Greeks, real, inherent, essential, present, and continuous—light showing up things in us and in the world that cannot stand the light. My soul! this is the judgment!

As we endeavor to discover the range and meaning of this truth, consider first that here lies the real significance of sin. There is no sin until light comes, and then there is. When men had only tom-toms it was not reprehensible in them to love that monotonous cacophony best of all, but now that Bach and Mozart and Beethoven and Brahms have come, it is artistic sin.

All sin, in a real sense, is thus belatedness, being behind the times, clinging to ancient darkness after the light has come. Once cannibalism was not wrong. It existed among our forefathers in northern Europe and Britain down to the fourth century A.D., and there was no guilt about it. But then the light came. After that it was sin. Once polygamy was not sin. Our early Old Testament is full of it. But then light came. The loveliest family relationship possible to man rose like dawn over the horizon—one man and one woman loving each other so much that they did not care to love anyone else in the same way at all, and so throwing around their children the affection and security of an abiding home. After that anything less was wrong. Always light makes the darkness visible.

This is the whole idea of sin in John's Gospel. All sin is the refusal of light. Jesus says in the fifteenth chapter: "If I had not come and spoken unto them, they had not had sin: but now they have no excuse for their sin." Just so! Christ by his coming created a whole new list of sins. They had not been sins before. They would not have been sins if he had not come, but now they were sins.

We constantly picture Christ as beautiful. He was beautiful, as light is, and there lies a difficulty—light shows things up.

Is it wrong, for example, to take vengeance on a personal enemy? Once it was not. Cicero was a good and conscientious man, but an enemy of his was killed in battle and a year and a half later Cicero was still dating his letters: "The 560th day after Bovillae." But not long after Cicero another kind of person came into the world who said: "Love your enemies," and in his life and death exemplified boundless, undiscourageable goodwill. And ever since, some men, at least, standing in the light of that life, have felt their vindictiveness condemned, until magnanimity has risen to great heights in some, saying even in the midst of a bitter war: "With malice toward none, with charity for all." Judgment is not so much being sentenced to punishment; judgement is being shown up by light. We sing "Walk in the Light," as though that were a glorious experience, but it is one of the most searching that any man can know. Ah Christ, in spite of yourself, just by being what you are, inevitably you are our judge!

The old story runs that a social worker, having tried in vain to persuade a slatternly family to clean up their home, brought to them the loveliest potted plant she could find and put it in their living room. There it sat in judgment on its slovenly surroundings. First they tidied up the living room to make it a fitter place for the new gift, and then the living room sat in judgment on the rest of the house, until they cleaned that up too. Beauty had come into the home and had condemned their slatternly ways. That was the judgment.

Whenever light comes anywhere, we at once begin being judged by the way we treat it. Tennyson sings:

> We needs must love the highest when we see it,
> Not Lancelot, nor another.

Alas, if that were only true! But it is not true. We need not love the highest when we see it. We can refuse to love it. So there it stands, judging us. Where is that happening in our lives today?

Consider, in the second place, that this truth reveals the deeper meaning of faith in Christ. The typical modern question about him is, What do we think about Christ? That is to say, we sit in judgment on him. We try to get all the historic data there is, to use our critical faculties as intelligently as we can, and so to make up our minds what we think about Christ. But whenever we come upon deeply Christian souls, always a profounder inquiry is present: not alone, What do I think about Christ? but, What does Christ think about me?

Forbes-Robertson, the actor, in his autobiography says that in his London club there was a rather vehement atheist named Crow, who constantly voiced his disbelief in Christ until he was stopped by a quatrain, written by one of the members, that soon became the common property of all the club.

> We've heard in language highly spiced,
> That Crow does not believe in Christ,
> But what we're more concerned to know,
> Is whether Christ believes in Crow.

We are not denying the importance of that first question, What think ye of Christ? but all profound faith in him involves the second also, and a great transformation could take place in some lives here were they to pass over that line. See how we sit upon our little judgment seats, passing sentence on what you will, and saying even that we think so-and-so about Christ. But what does he think about us?

Dr. Zinsser, one of the finest-spirited scientists of our time, during his last years, as he faced death, wrote his autobiography in the third person, as though it were about another man. He was an agnostic. He had no clear idea of God, or faith in him. Yet at the end he wrote this about himself: "He became more firm in his determination to see things out consistently along his own lines of resignation to agnostic uncertainty—as his father had done before him. Moving further away, therefore, from faith in any comprehensible conception of God, he yet grew closer in conviction of the wisdom and guiding integrity of the compassionate philosophy of Christ." So even the agnostic acknowledges the light that came in him, as though to say that the test of life would be to know what he thinks of us.

Once war was not sin. The light had not come. Even today on all sides of the battle line multitudes of men and women would say, I believe in Christ. But what if all of us together, out of every tribe, tongue, people, and nation, ruining with our insensate brutality the hopes of generations yet unborn, could genuinely face that higher judgment seat and ask, What does Christ think of us?

As for more private matters, somewhere in this congregation some individual needs this truth.

Let us now go further, to face a strange new aspect of our truth, namely, that when one thus thinks of Christ in terms of light, it is difficult to separate his activity as a judge from his activity as a savior. Light condemns, we have said; but light also saves; it is the source of every lovely and redeeming thing we know. So John says, on one side, as Dr. Moffatt translates him: "This is the sentence of condemnation, that the Light has entered the world," but on the other side, he says: "In him was life; and the life was the light of men." Here is a mystery, that condemnation of sin and salvation from it should come commingled together.

The trouble with all lesser ideas of judgment is that they are negative, unredeeming, crushing. They are like some unskilled psychiatrists who can take you all apart and tell you what is wrong with you, but cannot put you together again. The Eternal Arbiter on his judgment seat, concerning whom Jonathan Edwards preached his awful sermon on "Sinners in the Hands of an Angry God" until women fainted and strong men clung to the pillars of the church in agony—what redeeming thing can he do for me? That idea of judgment blasts the soul with terror and dismay.

Has someone here been thinking that the entire concept of judgment anyway is an outgrown superstition? No, my friend, we cannot get away with that, not in the new scientific world of the reign of law—immutable, irrefragable, cause and consequence linked in an enforced companionship that is never broken. A momentous doctrine of judgment is at the center of the whole scientific view of the world, so that while ministers have dropped it from their preaching, scientists everywhere have been taking it up, physicians, economists, sociologists, physicists all saying, If you do this, you will get that; "Whatsoever a man soweth, that shall he also reap." How terrific even our modern scientific ideas of judgment can be!

Then this New Testament idea appears, saying to us, Light comes into the world; it does show our evil up, make our darkness visible, leave us without excuse, but light is also life-giving. It shines not alone upon our sins, but upon our possibilities; it makes luminous not only the shadowed selves we are, but the finer selves we might grow to be; it convicts us not simply of our evil, but of our potentialities; it reveals the winter of our sin, but it makes possible our spring, for, being light, warmth comes with it. The very light that judges us, saves us—that is a great gospel.

These are dark days in which we are living now. But how do we know that they are dark? Because light has come. That is something. Until 5000 years ago, says Dr. Breasted, there was no such thing as social conscience at all, no light to make even the darkness visible. But now there is. There are Christian souls in whom Christ's way of living has been gloriously exemplified. There are Christian families where the beauty of boundless goodwill has made a heaven on earth. There are Christian friendships and communities where, being members one of another, we have proved that we never find our lives until we lose them in the larger life of the fellowship. Light has come that today both shows up this hideous madness of our fratricidal strife for the brutality and insanity it is, and, being thus our judgment, is the hope of our salvation too.

For mark this: When light once comes it stays. Recall in John's Gospel the verse as the King James version gives it: "And the light shineth in darkness; and the darkness comprehended it not." No, that is not what the Greek means. Listen to Moffatt: "Amid the darkness the Light shone, but the darkness did not master it." Listen to Goodspeed: "The light is still shining in the darkness, for the darkness has never put it out." That is what it means. There is a magnificent phrase in an old prayer which addresses God as the "true sun of the world, evermore rising, and never going down!" See the historic truth in that! Christ came, and they crucified him, but he was light, and you cannot stop that with a cross. Bach was forgotten for a hundred years after his death, but he was light, and that cannot be stopped by a century of neglect. Even a feeble light like the dawning idea that the earth may be round, at first only a pinprick of illumination, can at last conquer a world of darkness. How small a candle Columbus had when he first sailed west, so that President Lowell of Harvard used to say: "When Columbus set out he did not know where he was going; when he arrived he did not know where he was; when he returned he did not know where he had been, but all the same he discovered America." One of the most impressive aspects of the story of evolution is the gradual emergence of friendship, for example. How timid its dawn, hardly a thread of radiance on the horizon! How slow its spread—Ruth and Naomi, David and Jonathan, Damon and Pythias—a strange new radiant idea of what human fellowship might be, until Greece came to her glory, that ancient illuminator of the race, and Aristotle in his great work on "Ethics" devoted two books to friendship, which, as he said, "holds mankind together." It is amazing to see that wherever light comes it stays—long neglected, yet it stays, shrouded in eras of gloom, but it grows, alike condemning and saving, judging men's evil and widening the area of radiance amid the dark.

This fact of commingled condemnation and salvation in Christ, the light of the world, is the explanation of a strange contradiction in the Gospel of John. For one can put over against each other two sets of texts from that Gospel that seem to cancel each other out. On the one side are sayings like this: "I came not to judge the world, but to save the world," and again: "God sent not the Son into the world to judge the world; but that the world should be saved through him." So Christ does not judge the world. But then come sayings like this: "For judgment came I into this world"; "If I judge, my judgment is true"; "The Father . . . hath given all judgment unto the Son." So he does judge the world. There is a head-on collision! Yet the explanation is as plain as day. Christ is light. He cannot help judging the world. Being what he is, he condemns it. But that is not what his coming was all about. His mission is not negative—positive! not condemnatory—redeeming! He is the physician who can show you what is the matter with you in order to cure it. He came not to judge, but to save.

Do not get one side of him without the other! If you let him, he can be the most discouraging figure in all history. Who can go into his presence and not be condemned? But he is not a judge sitting on the bench; he is not a mere exemplar of the inexorable reign of law. To each of us here he can mean what he meant to Peter. For when Peter first faced him he felt and said the inevitable thing: "Depart from me; for I am a sinful man, O Lord." There he stood, judged. And Jesus answered: "Come ye after me, and I will make you—I will make you—fishers of men."

An Unavoidable Choice Faces Our Jerusalem Too*

As JERUSALEM confronts Christ that week before Easter long ago, one fact stands plainly out: what a relief it would have been if they had not had to confront him! The city as a whole did not want to accept him; they did not want to crucify him; if only they could have dodged the issue and done nothing about him, what a relief! The inside of Pilate's mind will always be a puzzle but surely this factor was present: he wished he could avoid responsibility. Accepting Christ was preposterous, crucifying Christ distasteful—why did he have to do anything with Christ? He even symbolized this desire to side-step decision by publicly washing his hands of the whole matter.

Indeed, Pilate's wife, we are told, sent him an anxious message which ran: "Have thou nothing to do with that righteous man." Most of all, Pilate desired that—to have nothing to do with Christ; free from the whole disturbing business, to make no decision about him. But although he was the Roman procurator and Jesus was a carpenter from Galilee, he stood confronted with an issue he could not dodge. For or against—that he could choose; but what his wife urged on him he could not choose: "Have thou nothing to do with that righteous man."

Let us begin by recognizing our kinship with Pilate in our instinctive desire to side-step issues. We are all escapists, wanting to run away from difficult decisions, and naturally so, for decision is the hardest work in the world. None may scoff at that Roman procurator,

* A Palm Sunday Sermon.

wishing he could retreat into neutrality. What a lotus land that is, to be neither for nor against, but neutral, having nothing to do with some difficult decision!

But alas! life is not made for neutrals. Life habitually presents us not with three choices—pro, con or indifference—but with two choices, pro or con, one or the other. When Jesus said, "He that is not with me is against me," and again, "He that is not against us is for us," he stated a kind of fact that forever defeats the Pilates, trying to wash their hands of some great matter.

In the psychological realm we face this. Habit, for example—what a nuisance to have to choose between habits! Sobriety or drunkenness, sexual self-control or the lack of it, harnessed temper or explosive anger, Christian altruism or self-centeredness—if one could only be neutral about such matters, what a relief! But something mightier than we are confronts us: "Sow an act and reap a habit; sow a habit and reap a character; sow a character and reap a destiny." Try as we may to wash our hands of the whole matter, one way or another we do become creatures of habit. We must choose.

As in the psychological, so in the social realm we face this. American isolationism was escapism. What a nuisance international interdependence and world government are! What troublesome responsibilities they involve us in! Let's have nothing to do with them, said isolationism. But now the international situation has walked up on us in so imperative a fashion that everyone knows neutrality is out, with not a chance left for any great nation to avoid decision between world government and war.

Palm Sunday dramatized in unforgettable fashion this impossibility of neutrality on great issues. When we read that Jesus "stedfastly set his face to go to Jerusalem," we generally think of what that meant to Jesus, but today we are thinking of what it meant to Jerusalem. If only he had stayed away, what a relief! Why did they have to face that decision which split the city wide open, some welcoming him with hosannas and palm branches and some convinced he must be liquidated? A disturbing nuisance Jesus was, coming thus to Jerusalem, and there is no use trying to keep ourselves out of that picture. Human nature being what it is, Christ is disturbing. We Christians commonly interpret him in terms of his loveliness; we call him glorious names; but he himself said he came to cast fire on the earth. Something incendiary about Jesus starts a conflagration wherever he appears. To our human nature he is upsetting. Why must we be haunted by his ideals so far above us, and made miserable by the necessity of choosing either for him or against? Would not life be easier if he had never come, so to challenge us with his demands?

If that sounds irreverent I appeal to a great Christian theologian of the last century, Kierkegaard, whose influence has powerfully revived in our time because he so forthrightly tells the truth about us: "Let us collect all the New Testaments there are in existence, let us carry them out to an open place or up upon a mountain, and then, while we all kneel down, let some one address God in this fashion: Take this book back again; we men, such as we are now, are no good at dealing with a thing like this, it only makes us unhappy. My proposal is that like the inhabitants of Gadara we beseech Christ to 'depart out of our coasts.' "

A man who has never felt like that about Christ has never, I suspect, taken him seriously. From the difficult decisions he forces on us our human nature gladly would escape. Let us see ourselves so today, in Pilate's shoes, escapists that we are, often trying to have nothing to do with him, while still, after nearly two thousand years, he confronts us, saying, For or against, you must decide.

In every realm there are personalities who so present the world with forced decisions, and they all have this quality—they are the great revealers. Copernicus as an individual could be side-stepped, but when he revealed the truth about the solar system mankind faced an issue where neutrality was impossible: either the sun circled about the earth, or the earth about the sun, one or the other. In the orthodox Moslem University in Cairo a professor some years ago was asked which type of astronomy they taught there, Copernican or pre-Copernican, and he answered, "We teach both." In vain, however, they tried thus to sit undecided on the fence. It is one or the other, and in the long run mankind must be for or against.

So Jesus was more than an individual; he was a revealer. We commonly picture him as teaching ideals, saying, This ought to be so; but what he really said was, This is so, the everlasting truth, the way God's moral order is. The Golden Rule—this is the law of life in God's world; the infinite value of every human soul in the sight of God—this is the truth; good will and brotherhood the precondition of mankind's welfare—this is the eternal fact. If someone here has been thinking that he can be neutral concerning Christ, I answer, Surely we can side-step decision about men whose greatness lies only in their self-centered genius, and can refuse to have anything to do with those who represent nothing beyond themselves, but the great revealers of truth, whether in the physical or spiritual realm, present us with forced decisions. For or against—mankind in the end must take sides.

That Christ is the revealer of eternal truth finds confirmation in a fact to which we Christians too seldom appeal, namely, that so many other seers have said some of the same things that Jesus said. "Whatsoever ye would that men should do to you, do ye even so to them," said Jesus. Yes, and Confucianism says, "Do not unto others what you would not they should do unto you." And Buddhism says, "Hurt not others with that which pains yourself." And Hinduism says, "Do naught to others which if done to thee, would cause thee pain." And Islam says, "No one of you is a believer until he loves for his brother what he loves for himself." And Judaism says, "What is hurtful to yourself do not to your fellow man. That is the whole law and the remainder is but commentary." Strangely enough, some Christians seem to think that this sort of fact detracts from Jesus' uniqueness and originality. Upon the contrary, when eternal truth, waiting to be revealed, breaks through the clouds and is glimpsed and welcomed by many seers, that confirms the revelation. So, long before Copernicus, Pythagoras guessed that the earth circled about the sun. What would you expect? If an everlasting truth is really there, shall not eyes other than one man's get a glimpse of it? Nevertheless it was Copernicus, not Pythagoras, who really confronted the world with what he saw, and it is Christ who supremely forces the issue on us now, saying about one great matter after another, This is the everlasting truth; are you for it or against?

Were Jesus only an individual we could side-step him. Pilate could even kill him as an individual. But the truth he revealed—no nails spiked them to the cross. Pilate little guessed what he was up against when he tried to have nothing to do with him.

To be sure, in one area where Christ's revelation runs many still think they can be neutral: namely, about Jesus' God. They suppose they can be agnostic about him and have nothing to do with him. Well, we can be neutral about God in theory, but the God-question is never seriously faced until, carried out of theory, we confront it in practical life. Every man has his God. A man may give his life to money, alcohol, lust, what you will—but every man has his God. We are born worshipers, always giving our lives to something. Have we not heard Hitler say, "We want no God but Germany"? The God-question is inescapable; no one avoids it. See idolatrous mankind today serving ruinous deities whose worship is the menace of the world, and is it not clear? No man is or can be neutral on the God-question; he chooses either Christ's God or some other. For or against the God and Father of our Lord Jesus Christ—on that issue no convenient fence exists on which, undecided, one can sit. What a troublesome personality Christ is still, as he was in old Jerusalem. If only we could dodge him—but we can't; if only we could have nothing to do with him—but we can't. "He that is not with me is against me."

See how vividly our present crisis in civilization lights up this truth. A long way off seem those youthful days of mine when I had my first struggles about faith in Christ. Those struggles were predominantly theoretical: was this theological statement or that about him the more credible—so ran debate in my troubled mind. That speculative debate has its place; I do not regret it. But now the issue about Christ rises in a form that thrusts all that into the background. Hold this theory or that about him, still there he stands, announcing a way of life for men and nations that this world must choose or else choose its opposite; and the opposite, in all its naked horror and calamity, is so intolerable that I would all mankind could be made to face the issue.

I am not talking about secondary things in Christianity. Many of them matter little, and about them one can be neutral. This theory or that, this ritual or that, this denomination or that—cannot the English king be a Presbyterian in Scotland, and an Episcopalian in England? What difference do such things make? One does not need to choose. But Christ's basic principles and way of life present a forced issue, an inescapable decision; that, or its opposite, we will choose. "Have nothing to do with that righteous man"—so Pilate tried, but alas! for centuries the grim words that curse his memory have been repeated by millions: "Crucified under Pontius Pilate." What a decision he made when he tried not to decide!

Christ is beautiful. I agree.

> Majestic sweetness sits enthroned
> Upon the Saviour's brow.

Any preacher would prefer to present him only so—the most glorious spirit earth has known, whom to choose is to choose abundant life. From all man's ugliness and cruelty one turns to him today and wonders why the world does not acclaim him with hosannas as God's best gift to man. But there is another side to Christ. He said so himself. Listen to him, speaking of his truth: "He that falleth on this stone shall be broken to pieces: but on whomsoever it shall fall, it will scatter him as dust." So the law of gravitation is marvelous to those who accept and use it well, but misused it is a stone on which men break themselves to pieces. Thus, too, the everlasting truth which Christ reveals is to those that accept it beautiful, but like all truth, when rejected, it becomes a rock on which men and nations can crash in ruin. The nations have been doing that—are doing it. Pilate did that long ago. He thought he was sitting in judgment on Jesus while all the time Jesus was sitting in judgment on him, and his name and memory have been broken in pieces on that rock. Friends, if this Palm Sunday our Jerusalem is to be represented, not by Pilate, not by the priestly claque that cried, "Crucify him!" in the Praetorium, but by the people in the streets who welcomed him with palm branches and hosannas, then a personal decision is presented to each of us. No man can avoid it. We are for or against.

Consider that personal fact for a moment now for it is the crux of the whole matter. Whenever an individual faced Jesus he faced a decision. Zacchaeus, the tax gatherer, with his dishonest exploitation, confronted in Jesus no theoretical matter he could hem and haw about, plead agnosticism and leave undecided. An ethical choice was presented to him, with yes or no for the answer—would he or would he not make restitution for his ill-gotten gains, and clean up his life? I am pleading with some one here now to go back behind the ecclesiastical Christ whom we often discuss in theory, to face the historic Christ as he confronted men. Dives, mishandling wealth; the woman of Samaria, mishandling sex; the Pharisees, with their race prejudice, hating all Samaritans; Nicodemus, needing to be born again; Pilate, trying to dodge the most critical choice of his life—these and many another the Master faced and always with a forced decision: will you or won't you? If they could have side-stepped him and been neutral, what a relief! But they had to choose.

My sympathy goes out especially to some young people here. You're up against it! You've got to choose! Trying not to choose is the fatalest choice of all. Seeing from the vantage point of elder years the far-off consequence of your decision now, I could almost wish that it were possible to relieve you of that necessity, discover for you, if I could, some safe neutrality to which you could escape, but you too, in the end, will either accept Christ or not. Even though you do not use his name in making your decision, you are up against the kind of life he stood for, the truth that he revealed—for or against that, you will be. Ah Jerusalem, Jerusalem, no ancient city only, but our world now, with Christ coming over the brow of Olivet, to confront you with his claims, God grant for our children's sake a different decision than was given then! Before this world finds peace and happiness, the cry that welcomed him to the city gates must swell to such unanimous accord that all opposing cries are drowned in its greeting, in which may our hearts join today: "Blessed is he that cometh in the name of the Lord: Hosanna in the highest."

The Cross, an Amazing Paradox*

IT IS one thing to preach a Christmas sermon about the radiant stories that light up the birth of Jesus; it is another to preach a Palm Sunday sermon about the tragic events that culminated in the cross. John Milton celebrated the birth of Jesus in his glorious ode, "On The Morning of Christ's Nativity," but when he tried to write a companion piece on Jesus' death he gave it up. In his published works one finds the uncompleted beginning, with a note appended saying: "This subject the Author finding to be above the years he had when he wrote it, and nothing satisfied with what was begun, left it unfinished." What preacher, trying to speak about the cross, does not share Milton's despair and his desire to surrender the endeavor? Quite apart from any recondite theology, the cross confronts us with some of the most perplexing paradoxes we can face.

One of the simplest of them is that the cross, with its associated events, presents an ancient historic spectacle on a grand and panoramic scale and yet it is an intimate, personal matter that involves us, everyone. Many spectacular events loom large in history such as the campaigns of Alexander and the fall of Rome, before which we stand as before some Niagara, some Grand Canyon of the Colorado—huge phenomena. Among them one of the most impressive is the last week of Jesus' earthly life. The characters of that drama are momentous. Rome was there with her imperial power; one of the world's great religions was there in an hour of critical decision; the most moving figure in man's spiritual record was there; and the total tragedy, as it worked itself out, was intensely dramatic and incalculably influential. Yet this historic spectacle in the grand manner, now nearly 2000 years old and in a far distant land, personally includes you and me.

* A Palm Sunday Sermon.

Recall that moving Negro spiritual, "When they crucified my Lord, were you there?" Even to ask that question is strange. Suppose it concerned the slaying of Julius Cæsar. That, too, was a momentous tragedy yet who ever thought of asking whether we were there? But this other question is asked and has been asked in manifold ways times without number across the centuries: "When they crucified my Lord, were you there?" Well, we were there; in a deep sense we are there. All the major factors in that tragedy involve you and me. The blindness of religious leaders who cannot see a new and larger truth, the selfishness of a business community that does not want the profitable traffic in the temple courts disturbed, the disloyalty of Judas, who cares more for himself than for Christ, the political shrewdness of Pilate, who does his best to free Jesus, but, finding it costs too much, washes his hands of it, the emotionalism of the crowd, stirred by effective propaganda to cry for they know not what, the fearfulness of disciples who run away—who of us was not there?

Not one unusual sin was involved in the crucifixion of Jesus. Say, as we will, that the tragic result was the towering crime of history, doing to a shameful death the "young Prince of Glory," still it was our small, familiar, day-by-day sins that did it. I have walked the streets of Jerusalem and recapitulated in detail the events of that last week, and alas, how easy for one to imagine oneself sharing in it all! When they crucified our Lord, we were there.

Consider, for example, the crowd's choice of Barabbas rather than of Jesus. Barabbas was no common criminal. He was, says Matthew's Gospel, "a notable prisoner." His name means "son of a rabbi." He was a patriot, an outstanding nationalist, tired of subjection to Roman rule, calling for violent insurrection. He himself had dared murder, trying to foment rebellion. He appealed to the admiration of the crowd; they wanted him released. But this Jesus, this idealist, this believer in spiritual forces, who even told them to love their enemies, "Away with him, crucify him!" That is not ancient history. That is the contemporary world in all its ruinous barbarity, its trust in force. Listen in the public places of the world, and it is as though echoes came from a far-off time, crying, "Release unto us Barabbas."

Every factor that sent Jesus to the cross involves our familiar, day-by-day iniquities. Recall how at the Last Supper Jesus said to the disciples, "One of you shall betray me," and they all asked, we read, Peter, James, John, and all the rest, "Is it I?" So one walks in imagination through the streets of Jerusalem that last week and at every step one has to say, "Is it I?"

A still deeper paradox follows. The crucifixion of Jesus was so cruel and unjust a crime that no worse thing, I think, can be said about man than that man is capable of doing *that*; yet the cross of Christ, more than any other influence in history, has elevated and dignified man's sense of his essential worth and possibility. That is a paradox.

Look at the cross in its stark horror. What happened there has been called "the loneliest death in all history." Jesus' nation had rejected him as a traitor; his church had rejected him as a heretic. He was alone. The Roman soldiers had spit upon him; Pilate had washed his hands of him; the crowd jeered at him; his friends forsook him. He was alone. The Fourth Gospel says, to be sure, that Jesus' mother was there, but the Fourth Gospel was not written before 100 A.D., and the first three Gospels, written earlier, say nothing of Jesus' mother at Calvary. I am afraid we will have to stand by the first three Gospels. I am afraid he really was alone, until his heart broke in the most desolate of all cries: "My God, my God, why hast thou forsaken me?" It was the loneliest death in all history.

Man did that. That is what man is capable of doing to the choicest soul that ever visited the earth. There the full measure of man's sin stands revealed, the abyss of baseness man can fall to. What a beast and devil man can be! How full of such barbarity his history is! How can one believe in man, hope anything from man, when one sees the cross as the exhibition of his stupidity, and his pitiless cruelty wreaked through all his history upon the innocent?

Well, here is the paradox. The cross of Christ, supremely in history, has elevated and dignified man's sense of his essential worth and possibility. Man, cries the New Testament, is the "brother for whose sake Christ died." So the same cross that revealed man at his worst made man believe in himself at his best. That is a strange paradox.

The humanist scholar, Muretus, in the seventeenth century, a fugitive from France, fell ill in Lombardy, and looking like a vagabond in rags asked aid of the doctors. The physicians discussed his case in Latin, not thinking that this bedraggled pauper could understand the learned tongue. *Faciamus experimentum in anima vili*, they said, "Let us try an experiment with this worthless creature." And to their amazement the "worthless creature" spoke to them in Latin: *Vilem animam appellas pro qua Christus non dedignatus est mori?*—"Will you call worthless one for whom Christ did not disdain to die?"

The influence of that idea has been incalculable. When a king stoops to pick up something it must have value. When Christ dies for someone there must be something in him worth dying for. Christ died for every man, says the New Testament. Let that idea once get really started and something is bound to happen to the estimate of man. Christianity has failed miserably in many ways but at its best it has reached out to those whom the world has commonly treated as worthless creatures—the wicked, the neglected, the insane, the blind, the prisoners; it has believed in the value of personality even in its bedraggled forms, and the story of its sacrificial philanthropy toward the lowly and the lost, its Elizabeth Fry, John Howard, David Livingstone, Sir Wilfred Grenfell, and all the rest, constitutes the noblest element, I think, in human history. And at the fountainhead of this stream of faith in man has been the cross with its insistent appeal: "Will you call worthless one for whom Christ did not disdain to die?"

The cross, where man is at his worst, has, more than any other influence, made man believe in his best. As Paul said: "Where sin abounded, grace did much more abound." That is a strange paradox. Surely there must be something real, potent, saving, victorious, at the heart of the spiritual world to achieve a consequence like that. When I so see the cross I believe afresh in God.

This, however, only leads to another paradoxical fact about Calvary: It was the most terrible thing that could have happened to Jesus and yet it was the best thing that happened to him. That is strange. The harrowing fact that it was the most dreadful thing that could have befallen him we need not expand upon. Suffice it to say that Jesus himself must have seen crucifixions. When he was a boy at Nazareth, the Jews broke out in insurrection in Sepphoris, barely five miles away, and Josephus tells us that two thousand were crucified by the Romans along the roadside. It is incredible that Jesus should not have seen many a crucified man hanging on a cross. He knew what the barbarity meant. No wonder he prayed in an agony: "If it be possible, let this cup pass away from me."

Yet this calamity, so much the worst thing that could happen to anyone in the Roman world, was the best thing that could have happened to Jesus. The New Testament says that. "It became him," says the Epistle to the Hebrews, "in bringing many sons unto glory, to make the author of their salvation perfect through sufferings." Ah Christ, it is easy enough for someone after the event, in retrospect, to see that, but the marvel is that you saw it yourself. It is no sufficient statement of the case to say that your enemies put you to death; you put yourself to death; you walked straight into it with your eyes open; that is what you said: "I lay down my life. . . . No one taketh it away from me, but I lay it down of myself." You set your face steadfastly to go to Jerusalem. You dared the cupidity of the temple ring and overturned their money tables. You prayed it out in Gethsemane when you might have run away. You put yourself on that cross. You knew—but how did you know—that this, the most appalling thing that could happen to you, was the best thing that could happen to you, your supreme chance to get at the heart of the world. How could anyone have known that 2000 years afterwards millions would be singing: "In the cross of Christ I glory"? Yet you did know that this, the worst that could befall you, was the best.

This mystery in the cross lights up many of our lesser mysteries. Browning has a phrase in one of his poems: "The worst turns the best to the brave." How often that happens, even in our lesser lives! Whistler failed at West Point. He was deeply humiliated, but it is the best thing that could have happened to him. Otherwise he never would have been an artist. Oliver Goldsmith failed an examination as hospital mate and he could get no clientele as a physician. He was grievously disappointed, but if he had not failed he might never have written *The Vicar of Wakefield.* Daniel Defoe failed in business at the price of humiliation and suffering, for which we may all be thankful, for otherwise he would never have written *Robinson Crusoe.* Often the worst turns the best to the brave. In the light of the cross it is clear that trouble, hardship, disappointment, tragedy, are not accidents and intruders in life but part and parcel of it and that no one is prepared to live at all who is not prepared to welcome them, walk up to them, take them in, sometimes in the service of a sacrificial cause deliberately seek them and transmute them into good.

In one of O. Henry's stories a shop girl keeps a picture of Lord Kitchener upon her bureau. She does not know much about him but she keeps his picture there and at times when her life is in danger of going weakly to pieces that stern face challenges and rallies her. Say as we will that Jesus was gentle, tender-hearted and friendly, be sure that he too had a stern face. He could confront the most dreadful thing that could happen, knowing that it was the best that could befall him.

We say we adore and love Christ. That is not the whole story. He is like the sea. I love it, but at times it is fearful. Then one stands in awe of it and wishes to see it only from a distance. So is Christ. Who that sees him clearly can help being drawn to him, but who that sees him clearly can help shrinking from him when with his stern face he says that some difficult and sacrificial thing we fear to do or suffer is the best thing that can befall us. He bought the right to say that in a hard market. He lived out that paradox himself. In a world where that can happen, there must be something like God.

This, however, leads us to a deeper paradox. The cross was a crushing defeat of righteousness and yet it was one of the greatest victories that righteousness ever won.

Here in this church today and throughout Christendom a mystery is present: Nearly 2000 years after the event, we are celebrating this week one of the most colossal failures of history. On Palm Sunday Jesus swung round the brow of Olivet amid the hosannas of the crowd but by Friday the crowd was crying, "Crucify him!" He had failed. In the sacred city of his faith he appealed for a reform of religion and the leaders of the people answered in Pilate's court, "Away with him." He had failed. He trusted his disciples to be the nucleus of the coming Kingdom of God, but one betrayed him, another denied him, and they all fled. He opposed violent revolt against Rome, differed not only from the Pharisees and Sadducees, but from the Zealots, those vehement nationalists and militarists of their day, and lo! he was accused of trying to make himself a king against Cæsar, and Rome crucified him. It was a complete, sardonic, and colossal failure. That Friday night Pilate and the leaders of the people and all Jerusalem, and the disciples too, thought that Jesus was done for.

What can we make of the enigma that the future belongs to that failure? Of course, in understanding that enigma one cannot leave the Easter message out, the exultant reassurance of the disciples as the conviction dawned upon them that Jesus was not dead, but alive. Along with that, however, is a companion fact that ever since has made not merely Easter morning but the cross itself a source of Christian triumph. Here is the mystery: the most potent and impressive factor in the moral experience of man is vicarious self-sacrifice. The cross itself has in it a paradoxical duality: on the one side it is failure complete and awful; on the other it is power, the most impressive and moving power in man's ethical experience, the potency of a life that gets at the heart of the world by caring enough about the world to die for it. So one of the most colossal defeats of righteousness in history became one of the greatest triumphs righteousness ever won.

See how the ancient situation is now reversed! Did Pilate condemn Jesus? Does not the whole world know that Pilate condemned himself? Did Judas betray his Lord? Does not the whole world know that Judas betrayed himself? When the people in the Praetorium, clamoring for his death, cried: "His blood be on us, and on our children," what merciful soul with any pity in him would not cry out to them, as it were, across the centuries, Unsay that! Unsay that before it is too late! There is an old legend that after Pilate died his body was cast into Lake Lucerne in Switzerland, under the shadow of Mt. Pilatus, and that every Good Friday his spirit is dragged by demons out of the waters and enthroned, while he still unavailingly washes his hands. So all who shared in Jesus' crucifixion, could they return, would, if they might, wash their hands of it. For the future belonged to the failure.

In days like these we may well be grateful for this paradox at the heart of the gospel. If the future belonged to the things that seem to succeed, then were all our hopes undone today, whether of democracy, or Christianity, or decent human brotherhood. But there is something in the world deeper and stronger than the things that succeed, namely, the things that fail, the things that are everlastingly right and that honorably and sacrificially fail. They are the strongest elements in the world. George Tyrrell, a brave soul fighting a hard battle for his truth against many enemies, wrote once: "Again and again I have been tempted to give up the struggle, but always the figure of that strange Man hanging on the cross sends me back to my task again." So! That "strange Man" hanging on the cross, that colossal failure, whose pierced hands still hold the future in their grasp!

To be sure, now long after the event, the principle on which all this is based has percolated into human thinking and the seers have voiced it. Says Ruskin: "It is better to prefer honorable defeat to a mean victory." Says George Eliot: "Failure after long perseverance is much grander than never to have a striving good enough to be called a failure." Says Browning:

> For thence,—a paradox
> Which comforts while it mocks,—
> Shall life succeed in that it seems to fail.

But ah, Christ, how did you know that to fail *as you did* would be the surest way to succeed? For you said: "Except a grain of wheat fall into the earth and die, it abideth by itself alone; but if it die, it beareth much fruit." So they killed you on Calvary but you had in your possession a power they did not reckon with, the potency of a life that gets into the heart of the world by caring enough for the world to die for it.

This, then, is the conclusion of the matter, the crowning paradox of all. The cross was a denial of God, a blatant, cruel denial of God, and yet it was supremely the revelation of God. Why across the centuries, through changing world views and theologies, has the cross of Christ so held the fascinated attention of mankind? This, I suspect, is the main reason: Our life itself is an enigma, and it takes an enigma to meet its need. What good would Christianity be to us today if it were centered and confined in the lovely stories of Bethlehem, with adoring wise men and shepherds and singing angels? That is no adequate representation of what life confronts us with. Life is a mysterious, baffling, often tragic enigma, and the cross, which is an enigma too, talks to our true estate—a huge, historic tragedy that yet takes in you and me, a revelation of man at his worst that yet awakens faith in man at his best, the worst that can happen that yet turns the best to the brave, a crushing defeat of righteousness that yet is one of the greatest victories righteousness ever won, and so a supreme denial of God that yet has supremely revealed him. Thus the enigma of human life is matched and illumined by the enigma of Calvary:

When I survey the wondrous cross
On which the Prince of glory died.

The Eternal Victorious Over the Temporal*

WHEN in his letter to the Corinthians Paul wrote, "The things which are seen are temporal; but the things which are not seen are eternal," he stated the proposition on which faith in immortality rests. The first part of his statement is beyond doubt—everything visible passes away. To us as children life looked secure and our plans reached down a long, long road that seemed to have no ending but, growing older, we awoke to the insecurity of mortal life. Someone whom we loved died; we read biography—how young Shelley sang songs more winsome than his own *Skylark*, when a squall of wind off the Italian coast ended his melody. We began to understand Shakespeare's lines:

> All the world's a stage,
> And all the men and women merely players:
> They have their exits and their entrances.

Moreover, life's transiency concerns not individuals alone but societies and nations. When first we thought of them, how secure they seemed! But Egypt, Babylon, Assyria, Greece, Rome, vast and stable, were in the end like sand houses on the shore which tides of destiny, moved by a higher heaven than man's hands can reach, rose up and swept away.

Even with nations this sense of transiency cannot stop. The successive generations of men, like snowstorms, multitudinous in flakes, fall on the earth only to melt and disappear. As children, death seemed strange to us, but as we grew older wars came, and news of

* An Easter Sermon.

famine and pestilence, and we perceived that death, like a reaper, mows millions down. Is some one here today eighty years old? Since you were born between two and three billion people have died. Martineau's prayer gains new significance as we grow older: "O God, . . . before whose face the generations rise and pass away."

Even here, however, the sense of transiency cannot stop. We call the stars eternal, but they are not eternal. Some of them in embryo are being born out of whirling nebulae; some are in their fierce and fiery youth; some, like our own sun, are past middle age; and some are growing old and soon will die. Everything seen is temporal—ourselves, our nations, the generations, the very stars.

Against this background it seems strange to hear some say, What difference does it make whether one believes in immortality? What difference! How can a thoughtful man face the transiency of the universe and all within it and not ask himself, Is there nothing that lasts? Is it all a passing shadow show leaving not a wrack behind? Is this first superficial description we just have given of it the final word? Then in this vast changefulness there is no permanence at all. The very thought of that makes a man hungry for something eternal. There must be something here that lasts, some strand of abiding unity upon which the changes all are strung; else, as William James said, this whole creation were no better than a silly moving picture film that might as well be run backward as forward, because it means nothing either way. We must not believe in a senseless universe like that if we can help it. Our Easter thought is serious business. We are pleading for the presence somewhere of something that abides.

As a matter of fact, almost everyone believes that there is something here that lasts. Some turn Paul's text upside down and say: The things which are seen are eternal, but the things which are not seen are temporal. They mean that the physical universe goes on forever; these special stars pass but new ones come; these solar universes die but others take their places. Personality, they think, passes away and is no more; spiritual life, love, character, honor, beauty—these, the thin fragrance of matter finely organized, are blown away and perish utterly. Only omnipotent matter crashes victoriously on its endless course. This, my friends, is what it means to deny immortality. There is something here that lasts, the deniers say, but it is the lowest that endures, the physical eternal, while the spiritual dies.

Here is evident the momentous meaning of the Easter message, proclaiming to all the world a gospel upon whose truth our best hopes depend, that not the lowest but the highest persists, spiritual life abiding, things seen, temporal, but things not seen, eternal.

Consider, to begin with, what deep meaning this message puts into the universe. Materialism oversimplifies even the physical cosmos, for there too the profoundest forces are unseen. Planets are marvelous, but not so marvelous as the invisible gravitation that holds them all together. Stars are wonderful, but not so wonderful as the invisible mathematical fomulae in accordance with which they are organized. The creative Power from which all things come, no man ever saw, but it weaves the fabric of everything that is. Even this physical cosmos, where all the seen comes from the unseen, is a thousand times more mysterious than materialists guess.

This marvel deepens when one thinks of living things. Amid the lofty Alps one stands thunderstruck at the towering peaks, thrusting their heads up into heaven, their shoulders caped with snow; and then to rest his eyes from this magnificence he looks down at the blue forget-me-nots, growing along the glacier's edge. Pick one of them, tiny, frail, perishable, yet one of them is more marvelous than all the Alps. For the Alps are dead, but this has life. They have been thrust up from without, but this developed from within. They stand static for centuries but this grows, and dies, and is reborn from seeds that it creates. Here is the real marvel of the universe—life, that no man ever yet has seen or been able to explain, in comparison with which the Alpine peaks are a simple thing.

Well, then, pick up not a forget-me-not but a little child, and is not he more marvelous than all the stars? For he lives, but they are dead. He thinks, but they do not even know they are thought about. He loves, but the rumors of it never reach them. He achieves character, but they never can. The stars do not meditate upon their transiency but even a child has dreams of life to come, and thinks he was not made to die. Surely, spiritual life is the supreme marvel and treasure of creation.

This, then, is at stake on Easter Day; Is this a universe that keeps its lowest and lets its highest go? Some people think we Christians believe in immortality because we clamorously insist upon the selfish continuance of our individual lives. How absurd! Who among us is sufficiently obsessed by his own importance to insist upon his going on forever, if that is all that is involved? What we are profoundly concerned about is the kind of creation we are living in. Is it a universe that saves its lowest, clinging to dust with tenacious eagerness and with careless fingers throwing spirit all away? What an irrational world! Suppose you had a magnificent house, and suppose that through the halls and up the stairs and around the galleries of that house there played a child, your child, and suppose that some day fire threatened and you had to choose which you would keep, your house or your child. If you chose to keep the house and lose the child, we should know you to be as insane as you are wicked, as wicked as you are insane. Well, is this an insane universe, that keeps the house and lets the children go, that clings to matter and cares not for spirit, that hugs dust and throws soul away? As Professor Palmer of Harvard said about his wife's death, who can fail to feel the irrationality of the universe "if out of deference to a few particles of disordered matter it excludes so fair a spirit?" Thank God for the Easter message, affirming that God's world is not thus mad, but that while the physical passes, the spiritual endures!

Consider not only the meaning this puts into the universe but the light it throws upon the nature of immortality itself. The details of life after death we cannot imagine. As Reinhold Niebuhr said, it is unwise for Christians to claim any knowledge of either the furniture of heaven or the temperature of hell. Of course it is! Paul, for one, never indulged in such folly, but when he summed up his thoughts of the world to come, cried, "Eye hath not seen, nor ear heard, neither have entered into the heart of man, the things which God hath prepared for them that love him." That is to say, immortality is a great adventure into the unseen and the unknown. Remember Peter Pan standing on the rock in the midst of the lagoon, while the waters rose about him until drowning seemed inevitable? "To die," cried Peter, "to die will be an awfully big adventure!"

Many people need this emphasis on death as an adventure. Faith in immortality, they think, is meant for the weak, to comfort them in feebleness; it is an opiate that makes death hurt less. That is a strange perversion of our actual experience. At any rate, when I, for one, am weak, I care least about immortality. When I am weak, I am willing to lie down, go to sleep and never wake. In hours of weakness I understand what Swinburne felt when he thanked

with brief thanksgiving
Whatever gods may be
That no life lives forever;
That dead men rise up never;
That even the weariest river
Winds somewhere safe to sea.

When we are weak we feel like that! But when we are strong, when the tides of life are mighty in us, when love powerfully insists on the deathless value of our friends, when possibilities open up within us too fine and deep for threescore years and ten ever to unfold, when we are at our best, it is then we crave the chance of going on. Faith in immortality is not the child of human feebleness seeking an opiate; it springs from human strength pounding against the too narrow bars of our mortality.

When the archeologists first began their investigations of ancient Roman cemeteries, they found everywhere tombstones with seven letters on them: NFFNSNC. These letters represented an old inscription, so familiar that the Romans put only the initials down, and these are the Latin words for which the initials stood: Non fui, fui, non sum, non curo. And this is the translation: I was not, I was, I am not, I do not care. So sons buried fathers, and fathers sons; wives interred husbands, and husbands wives; and over their graves, this cynical, hopeless summary of life was put: I was not, I was, I am not, I do not care. Do you call that an expression of strength? Is it not the quintessence of surrender? Over against those ancient Roman cemeteries, put just one Christian grave, Dean Alford's, who wrote,

Ten thousand times ten thousand
In sparkling raiment bright.

He lies buried in Canterbury, England, and on his grave are inscribed these words: "The inn of a traveler on his road to Jerusalem."

For lack of this emphasis upon adventurousness in our thought of life after death, many come not only to doubt immortality but not really to desire it. Who wants to go to the conventional heaven? It would be intolerable. No live man could stand it for a week! Say to that grammar school son of yours with an earnest and aspiring mind, You can go on forever and forever being a grammar school pupil. Annihilation would be far better. But say to him, You can graduate from grammar school to high school, from high school to college, and from college to life. Always there will be new modes of thinking and new opportunities to learn, and when at last you fall on sleep like Goethe, crying, "More light!" more light will be waiting beyond your power to guess. Minds can grow, spirits can expand, life can move into new dimensions, personality can mount from plane to plane of being beyond the reach of our imaginations' fingertips. That is gospel, not for the feeble, but for the strong, the courageous, the venturesome, who trust God enough to "greet the unseen with a cheer." Do you believe *that* this morning, that God will never let the best in this universe, spiritual life, slip through his fingers, but will always give it infinite opportunity to expand and grow? Believe it! For unless one can think this universe to be utterly insane, it is true: the things seen, temporal, but the things not seen, eternal.

Come further now and see the light this throws upon the special Easter message that Jesus is alive. Once, when accumulating troubles were disturbing Martin Luther, his friends saw him writing with his fingers on the dust of a table top: "Vivit, vivit"—he lives, he lives. Let us say it to ourselves this morning: Christ is alive! Some here may have been disturbed by what we just have said about our inability to know details concerning life to come. They still are curious; they urgently wish they knew. But of course we cannot. How can an unborn babe picture the world he is going to be born into? Nevertheless, from adventuring into an unknown world, many shrink. They are afraid of death. We are not all daring Columbuses, eager to slip our caravels loose from a friendly coast and send them out upon an unknown sea. Turn again, then, to the Easter message. One great thing we do know about the future world—we know who is there. Some spiritual lives whom we have loved make it homelike today, and most of all, he is there, whom Easter celebrates.

In this audience now there may be some young lad whose mother lives far out upon the western plains. She has never seen New York. Until you came here she thought little of it, but now she thinks of it much of the time. What is New York to her? Not the town of skyscrapers and thronging multitudes, but most of all the place where you are, all else dim except the vivid thought that you are here. And were she to cross the continent, one song would be singing in her heart all the way—not the thought of outward grandeur but the thought of seeing you, where you live.

If someone says that that, like all human analogies, cannot possibly be adequate to fit the circumstances of life to come—too childlike, too simple—I answer, Granted! Yet consider: centuries before Jesus, Plato the philosopher believed in immortality—his *Phaedo* still one of the most magnificent memorials of faith in life eternal man ever wrote—and what Plato meant by it stands clearly out when he says that he would gladly die often to have a chance to talk with Hesiod and Homer. Well, we do not know details about the life to come. Right! Even John Bunyan says that when Pilgrim came within sight of the eternal city he tried to look at it through his glass but his hands shook so that he could not clearly see. We do know something, however—granting life immortal, we know who is there. Lives we loved once were among us here, the seen in them temporal, too temporal and too soon fled; but the unseen in them—we cannot believe *that* will have no end but the grave. And as the years pass and the majority of our friends slip over into the world unseen, the world unseen becomes populous and inviting.

Friends, I appeal to you this Easter morning. You do not really believe that this is so irrational a universe that it keeps the physical forever and lets the spiritual go. Deeper than your doubts is your invincible surmise that death must somehow be an open door through which the unseen and eternal in us pass into life abiding. Science says that all the physical in us is ninety-eight cents worth of chemical material. Is that the last word about us? And when we lift our thought to him through whom the Divine so gloriously shone, can you believe that as the last word about him—ninety-eight cents worth of chemical material, and when that dissolved, all was gone? No! The deeper difficulty lies not in believing an immortality but in disbelieving it, in reducing the imperishable values of the spirit in us to perishable dust. This mortal must put on immortality. Let that faith this Easter morning dignify our lives, ground our characters, on unshakable foundations, devote our service to abiding aims, and keep our hope invincible. Hallelujah! The Lord God Omnipotent reigneth!

God Talks to a Dictator

THIS is not the first time in history that the world has faced the military conquests of dictators. Long ago a Hebrew prophet lived through an era like ours, when his people were assailed by the Assyrians, but unlike most of us he achieved a standpoint from which to view the scene, that was distinctive of his religious prophethood—he heard God talking to the dictator.

Granted that in an absolute and literal sense no man can know what God would say to anyone! Yet this is one of man's distinctive attributes, that he can erect himself higher than himself and see the situations that confront him, not simply from a level stance but from above, as they might look to God. That is what a prophet is for—to help people see their contemporary world in wide perspective from a height, as God might see it. So Isaiah heard God talking to the dictator. "The Assyrian came down like the wolf on the fold," so that Judea lay under the thralldom of a conqueror, and in distress and confusion, as among us now, everyone was talking about him and to him. But history has thought it worth-while to record only what the prophet heard God say to him: "Ho Assyrian, the rod of mine anger, the staff in whose hand is mine indignation!"

The Jews hated that conqueror. He seemed altogether wild and lawless; he threatened their temple and their culture; his victory meant to them the downfall of their choicest values; he was to them anti-God, as though some volcanic evil, some demonic force, had escaped from God's control and was running amuck in the world. They felt about him as we feel about Hitler. Then Isaiah heard God talking to him, calling him, as Dr. Moffatt translates it, "my club in anger, the rod I wield in wrath." So that dictator was not merely wild and lawless; he had not escaped the sovereignty of God; he was a rod in God's hands; God had picked him up; God was using him; God could lay him down again. The dictator himself did not know this. Says Isaiah, "other plans has he, and other aims!" But even amid his devastations God talked to him as though to say, You are my instrument; I am using you; I took you up, and I can throw you down.

Like all typical religious language this is picturesque metaphor and simile. We may not interpret it to mean that God uses evil means to good ends. In two ways we deal with evil, sometimes choosing it as a method, as Jesus' enemies chose his crucifixion to secure a result they wanted, sometimes confronting it, as Jesus himself confronted the cross, not choosing it but forced to face it, and turning it to the purposes of man's salvation. The choice of evil for good ends is always wrong; the use of evil, when it is thrust upon us, to high purposes is one of the noblest forms of moral victory. It is in the second category, not the first, that we should place Isaiah's vision of God as he says to the Assyrian conqueror, You are my rod.

In the first place, Isaiah saw God using that conqueror as a just punishment on Judea for its sins. "Ho Assyrian, the rod of mine anger." That was a dreadful thing for the prophet to have to say to his own people, but he said it. He was like a faithful psychiatrist dealing with one of us when we blaze out with indignation against someone who, we think, is wronging us. For the psychiatrist says, Wait a moment; that was your own fault; you brought that on yourself. So Isaiah spoke to the people. They suffered their tragedy, he said, because they deserved it.

Unless we can see that truth about ourselves today, I am sure we have missed one of the major meanings of our catastrophe. We brought this disaster upon ourselves.

As a matter of historic fact, it was only by giving that interpretation to the conquerors that the Jewish prophets achieved the monotheism they have bequeathed to us. For in those days the theory was that there were many gods, each nation having it own deities, and the theological question then was which nation's gods were most real and powerful. The answer to that polytheistic question was naturally made evident in war. If one nation conquered another, clearly the gods of the conquerors were real and strong, and the gods of the conquered weak. So when Assyria triumphed over Judea, the popular conclusion was swift and clear—the gods of Assyria must be real; the gods of Israel must be futile. Monotheism never could have come from that interpretation of the conqueror.

The great prophets gave us monotheism because they saw the conqueror from another point of view. They said not that he disproved the one true God, but that he represented the inevitable punishment of the one true God on his people's sin. The victory of Assyria was to the prophets not evidence of God's weakness or abdication, but of God's terrific reality as the impartial administrator of ethical cause and consequence. The one God of Israel, they cried, is still the God of all the world, but he is a God of moral law; not even a chosen people can escape his punishments! When, then, the Assyrian conquered Judea, and all the people were tempted to cry, That proves the gods of Assyria to be real! the prophet said, Rather that proves that we have sinned, and that the Eternal God of righteousness plays no favorites in this world, but brings down his judgment even on Judea when she rebels.

As a matter of historic fact that is the way we got monotheism—from prophets penitent enough to acknowledge that their catastrophe was the one God's just punishment on their own people's sin. And that is not ancient history. Some today say that Hitler and Mussolini prove that the gods of naziism and fascism are the true gods. Others say that these conquerors with their cruel devastations prove that there is no God at all. The prophetic vision is needed afresh to see that what the dictators really prove is that we all have sinned, that this is a morally law-abiding world, that cause does bring consequence, that our present tragedy is the inevitable result of our joint guilt.

There are many things in these troubled days that the church cannot do to help, but some things are the church's special business, and none, I think, more crucial and important than to keep penitence alive in this situation. Said a wise friend to me recently: "If all of us could go to the council table after this war is over in the spirit of penitence, there might be some hope." Well, without that there can be no hope at all.

Moreover, we of the democracies should be especially penitent. We won the last war. With utter and crushing completeness we won it.

Never forget that. Endure, if you can, the reading of one paragraph from President Wilson's announcement of the Armistice to Congress in 1918: "We know that the object of the war is attained; the object upon which all free men had set their hearts; and attained with a sweeping completeness which even now we do not realize. Armed imperialism such as the men conceived who were but yesterday the masters of Germany is at an end, its illicit ambitions engulfed in black disaster. Who will now seek to revive it? The arbitrary power of the military caste of Germany which once could secretly and of its own single choice disturb the peace of the world is discredited and destroyed. And more than that—much more than that—has been accomplished." So completely did we, the democracies, win the war. We were in charge of the world. We could do what we would. As to what we did and did not do, the bill of particulars has been written again and again, and I know no judgment more unanimous than this —that we of the democracies are more responsible for the rise of the dictators than the plain people of the dictatorships themselves. Penitence becomes us well.

There are many angles from which one can look at Hitler and Mussolini today. I am not denying the truth in any of them, but they are partial and incomplete unless we humbly and penitently recognize that the dictators have come as an inevitable consequence of our joint sin, unless we hear, as it were, the moral order of this universe talking to them, saying: "Ho Assyrian, the rod of mine anger."

Now such penitence is not at home in wartime. In wartime pride is at home. Today pride rules our wills. In picking out sin and distributing blame we practice selective attention. We can easily see the iniquities of everyone except ourselves and our friends. We Christians should do better than that, as Lincoln did during the Civil War. I commend his spirit to you. "If God wills that . . . all the wealth piled by the bondman's two hundred and fifty years of unrequited toil shall be sunk, and . . . every drop of blood drawn with the lash shall be paid by another drawn with the sword; as was said three thousand years ago, so still it must be said, 'The judgments of the Lord are true and righteous altogether.' "

In the second place, however, this address of God to the dictator implies another meaning, namely, that God is employing the dictator to some good purpose of his own. When the populace upon the common levels saw the conqueror's victory, they cried, All is lost! But the prophets did not. God had picked up that rod of Assyria, they said; he would do something with it before he laid it down. They found, that is, not only humility and penitence, but courage and hope in the sovereignty of God.

There is a strange verse in one of the Psalms addressed to the Lord which says, "the wrath of man shall praise thee." How can that be true? It says that God can take man's evil and use it, that in his hands even man's wrath and iniquity are not a total loss. It says that God can use downright sin, as though a piece of grit that did not belong there, getting into an oyster shell, the oyster could make into a pearl after all. How can that be true about sin? Yet, where would we be in personal life if that were not true? When a man sins, need that be a total loss? No, not necessarily a total loss. It may seem dangerous for a preacher to give that answer, but it is the true one. Even downright wickedness need not be a total loss.

Did that Prodigal Son, for example, learn nothing in the far country that God could put to good use afterwards? He learned a lot that boys who stay at home never know. It was dreadful. Only a fool would go through what he went through for the sake of learning it. But when in after days some boy was tempted to seek the far country, who was it in that Jewish town that best could help him? That Prodigal. He knew. He could put his very sin to use for the sake of God and of that other boy now tempted. We are often told that we ought to capitalize our troubles, and transform them into sympathy, understanding, and increased usefulness. That is true also about our sin. Here it is, a great mistake, a wrong committed. It is a loss, but thank God it need not be a total loss. Capitalize it. There are some people we especially can help because of it. God can use it. He can make even the wrath of men praise him.

Even unredeemed sinners God uses. We constantly and rightly exalt the ways in which God has used Christ, his perfect instrument. Yes, but he has used Judas Iscariot too. Someone, I suppose, had to try that experiment of betraying Christ, and stand there, an example of the way such betrayal looks when seen in the retrospect of history. How many of us, then, in some pinch in our lives when we have been tempted to betray Christ, have thought of Judas, and have said, No! not that! I'll not do that! God can use even Judas.

I am pleading for what our fathers called an overruling Providence, as though man's wickedness, like a stream, could indeed go wild, break its banks, and let loose a torrential flood, but lo! there is a lie of the land that gets control in the end, a limit beyond which no stream's wildness can go, a contour to the landscape, a shape to the eternal hills, a declivity in the valleys, that at last bring even the wildest streams to terms and force them into channels that they did not choose. That fact about the world the great prophets saw. "Ho Assyrian!"

As a matter of history, this has been true in man's public affairs. The Roman Empire was a vast imperialism, cruel, selfish, bloody. Was it a total loss? Far from it! God used Rome for an overriding of racial and national boundaries, a unifying of the known world, a creative building of law and order, to which we still are incalculably indebted. The French Revolution was terrible, with tumbrils rolling down Parisian streets, and heads falling daily beneath the guillotine. Was it a total loss? Far from it! In the retrospect of history it left gains that cannot be measured. Hitler and Mussolini represent everything that most we fear and hate in public life. Will they be a total loss? Not unless history reverses itself. My friends, a radical change in the world order has been long overdue. Our military and economic imperialisms, our subjugation of native peoples, our insane tariff barriers, our unjust division of the world's resources, have long cried out for change. We the democracies might have done it peacefully, but alas! we failed. Now the dictators come. They are to me as terrible as they are to you, but be sure of this, in the retrospect of history they will not be a total loss. God is saying to them today: Ho Assyrian, my rod!

Indeed, has it not occurred to us that Hitler may turn out to be a powerful, even though unintentional, friend of democracy? For consider! We in the democracies were slipping. Indeed, we were! We were taking democracy for granted. Was it not a lovely way of living that our fathers had bequeathed to us? What we could get out of it, not what we should dedicate to it, was foremost in our thoughts. Our life in this country had become undisciplined, soft, indulgent, careless, and what we took so easily for granted we had forgotten deeply and sacrificially to value. But now democracy is in danger, and there has been in the United States more care about it, more study of what it means, more concern over its foundations, more sense of its value in the last year than in many a year before. Alas! we never value anything as we should until we face the peril of losing it. That is true even in the family, where some loved person who for years has been safely at our side, who has been assumed as part of the scenery of our life, falls ill, and we wake up to see how carelessly we have been taking for granted one whom we so easily might lose. So today we feel about democracy. It has become to us a very dear thing. We have faced the possibility of seeing democracy crushed, and we have said that democracy should not die as long as free spirits were left in the world. Who has wrought this change? Hitler. What then? Am I saying, Thank God for Hitler? Far from it, but thank God for God, who towers above Hitler, who can use him, despite himself, for causes that he has no mind to serve. Thank God for that lie of the land that no overflowing flood can ultimately escape, but that will turn the wildest currents to channels that not they but God chooses!

See what I am pleading for—faith in the God of history. Throughout my ministry two aspects of God have been predominant in my thought and preaching—the God of nature, and the God of inner personal experience. But in these days another aspect of deity grows imperative—the God of history. Not to be identified with any national policy, not even with our own, the God of history sitteth above the circle of the earth, and the nations are accounted as a drop in the bucket. And there he is today, and his word to the dictators has not lost its power: Ho Assyrian, my rod!

This leaves us a brief moment for the final truth involved in the prophet's insight. When God picks up a rod, he can throw it down again. He always has. These rods of his, these conquerors that seem so strong, one by one have been thrown down. God picked them up. Well, then, "Shall the axe boast itself against him that heweth therewith? shall the saw magnify itself against him that wieldeth it?"

One of the great passages in Victor Hugo's *Les Misérables* is his description of the Battle of Waterloo. Recall how it ends: "Was it possible for Napoleon to win the battle? We answer in the negative. Why? On account of Wellington, on account of Blücher? No; on account of God. . . . When the earth is suffering from an excessive burden, there are mysterious groans from the shadow, which the abyss hears. Napoleon had been denounced in infinitude, and his fall was decided. He had angered God." Napoleon himself had an intimation of this fact, for he said once: "As long as I am necessary, no power in the world will be able to brush me aside. But the moment I become unnecessary, an atom will be enough to smash me."

I am not saying that in this grim crisis that confronts the world we can shoulder off on God all the responsibility of getting rid of the conquerors, as though he would settle everything. We have our tasks, many and imperative, to make these dictators unnecessary and impossible. But if we are to have strength for them, we need to see and hear more than the daily news brings to our eyes and ears. Not we humans alone, but God also is talking to the dictators, and in the broad perspective of history it is not too difficult to discover what he is saying: Ho Assyrian! the rod of mine indignation, the punishment of the world's sins—he is saying that. I am using you, and, far beyond your will, you will serve my purposes and not be a total loss—he is saying that. But he is saying also, When I am through with you, you are done! No wild stream, however madly it grows turbulent, can in the end escape the lie of my land.

Ah Christ! How utterly different you are from the dictators! How weak today you often seem in comparison with them! Yet the long perspectives of history suggest another judgment.

> I saw the conquerors riding by
> With cruel lips and faces wan:
> Musing on kingdoms sacked and burned
> There rode the Mongol Genghis Khan;
>
> And Alexander, like a god,
> Who sought to weld the world in one;
> And Caesar with his laurel wreath;
> And like a thing from Hell the Hun;
>
> And, leading like a star, the van,
> Heedless of upstretched arm and groan,
> Inscrutable Napoleon went,
> Dreaming of empire, and alone . . .

Then all they perished from the earth,
As fleeting shadows from a glass,
And, conquering down the centuries,
Came Christ the Swordless on an ass.

The Unknown Soldier

IT WAS an interesting idea to deposit the body of an unrecognized soldier in the national memorial of the Great War, and yet, when one stops to think of it, how strange it is! Yesterday, in Rome, Paris, London, Washington, and how many capitals beside, the most stirring military pageantry, decked with flags and exultant with music, centered about the bodies of unknown soldiers. That is strange. So this is the outcome of Western civilization, which for nearly two thousand years has worshiped Christ, and in which democracy and science have had their widest opportunity, that the whole nation pauses, its acclamations rise, its colorful pageantry centers, its patriotic oratory flourishes, around the unrecognizable body of a soldier blown to bits on the battlefield. That is strange.

It was the war lords themselves who picked him out as the symbol of war. So be it! As a symbol of war we accept him from their hands.

You may not say that I, being a Christian minister, did not know him. I knew him well. From the north of Scotland, where they planted the sea with mines, to the trenches of France, I lived with him and his fellows—British, Australian, New Zealand, French, American. The places where he fought, from Ypres through the Somme battlefield to the southern trenches, I saw while he still was there. I lived with him in his dugouts in the trenches, and on destroyers searching for submarines off the shores of France. Short of actual battle, from training camp to hospital, from the fleet to No Man's Land, I, a Christian minister, saw the war. Moreover, I, a Christian minister, participated in it. I too was persuaded that it was a war to end war. I too was a gullible fool and thought that modern war could somehow make the world safe for democracy. They sent men like me to explain to the army the high meanings of war and, by every argument we could command, to strengthen their morale. I wonder if I ever spoke to the Unknown Soldier.

One night, in a ruined barn behind the lines, I spoke at sunset to a company of hand-grenaders who were going out that night to raid the German trenches. They told me that on the average no more than half a company came back from such a raid, and I, a minister of Christ, tried to nerve them for their suicidal and murderous endeavor. I wonder if the Unknown Soldier was in that barn that night.

Once in a dugout which in other days had been a French wine cellar I bade Godspeed at two in the morning to a detail of men going out on patrol in No Man's Land. They were a fine company of American boys fresh from home. I recall that, huddled in the dark, underground chamber, they sang,

> Lead, kindly Light, amid th' encircling gloom,
> Lead thou me on.
> The night is dark, and I am far from home,—
> Lead thou me on.

Then, with my admonitions in their ears, they went down from the second- to the first-line trenches and so out to No Man's Land. I wonder if the Unknown Soldier was in that dugout.

You here this morning may listen to the rest of this sermon or not, as you please. It makes much less difference to me than usual what you do or think. I have an account to settle in this pulpit today between my soul and the Unknown Soldier.

He is not so utterly unknown as we sometimes think. Of one thing we can be certain: he was sound of mind and body. We made sure of that. All primitive gods who demanded bloody sacrifices on their altars insisted that the animals should be of the best, without mar or hurt. Turn to the Old Testament and you find it written there: "Whether male or female, he shall offer it without blemish before Jehovah." The god of war still maintains the old demand. These men to be sacrificed upon his altars were sound and strong. Once there might have been guessing about that. Not now. Now we have medical science, which tests the prospective soldier's body. Now we have psychiatry, which tests his mind. We used them both to make sure that these sacrifices for the god of war were without blemish. Of all insane and suicidal procedures, can you imagine anything madder than this, that all the nations should pick out their best, use their scientific skill to make certain that they are the best, and then in one mighty holocaust offer ten million of them on the battlefields of one war?

I have an account to settle between my soul and the Unknown Soldier. I deceived him. I deceived myself first, unwittingly, and then I deceived him, assuring him that good consequence could come out of that. As a matter of hard-headed, biological fact, what good can come out of that? Mad civilization, you cannot sacrifice on bloody altars the best of your breed and expect anything to compensate for the loss.

Of another thing we may be fairly sure concerning the Unknown Soldier—that he was a conscript. He may have been a volunteer but on an actuarial average he probably was a conscript. The long arm of the nation reached into his home, touched him on the shoulder, saying, You must go to France and fight. If some one asks why in this "land of the free" conscription was used, the answer is, of course, that it was necessary if we were to win the war. Certainly it was. And that reveals something terrific about modern war. We cannot get soldiers —not enough of them, not the right kind of them—without forcing them. When a nation goes to war now, the entire nation must go. That means that the youth of the nation must be compelled, coerced, conscripted to fight.

When you stand in Arlington before the tomb of the Unknown Soldier on some occasion, let us say, when the panoply of military glory decks it with music and color, are you thrilled? I am not—not any more. I see there the memorial of one of the saddest things in American history, from the continued repetition of which may God deliver us!—the conscripted boy.

He was a son, the hope of the family, and the nation coerced him. He was, perchance, a lover and the deepest emotion of his life was not desire for military glory or hatred of another country or any other idiotic thing like that, but love of a girl and hope of a home. He was, maybe, a husband and a father, and already, by that slow and beautiful gradation which all fathers know, he had felt the deep ambitions of his heart being transferred from himself to his children. And the nation coerced him. I am not blaming him; he was conscripted. I am not blaming the nation; it never could have won the war without conscription. I am simply saying that *that* is modern war, not by accident but by necessity, and with every repetition that will be more and more the attribute of war.

Last time they coerced our sons. Next time, of course, they will coerce our daughters, and in any future war they will conscript property. Old-fashioned Americans, born out of the long tradition of liberty, some of us have trouble with these new coercions used as short cuts to get things done, but nothing else compares with this inevitable, universal, national conscription in time of war. Repeated once or twice more, it will end everything in this nation that remotely approaches liberty.

If I blame anybody about this matter, it is men like myself who ought to have known better. We went out to the army and explained to these valiant men what a resplendent future they were preparing for their children by their heroic sacrifice. O Unknown Soldier, however can I make that right with you? For sometimes I think I hear you asking me about it:

> Where is this great, new era that the war was to create? Where is it? They blew out my eyes in the Argonne. Is it because of that that now from Arlington I strain them vainly to see the great gains of the war? If I could see the prosperity, plenty, and peace of my children for which this mangled body was laid down!

My friends, sometimes I do not want to believe in immortality. Sometimes I hope that the Unknown Soldier will never know.

Many of you here knew these men better, you may think, than I knew them, and already you may be relieving my presentation of the case by another picture. Probably, you say, the Unknown Soldier enjoyed soldiering and had a thrilling time in France. The Great War, you say, was the most exciting episode of our time. Some of us found in it emotional release unknown before or since. We escaped from ourselves. We were carried out of ourselves. Multitudes were picked up from a dull routine, lifted out of the drudgery of common days with which they were infinitely bored, and plunged into an exciting adventure which they remember yet as the most thrilling episode of their careers.

Indeed, you say, how could martial music be so stirring and martial poetry so exultant if there were not at the heart of war a lyric glory? Even in the churches you sing,

> Onward, Christian soldiers,
> Marching as to war.

You, too, when you wish to express or arouse ardor and courage, use war's symbolism. The Unknown Soldier, sound in mind and body—yes! The Unknown Soldier a conscript—probably! But be fair and add that the Unknown Soldier had a thrilling time in France.

To be sure, he may have had. Listen to this from a wounded American after a battle. "We went over the parapet at five o'clock and I was not hit till nine. They were the greatest four hours of my life." Quite so! Only let me talk to you a moment about that. *That* was the first time he went over the parapet. Anything risky, dangerous, tried for the first time, well handled, and now escaped from, is thrilling to an excitable and courageous soul. What about the second time and the third time and the fourth? What about the dreadful times between, the long-drawn-out, monotonous, dreary, muddy barrenness of war, concerning which one who knew said, "Nine-tenths of War is Waiting"? The trouble with much familar talk about the lyric glory of war is that it comes from people who never saw any soldiers except the American troops, fresh, resilient, who had time to go over the parapet about once. You ought to have seen the hardening-up camps of the armies which had been at the business since 1914. Did you ever see them? Did you look, as I have looked, into the faces of young men who had been over the top, wounded, hospitalized, hardened up—over the top, wounded, hospitalized, hardened up—over the top, wounded, hospitalized, hardened up—four times, five times, six times? Never talk to a man who has seen that about the lyric glory of war.

Where does all this talk about the glory of war come from, anyway?

"Charge, Chester, charge! On, Stanley, on!"
Were the last words of Marmion.

That is Sir Walter Scott. Did he ever see war? Never.

And how can man die better
Than facing fearful odds,
For the ashes of his fathers,
And the temples of his Gods?

That is Macaulay. Did he ever see war? He was never near one.

Storm'd at with shot and shell,
Boldly they rode and well,
Into the jaws of Death,
Into the mouth of Hell,
Rode the six hundred.

That is Tennyson. Did he ever see war? I should say not.

There is where the glory of war comes from. We have heard very little about it from the real soldiers of this last war. We have had from them the appalling opposite. They say what George Washington said: it is "a plague to mankind." The glory of war comes from poets, preachers, orators, the writers of martial music, statesmen preparing flowery proclamations for the people, who dress up war for other men to fight. They do not go to the trenches. They do not go over the top again and again and again.

Do you think that the Unknown Soldier would really believe in the lyric glory of war? I dare you; go down to Arlington and tell him that *now*.

Nevertheless, some may say that while war is a grim and murderous business with no glory in it in the end, and while the Unknown Soldier doubtless knew that well, we have the right in our imagination to make him the symbol of whatever was most idealistic and courageous in the men who went out to fight. Of course we have. Now, let us do that! On the body of a French sergeant killed in battle was found a letter to his parents in which he said, "You know how I made the sacrifice of my life before leaving." So we think of our Unknown Soldier as an idealist, rising up in answer to a human call and making the sacrifice of his life before leaving. His country seemed to him like Christ himself, saying, "If any man would come after me, let him deny himself, and take up his cross daily, and follow me." Far from appealing to his worst, the war brought out his best—his loyalty, his courage, his venturesomeness, his care for the downtrodden, his capacity for self-sacrifice. The noblest qualities of his young manhood were aroused. He went out to France a flaming patriot and in secret quoted Rupert Brooke to his own soul:

> If I should die, think only this of me:
> That there's some corner of a foreign field
> That is for ever England.

There, you say, is the Unknown Soldier.

Yes, indeed, did you suppose I never had met him? I talked with him many a time. When the words that I would speak about war are a blistering fury on my lips and the encouragement I gave to war is a deep self-condemnation in my heart, it is of that I think. For I watched war lay its hands on these strongest, loveliest things in men and use the noblest attributes of the human spirit for what ungodly deeds! Is there anything more infernal than this, to take the best that is in man and use it to do what war does? This is the ultimate description of war—it is the prostitution of the noblest powers of the human soul to the most dastardly deeds, the most abysmal cruelties of which our human nature is capable. That *is* war.

Granted, then, that the Unknown Soldier should be to us a symbol of everything most idealistic in a valiant warrior, I beg of you, be realistic and follow through what war made the Unknown Soldier do with his idealism. Here is one eye-witness speaking:

"Last night, at an officers' mess there was great laughter at the story of one of our men who had spent his last cartridge in defending an attack. 'Hand me down your spade, Mike,' he said; and as six Germans came one by one round the end of a traverse, he split each man's skull open with a deadly blow." The war made the Unknown Soldier do *that* with his idealism.

"I can remember," says one infantry officer, "a pair of hands (nationality unknown) which protruded from the soaked ashen soil like the roots of a tree turned upside down; one hand seemed to be pointing at the sky with an accusing gesture. . . . Floating on the surface of the flooded trench was the mask of a human face which had detached itself from the skull." War harnessed the idealism of the Unknown Soldier to *that*!

Do I not have an account to settle between my soul and him? They sent men like me into the camps to awaken his idealism, to touch those secret, holy springs within him so that with devotion, fidelity, loyalty, and self-sacrifice he might go out to war. O war, I hate you most of all for this, that you do lay your hands on the noblest elements in human character, with which we might make a heaven on earth, and you use them to make a hell on earth instead. You take even our science, the fruit of our dedicated intelligence, by means of which we might build here the City of God, and, using it, you fill the earth instead with new ways of slaughtering men. You take our loyalty, our unselfishness, with which we might make the earth beautiful, and, using these our finest qualities, you make death fall from the sky and burst up from the sea and hurtle from unseen ambuscades sixty miles away; you blast fathers in the trenches with gas while you are starving their children at home by blockades; and you so bedevil the world that fifteen years after the Armistice we cannot be sure who won the war, so sunk in the same disaster are victors and vanquished alike. If war were fought simply with evil things, like hate, it would be bad enough but, when one sees the deeds of war done with the loveliest faculties of the human spirit, he looks into the very pit of hell.

Suppose one thing more—that the Unknown Soldier was a Christian. Maybe he was not, but suppose he was, a Christian like Sergeant York, who at the beginning intended to take Jesus so seriously as to refuse to fight but afterward, otherwise persuaded, made a real soldier. For these Christians do make soldiers. Religion is a force. When religious faith supports war, when, as in the Crusades, the priests of Christ cry, "Deus Vult"—God wills it—and, confirming ordinary motives, the dynamic of Christian devotion is added, then an incalculable resource of confidence and power is released. No wonder the war departments wanted the churches behind them!

Suppose, then, that the Unknown Soldier was a Christian. I wonder what he thinks about war now. Practically all modern books about war emphasize the newness of it—new weapons, new horrors, new extensiveness. At times, however, it seems to me that still the worst things about war are the ancient elements. In the Bible we read terrible passages where the Hebrews thought they had command from Jehovah to slaughter the Amalekites, "both man and woman, infant and suckling, ox and sheep, camel and ass." Dreadful! we say, an ancient and appalling idea! Ancient? Appalling? Upon the contrary, that is war, and always will be. A military order, issued in our generation by an American general in the Philippines and publicly acknowledged by his counsel afterwards in a military court, commanded his soldiers to burn and kill, to exterminate all capable of bearing arms, and to make the island of Samar a howling wilderness. Moreover, his counsel acknowledged that he had specifically named the age of ten with instructions to kill every one over that. Far from launching into a denunciation of that American general, I am much more tempted to state his case for him. Why not? Cannot boys and girls of eleven fire a gun? Why not kill everything over ten? That is war, past, present, and future. All that our modern fashions have done is to make the necessity of slaughtering children not the comparatively simple and harmless matter of shooting some of them in Samar, one by one, but the wholesale destruction of children, starving them by millions, impoverishing them, spoiling the chances of unborn generations of them, as in the Great War.

My friends, I am not trying to make you sentimental about this. I want you to be hard-headed. We can have this monstrous thing or we can have Christ, but we cannot have both. O my country, stay out of war! Coöperate with the nations in every movement that has any hope for peace; enter the World Court, support the League of Nations, contend undiscourageably for disarmament, but set your face steadfastly and forever against being drawn into another war. O church of Christ, stay out of war! Withdraw from every alliance that maintains or encourages it. It was not a pacifist, it was Field-Marshal Earl Haig who said, "It is the business of the churches to make my business impossible." And O my soul, stay out of war!

At any rate, I will myself do the best I can to settle my account with the Unknown Soldier. I renounce war. I renounce war because of what it does to our own men. I have watched them coming gassed from the front-line trenches. I have seen the long, long hospital trains filled with their mutilated bodies. I have heard the cries of the crazed and the prayers of those who wanted to die and could not, and I remember the maimed and ruined men for whom the war is not yet over. I renounce war because of what it compels us to do to our enemies, bombing their mothers in villages, starving their children by blockades, laughing over our coffee cups about every damnable thing we have been able to do to them. I renounce war for its consequences, for the lies it lives on and propagates, for the undying hatreds it arouses, for the dictatorships it puts in the place of democracy, for the starvation that stalks after it. I renounce war and never again, directly or indirectly, will I sanction or support another! O Unknown Soldier, in penitent reparation I make you that pledge.

The Church Must Go Beyond Modernism

IF WE are successfully to maintain the thesis that the church must go beyond modernism, we must start by seeing that the church had to go as far as modernism. Fifty years ago, a boy seven years of age was crying himself to sleep at night in terror lest, dying, he should go to hell, and his solicitous mother, out of all patience with the fearful teachings which brought such apparitions to the mind, was trying in vain to comfort him. That boy is preaching to you today and you may be sure that to him the achievements of Christian modernism in the last half century seem not only important but indispensable.

Fifty years ago the intellectual portion of Western civilization had turned one of the most significant mental corners in history and was looking out on a new view of the world. The church, however, was utterly unfitted for the appreciation of that view. Protestant Christianity had been officially formulated in prescientific days. The Augsburg Confession was a notable statement but the men who drew it up, including Luther himself, did not even believe that the earth goes round the sun. The Westminster Confession, for the rigorous acceptance of which the Presbyterian rear-guard still contends, was a memorable document but it was written forty years before Newton published his work on the law of gravitation. Moreover, not only were the mental patterns of Protestant Christianity officially formulated in prescientific days but, as is always true of religion, those patterns were sacred to their believers and the changes forced by the new science seemed impious and sacrilegious.

Youths like myself, therefore, a half century ago faced an appalling lag between our generation's intellect on one side and its religion on the other, with religion asking us to believe incredible things. Behind his playfulness the author of *Through the Looking Glass* had this serious matter in mind when he represented the White Queen as saying to Alice, "I'm just one hundred and one, five months and a day." Said Alice, "I can't believe *that!*" Said the Queen pityingly, "Can't you? Try again: draw a long breath, and shut your eyes." So the church seemed to be speaking to us.

Modernism, therefore, came as a desperately needed way of thinking. It insisted that the deep and vital experiences of the Christian soul with itself, with its fellows, with its God, could be carried over into this new world and understood in the light of the new knowledge. We refused to live bifurcated lives, our intellect in the late nineteenth century and our religion in the early sixteenth. God, we said, is a living God who has never uttered his final word on any subject; why, therefore, should prescientific frameworks of thought be so sacred that forever through them man must seek the Eternal and the Eternal seek man? So we said, and, thanks to modernism, it became true of many an anxious and troubled soul in our time that, as Sam Walter Foss expressed it,

> He saw the boundless scheme dilate,
> In star and blossom, sky and clod;
> And as the universe grew great,
> He dreamed for it a greater God.

The church thus had to go as far as modernism but now the church must go beyond it. For even this brief rehearsal of its history reveals modernism's essential nature; it is primarily an adaptation, an adjustment, an accommodation of Christian faith to contemporary scientific thinking. It started by taking the intellectual culture of a particular period as its criterion and then adjusted Christian teaching to that standard. Herein lies modernism's tendency toward shallowness and transiency; arising out of a temporary intellectual crisis, it took a special type of scientific thinking as standard and became an adaptation to, a harmonization with, the intellectual culture of a particular generation. That, however, is no adequate religion to represent the Eternal and claim the allegiance of the soul. Let it be a modernist who says that to you! Unless the church can go deeper and reach higher than that it will fail indeed.

In the first place, modernism has been excessively preoccupied with intellectualism. Its chosen problem has been somehow to adjust Christian faith to the modern intellect so that a man could be a Christian without throwing his reason away. Modernism's message to the church has been after this fashion: When, long ago, the new music came, far from clinging to old sackbuts and psalteries, you welcomed the full orchestra and such composers as Palestrina, Bach, Beethoven, to the glory of God; when the new art came you did not refuse it but welcomed Cimabue, Giotto, Raphael, and Michelangelo, to the enrichment of your faith; when the new architecture came, far from clinging to primitive catacombs or the old Romanesque, you greeted the Gothic with its expanded spaces and aspiring altitudes; so now, when the new science comes, take that in too, and, however painful the adaptations, adjust your faith to it and assimilate its truths into your Christian thinking.

Surely, that has been a necessary appeal but it centers attention on one problem only—intellectual adjustment to modern science. It approaches the vast field of man's experience and need head first, whereas the deepest experiences of man's soul, whether in religion or out of it, cannot be approached head first. List as you will the soul's deepest experiences and needs—friendship, the love that makes a home, the enjoyment of music, delight in nature, devotion to moral causes, the practise of the presence of God—it is obvious that, whereas, if we are wise, we use our heads on them, nevertheless we do not approach them mainly head first, but heart first, conscience first, imagination first. A man is vastly greater than his logic, and the sweep and ambit of his spiritual experience and need are incalculably wider than his rational processes. So modernism, as such, covers only a segment of the spiritual field and does not nearly compass the range of religion's meaning.

Indeed, the critical need of overpassing modernism is evident in the fact that our personal spiritual problems do not lie there any more. When I was a student in the seminary, the classrooms where the atmosphere grew tense with excitement concerned the higher criticism of the Bible and the harmonization of science and religion. That, however, is no longer the case. The classrooms in the seminary where the atmosphere grows tense today concern Christian ethics and the towering question whether Christ has a moral challenge that can shake this contemporary culture to its foundations and save us from our deadly personal and social sins. So the world has moved far to a place where mere Christian harmonizers, absorbed with the intellectual attempt to adapt faith to science and accommodate Christ to prevalent culture, seem trivial and out of date. Our modern world, as a whole, cries out not so much for souls intellectually adjusted to it as for souls morally maladjusted to it, not most of all for accommodators and adjusters but for intellectual and ethical challengers.

When Paul wrote his first letter to the Corinthians, he said that he had become a Jew to the Jews that he might win the Jews, and he intimated that he had become a Greek to the Greeks that he might win the Greeks. "I am become," he said, "all things to all men, that I may by all means save some." That is a modernistic passage of adjustment and accommodation. But that is not all Paul said. Had it been all, Paul would have sunk from sight in an indistinguishable blend with the Greco-Roman culture of his day and we should never have heard of him. When he wrote the second time to the Corinthians he said something else:

> Come ye out from among them, and be ye separate, saith the Lord,
> And touch no unclean thing.

Church of Christ, take that to yourself now! Stop this endeavor to harmonize yourself with modern culture and customs as though they were a standard and criterion. Rather, come out from among them. Only an independent standing-ground from which to challenge modern culture can save either it or you.

In the second place, not only has modernism been thus predominantly intellectualistic and therefore partial, but, strange to say, at the same time it has been dangerously sentimental. The reason for this is easy to explain. One of the predominant elements in the intellectual culture of the late nineteenth and early twentieth centuries, to which modernism adjusted itself, was illusory belief in inevitable progress. So many hopeful and promising things were afoot that two whole generations were fairly bewitched into thinking that every day in every way man was growing better and better. Scientific discovery, exploration and invention, the rising tide of economic welfare, the spread of democracy, the increase of humanitarianism, the doctrine of evolution itself, twisted to mean that automatically today has to be better than yesterday and tomorrow better than today—how many elements seduced us in those romantic days into thinking that all was right with the world!

In the intellectual culture to which modernistic Christianity adapted itself, such lush optimism was a powerful factor, and the consequences are everywhere present in the natural predispositions of our thought today. In the little village of Selborne, England, the visitor is shown some trees planted by a former minister near his dwelling, so that he might be spared the view of the village slaughterhouse. Those trees are suggestive and symbolic of the sentimental illusions we plant to hide from our eyes the ugly facts of life. Especially we modernistic Christians, dealing, as we were, with thoughts of a kindly God by evolution lifting everything and everybody up, were deeply tempted to live in a fool's paradise behind our lovely trees!

For example, modernistic Christianity largely eliminated from its faith the God of moral judgment. To be sure, in the old theology, the God of moral judgment had been terribly presented so that little children did cry themselves to sleep at night for fear of him and of his hell. Modernism, however, not content with eliminating the excrescences of a harsh theology, became softer yet and created the general impression that there is nothing here to fear at all. One of the most characteristic religious movements of the nineteenth century heralded this summary of faith:

> The Fatherhood of God.
> The Brotherhood of Man.
> The Leadership of Jesus.
> Salvation by Character.
> The Progress of Mankind—
> onward and upward forever.

Well, if that is the whole creed, this is a lovely world with nothing here to dread at all.

But there *are* things here to dread. Ask the physicians. They will tell us that in a law-abiding world are stern conditions whose fulfilment or non-fulfilment involve bodily destiny. Ask the novelists and dramatists, and at their best they are not lying to us as they reveal the inexorable fatality with which character and conduct work out their implied consequence. Ask the economists. They will tell us there are things to dread which lead to an inevitable economic hell. Ask even the historians and they will talk at times like old preachers about the God of moral judgment, as James Anthony Froude did when he said, "One lesson, and only one, history may be said to repeat with distinctness: that the world is built somehow on moral foundations; that, in the long run, it is well with the good; in the long run, it is ill with the wicked."

Indeed, cannot we use our own eyes to see that there are things here to fear? For this is no longer the late nineteenth and early twentieth centuries. This is the epoch after the first world war shook the earth to its foundations, and the God of judgment has spoken. My soul, what a world, which the gentle modernism of my younger ministry, with its kindly sentiments and limitless optimism, does not fit at all! We must go beyond that. Because I know that I am speaking here to many minds powerfully affected by modernism, I say to you as to myself: Come out of these intellectual cubicles and sentimental retreats which we built by adapting Christian faith to an optimistic era. Underline this: *Sin is real.* Personal and social sin is as terribly real as our forefathers said it was, no matter how we change their way of saying so. And it leads men and nations to damnation as they said it did, no matter how we change their way of picturing it. For these are times, real times, of the kind out of which man's great exploits have commonly been won, in which, if a man is to have a real faith he must gain it from the very teeth of dismay; if he is to have real hope, it must shine, like a Rembrandt portrait, from the dark background of fearful apprehension; if he is to have real character, he must achieve it against the terrific downdrag of an antagonistic world; and if he is to have a real church, it must stand out from the world and challenge it, not be harmonized with it.

In the third place, modernism has even watered down and thinned out the central message and distinctive truth of religion, the reality of God. One does not mean by that, of course, that modernists are atheists. One does mean, however, that the intellectual culture of the late nineteenth and early twentieth centuries, to which modernism adjusted itself, was predominantly man-centered. Man was blowing on his hands and doing such things at such a rate as never had been done or dreamed on earth before. Man was pioneering new truth and building a new social order. You young people who were not here then can hardly imagine with what cheerful and confident trust we confided to man the saving of the world. So the temptation was to relegate God to an advisory capacity, as a kind of chairman of the board of sponsors of our highly successful human enterprise. A poet like Swinburne could even put the prevailing mood into candid words:

> Thou art smitten, thou God, thou art smitten; thy death is upon thee, O Lord.
> And the love-song of earth as thou diest resounds through the wind of her wings—
> Glory to Man in the highest! for Man is the master of things.

Look out on the world today and try, if you can, to repeat those words of Swinburne and still keep your face straight! At any rate, if ever I needed something deeper to go on than Swinburne's sentimental humanism, with man as the master of things, it is now—a philosophy, namely, a profound philosophy about what is ultimately and eternally real in this universe. We modernists were so disgusted with the absurdities of the old supernaturalistic theology that we were commonly tempted to visit our distaste on theology as a whole and throw it away. But theology means thinking about the central problem of existence—what is ultimately and eternally real in this universe. And in the lurid light of days like these it becomes clearer, as an increasing number of atheists are honestly saying, that if the eternally real is merely material, if the cosmos is a physical fortuity and the earth an accident, if there is no profounder reason for mankind's being here than just that at one stage in the planet's cooling the heat happened to be right, and if we ourselves are "the disease of the agglutinated dust," then to stand on this temporary and accidental earth in the face of this vast cosmos and try lyrically to sing,

> Glory to Man in the highest! for Man is the master of things,

is an absurd piece of sentimental tomfoolery. And because I have been and am a modernist it is proper that I should confess that often the modernistic movement, adjusting itself to a man-centered culture, has encouraged this mood, watered down the thought of the Divine, and, may we be forgiven for this, left souls standing, like the ancient Athenians, before an altar to an Unknown God!

On that point the church must go beyond modernism. We have been all things to all men long enough. We have adapted and adjusted and accommodated and conceded long enough. We have at times gotten so low down that we talked as though the highest compliment that could be paid Almighty God was that a few scientists believed in him. Yet all the time, by right, we had an independent standing-ground and a message of our own in which alone is there hope for humankind. The eternally real is the spiritual. The highest in us comes from the deepest in the universe. Goodness and truth and beauty are not accidents but revelations of creative reality. God is! On that point come out from among them and be ye separate! As the poet imagined Paul saying:

> Whoso has felt the Spirit of the Highest
> cannot confound nor doubt Him nor deny:
> yea with one voice, o world, tho' thou deniest,
> Stand thou on that side, for on this am I.

Finally, modernism has too commonly lost its ethical standing-ground and its power of moral attack. It is a dangerous thing for a great religion to begin adjusting itself to the culture of a special generation. Harmonizing slips easily into compromising. To adjust Christian faith to the new astronomy, the new geology, the new biology, is absolutely indispensable. But suppose that this modernizing process, well started, goes on and Christianity adapts itself to contemporary nationalism, contemporary imperialism, contemporary capitalism, contemporary racialism—harmonizing itself, that is, with the prevailing social *status quo* and the common moral judgments of our time—what then has become of religion, so sunk and submerged in undifferentiated identity with this world?

This lamentable end of a modernizing process, starting with indispensable adaptations and slipping into concession and compromise, is a familiar phenomenon in religious history. For the word "modernism" may not be exclusively identified with the adjustment of Christian faith and practise to the culture of a single era. Modernization is a recurrent habit in every living religion. Early Protestantism, itself, emerging along with a new nationalism and a new capitalism, was in its day modernism, involving itself and us in entanglements and compliances with political and economic ideas in whose presence we still are tempted to be servile. Every era with powerful originative factors in it evokes from religion indispensable adaptation, followed by further concessive acquiescences, which in time must be superseded and outgrown. Early Christianity went out from an old Jewish setting into a new Greek culture and never would have survived if it had not assimilated into its faith the profound insights of Greek philosophy. So in the classic creeds, like that of Nicæa, we have a blending of the old faith with the new philosophy, and in that process John and Paul themselves had already played a part. But, alas, early Christianity in its adjustment of its faith to Greek culture did not stop with adaptation to the insights of philosophy. At last it adapted itself to Constantine, to the licentious court, to war, to the lucrative enjoyment of imperial favors, to the use of bloody persecutions to coerce belief. One after another, it threw away the holiest things that had been entrusted to it by its Lord until, often hardly distinguishable from the culture it lived in, it nearly modernized itself into moral futility. Lift up that history, as it were a mirror, in which to see the peril of our American churches.

It is not in Germany alone that the church stands in danger of being enslaved by society. There the enslavement is outward, deliberate, explicit, organized. Here it is secret, quiet, pervasive, insidious. A powerful culture—social, economic, nationalistic, militaristic—impinging from every side upon the church, cries with persuasive voices, backed by all the sanctions and motives most urgent to the self-interest of man, Adjust yourself, adapt yourself, accommodate yourself!

When Great Britain was as mad about the Boer War as Italy is mad today about the Ethiopian War and all the forces of propaganda had whipped up the frenzy of the people to a fever heat, John Morley one night in Manchester faced an indignant, antagonistic crowd, and pleaded with his countrymen against the war. This is part of what he said: "You may carry fire and sword into the midst of peace and industry: it will be wrong. A war of the strongest government in the world with untold wealth and inexhaustible reserves against this little republic will bring you no glory: it will be wrong. You may make thousands of women widows and thousands of children fatherless: it will be wrong. It may add a new province to your empire: *it will still be wrong.*" John Morley did not call himself a Christian. He called himself an agnostic. But he was far nearer standing where Christ intended his church to stand than the church has often been.

We modernists had better talk to ourselves like this. So had the fundamentalists—but that is not our affair. We have already largely won the battle we started out to win; we have adjusted the Christian faith to the best intelligence of our day and have won the strongest minds and the best abilities of the churches to our side. Fundamentalism is still with us but mostly in the backwaters. The future of the churches, if we will have it so, is in the hands of modernism. Therefore let all modernists lift a new battle cry: We must go beyond modernism! And in that new enterprise the watchword will be not, Accommodate yourself to the prevailing culture! but, Stand out from it and challenge it! For this inescapable fact, which again and again in Christian history has called modernism to its senses, we face: we cannot harmonize Christ himself with modern culture. What Christ does to modern culture is to challenge it.